What Makes

Last?

How to Build Trust and Avoid Betrayal

John Gottman, Ph.D., and Nan Silver

Simon & Schuster Paperbacks

New York   London   Toronto   Sydney   New Delhi

Simon & Schuster Paperbacks
A Division of Simon & Schuster, Inc.
1230 Avenue of the Americas
New York, NY 10020

First Simon & Schuster trade paperback edition September 2013

SIMON & SCHUSTER PAPERBACKS and colophon are registered trademarks
of Simon & Schuster, Inc.

For information about special discounts for bulk purchases,
please contact Simon & Schuster Special Sales at
1-866-506-1949 or business@simonandschuster.com.

The Simon & Schuster Speakers Bureau can bring authors
to your live event. For more information or to book an event,
contact the Simon & Schuster Speakers Bureau at
1-866-248-3049 or visit our website at www.simonspeakers.com.

Designed by Ruth Lee-Mui

Manufactured in the United States of America

23 25 27 29 30 28 26 24

The Library of Congress had cataloged the hardcover edition as follows:
Gottman, John Mordechai.
What makes love last? : how to build trust and avoid betrayal / John Gottman and Nan Silver.
p.   cm.
Summary: "One of the foremost relationship experts at work today offers creative insight on
building trust and avoiding betrayal, helping readers to decode the mysteries of healthy love
and relationships"—Provided by publisher.
1. Love 2. Trust. 3. Betrayal. 4. Man-woman relationships. 5. Marriage.
I. Silver, Nan. II. Title.
HQ801.G5983 2012
306.7—dc23   2012018203
ISBN 978-1-4516-0847-2
ISBN 978-1-4516-0848-9 (pbk)
ISBN 978-1-4516-0849-6 (ebook)

For my wife, Julie,
who really understands trust.
—John

For my children,
Will and Elisabeth
—Nan

Authors' Note

The anecdotes and dialogue in this book are based on Dr. Gottman's years of experience studying and counseling couples. All names and identifying information have been changed. Transcripts have been edited for brevity and clarity. Some anecdotes use composite or fictive couples to illustrate Dr. Gottman's theories.

Contents

Contents

What Makes *Love* Last?

Introduction

Angel: I have something to say—

George: Hold on. I'm not finished.

Angel: What I am trying to say—

George: See and this is what I'm talking about—

Angel: Right, I know, because I do not—

George: You cut in—

Angel: I have to say something now—

George: No. Because when you *cut in*—

Angel: I have something to say here.

George: SHUT UP!

Angel and George were newlyweds juggling long work hours while raising two toddlers. That's a situation tough enough to put pressure on any marriage, but you wouldn't need a background in research psychology to recognize that this one was in trouble. The dialogue above is a snippet of the argument they had in my research lab. They sparred without end over who worked harder, who did more housework and who said what when. Angel and George, like many embattled couples, gave up on their marriage and divorced. This outcome was not unexpected considering how damaged their relationship was. When I met with them, they could barely look at each other without scowling and rolling their eyes.

For years I have invited couples like Angel and George to take part in experiments at my "Love Lab," the media's nickname for the facility at the University of Washington in Seattle, where I subject long-term romance to scientific scrutiny. In a typical study I analyze couples while they converse about everyday topics as well as when they argue. I interview them together and individually. I've even observed couples while they spend an entire day at the Love Lab's studio apartment, which comes complete with sofa, loveseat, TV, kitchen, a lake view, and video cameras hooked to the walls, which record every moment of their interactions. (The bathroom, of course, is off limits.) Thanks to these studies, I have accumulated nearly four decades' worth of data— a library of how and what partners say to and about each other, and their physiological reactions. These days I also conduct similar exercises with couples who are not part of any study but wish to receive a scientific assessment of their relationship's staying power.

When couples like Angel and George enter the Love Lab, we hook them up to enough sensors and wires to elicit quips about Dr. Frankenstein. While they adjust to the equipment and their surroundings, information begins to stream from the sensors, indicating their blood velocities, heart and pulse rates, the amount their palms sweat, and even how much they squirm in their chairs. A video camera records all of their words and body movements. On the other side of a one-way mirror, my assistants, surrounded by equipment readouts, and the requisite collection of empty cola cans, scrutinize the subtle interplay between the couple's biological reactions, body language, facial expressions, and words.

The most frequent experiment I conduct is called the conflict discussion, in which we ask the couple to converse about an area of disagreement for fifteen minutes. To facilitate the analysis of their facial expressions during their disputes, I train a separate video camera on each of them so I can view their faces in real time on a split screen.

It no longer surprises me when our couples are able to relax and "let it rip" despite the staring cameras. Still, I find that most people do curb their behavior in the lab compared to when they squabble at home. But even when partners are acting "camera ready," they can't hide from the accuracy of my sensors.

Close analysis of so many couples over the years led me to formulate seven key principles that can improve the odds of maintaining a positive relationship. Described in *The Seven Principles for Making Marriage Work*, they emphasize the value of friendship between partners, accepting each other's influence, and being gentle during disagreements. These fundamentals remain a powerful tool set for all relationships. But the sad fate of couples like Angel and George indicated to me that these principles did not reach deep enough to salvage many damaged romances. I could not accept that these partners were somehow fated to be losers at love. To aid these despairing couples, I needed to better understand what was going wrong between them.

Perhaps what puzzled me most about the unhappy couples I studied or counseled was their sincere insistence that they were deeply in love and committed to their relationship—even as they were ordering each other to "shut up" in the Love Lab. Why did so many self-proclaimed devoted couples engage in constant warfare? It made no sense. They derived no relationship benefits from their quarrels. They reported more distress over fighting than did happy couples—and yet *they went at it more often*.

It would be easy to assume that the unhappy couples argued more than others because, well, they disagreed more. What could be more logical? But as a scientist, I know that "obvious" conclusions are not always accurate. In my lab, computer scientist Dr. Tara Madyhastha helped me find the answer. To trace the anatomy of interactions between unhappy partners, she used what are called "hidden Markov models." These types of computer analyses, often implemented to decode languages or DNA sequences, can detect underlying patterns. Her results indicated that couples who seem to act like adversaries rather than lovers are trapped by what is known, in technical terms, as an *absorbing state of negativity*. This means the probability that they will enter the state is greater than the odds that they will exit it. In other words, they get stuck. These unlucky partners are imprisoned in a roach motel for lovers: They check in, but they can't check out. Consumed by negativity, their relationships die there.

Understanding why some couples wind up in this terrible trap while others are able to sidestep it has been at the heart of my recent research. As a result, I have developed a new understanding of couple dynamics and an enhanced approach to bettering all romantic relationships—not just the ones in distress.

If you listened to trapped couples argue in my lab, you would hear a litany of complaints that wouldn't seem to have much in common. Tim grouses that Jane cares more about her mother's opinion than his. Alexis keeps stalling on starting a family, to the frustration of her husband. Jimmy doesn't like it that Pat wants to switch churches. But when I speak to these unhappy partners, I am struck by an underlying similarity. They are all talking (or shouting) past each other or not even bothering to communicate at all.

Despite their commitment to sticking it out, they have lost something fundamental between lovers, a quality often termed "magic" or "passion," that exists at a primitive, "animal" level. That's why they end up in the roach motel.

I now know that a specific poison deprives couples of this precious "something" and drives them into relentless unhappiness. It is a noxious invader, arriving with great stealth, undermining a seemingly stable romance until it may be too late. You'll think at first that I'm stating the obvious when I tell you that the name of this toxin is *betrayal*. I recognize that some of the harm wrought by betrayal is common knowledge. We face a constant onslaught of tabloid "gotcha!" stories about celebrities and politicians with sex addictions and broken marriage vows. These morality tales of distrust and disloyalty underline how common and devastating infidelity can be. Yet I have good reason for calling betrayal a "secret" relationship killer. The disloyalty is not always expressed through a sexual affair. It more often takes a form that couples do not recognize as infidelity. In my lab, partners will insist that despite their troubles they have been faithful to each other. But they are wrong. Betrayal is the secret that lies at the heart of *every* failing relationship—it is there *even if the couple is unaware of it*. If a husband always puts his career ahead of his relationship, that is betrayal. When a wife keeps breaking her promise to start a family, that is also betrayal. Pervasive coldness, selfishness, unfairness, and other destructive behaviors are also evidence of disloyalty and can lead to consequences as equally devastating as adultery.

Despite how dangerous and widespread betrayal is, I can offer couples hope. By analyzing the anatomy of this poison, I have figured out how to defeat it. I now know that there is a *fundamental principle for making relationships work* that serves as an antidote to unfaithfulness. That principle is *trust*. Once again it might sound like I'm trumpeting the obvious! Happy couples tell me all the time that mutual trust is what lets them feel safe with each other, deepens their love, and allows friendship and sexual intimacy to blossom. Unhappy partners complain that their relationship lacks this element. But all couples tend to think of trust as an intangible quality that can't be pinned down or measured in a concrete way. In fact, it is now possible to calculate a couple's trust and betrayal levels mathematically and subject them to scientific study. This new analytical approach allows me to identify a couple's strengths and vulnerabilities, and to devise strategies that can rescue miserable relationships from the roach motel and keep others from going there.

In addition to benefitting couples, this new understanding of trust and betrayal has profound cultural implications. It has become commonplace for us to increase the complexity of our lives until we almost reach the breaking point. With our emails, cell phones, and intricate juggling of responsibilities, we live on the edge of a catastrophic stress response. We each have our own "carrying capacity" for stress and tend to pile it on till we come just shy of overload. Headlines that hawk "stress cures" are rife on the internet, on newsstands, and in bookstores. But I believe trust is the greatest stress buster of all.

In relationships where there is a high potential for betrayal, people waste time and emotional energy. Whether the fear concerns adultery or other faithlessness, suspicious people act like detectives or prosecuting attorneys, interrogating their partners, looking for verification that their insecurity is justified. Decision making becomes exhaustive and exhausting: If I go out of town, will he leave the kids with that babysitter I don't trust? If I check her closet, am I going to find new clothes despite our austerity budget? Should I risk confrontation by checking out his story? One man who suspected his wife of cheating put chalk marks on her rear tires before he left for work one morning. Later, when he discovered that the chalk marks were no longer visible, indicating the car wheels had turned, he asked whether she had left the house. Forgetting about her morning dash to the post office, she said no. This prompted a jealous rage, which put both of their stress levels into hyperdrive.

In sharp contrast, trust removes an enormous source of stress because it allows you to *act with incomplete information*. You don't subject your mind and body to constant worry, so the complexity of your decision making plummets. You don't need to put chalk on tires or otherwise test your partner. Implicit trust saves you a lot of time and leaves you free to grapple with less tumultuous concerns.

I always strive to increase the understanding of long-term relationships and to help couples navigate their way to happier and healthier romance. Still, I know that not all relationships can, or should, survive betrayal. Even when a long-term partnership ends for good reason, the shattered faith in love can be devastating. The loss must be acknowledged and confronted before moving on. If you are recovering from a breakup, the findings and exercises in the pages ahead may offer a deeper understanding of what went wrong and help prepare you to try again with somebody new.

Charting a way forward after a deep wound is just as important as learning to make a relationship work. If your last relationship failed, you may fear trusting someone again. But this wariness can leave you vulnerable to lifelong and profound loneliness. This isolation has not only serious psychological repercussions but physical ones as well. By fine-tuning your radar for deception, this book can help you develop the courage, strength, and wisdom to search for a trustworthy partner.

Throughout my career I have met skeptics who do not believe that sensors, computers, video cameras, and other lab equipment can assess something as mysterious and seemingly indefinable as love. Of course, scientists cannot create a love potion or a solution to all relationship woes. But I *can* offer advice founded on objective data rather than unproven theory or just the subjective experience of a particular therapist. The pages that follow offer the fruit of my research. They explain why romances can fail for reasons that seem as elusive as love itself. I hope you'll use my findings to protect a thriving relationship or to rescue one already in danger.

1

Assessing Your Trust Metric

You never know when scientific insight might strike. I certainly didn't expect a "eureka!" moment to arrive while I was watching a TV crime show. This particular episode of the program *Numb3rs* had the good guys prevent a terrorist attack after their resident genius devised a mathematical measurement, or "trust metric," to calculate the loyalty level among various suspected terrorists. The notion that you could precisely gauge the trust between potential terrorists was an intriguing plot twist. It was also nothing but a fantasy that I presume a creative script writer concocted with the show's mathematics consultant.

But it occurred to me that *my* data might be the key to calculating a real trust metric—not among violent extremists, of course, but between a couple in a committed relationship. A mathematical definition would allow me not only to confirm my theory that trust is the foundation of love, but also to study it in the lab. I could then identify when a relationship was suffering from its lack, even before it was apparent to the partners. I would be able to devise a GPS for the heart to keep happy couples from losing their way and guide those already adrift back to each other.

So often in science we make new discoveries by building on the work of others. But in my exploration of trust, I did not benefit from such support because, as far as I could tell, no previous research into a mathematical trust metric existed. A couple's loyalty level hasn't been considered important enough for this intensive number-crunching. Most psychologists and other social-science researchers regard trust as just one of many qualities that determine a relationship's strength, rather than its foundation. Some experts even consider trust a character trait—you either have it in you or you don't. But I don't believe that. I am certain that the majority of couples can maximize their loyalty level and therefore guard against betrayal and improve their odds of a happy future together.

I formulated my trust metric by thinking of the faithfulness between partners in terms of game theory. This is an approach to mathematics that delves deeply into questions of trust. But traditionally, its goals have not included saving relationships! Game Theory was popular during the Cold War, when analysts hoped that scrutinizing decision making would let them better predict the behavior of hostile groups or nations during confrontations. Game theory is based on the mathematics put forth by Drs. John von Neumann and Oskar Morgenstern in their pivotal book *Theory of Games and Economic Behavior*.* Mathematicians now recognize

---

*Von Neumann was responsible for many innovative ideas that we now take for granted, including a computer's internal architecture, computer programs, and the

game theory's limitations, but its development led to Nobel prizes and inspired a generation of Cold Warriors to foresee a future in which computers could assess the advantages of various diplomatic tactics. I doubt its proponents envisioned how useful a tool it would become for couples wishing to triumph at love, not war!

Shakespeare asserted that "all the world's a stage." But to game theorists, the world is a stadium, and we are all players. Whether we confront each other during a football game, a war, or a marital spat over dirty dishes, we follow certain rules, some spelled out, others unspecified. Underlying these rules is the assumption that we are all rational and therefore aspire to maximize our own benefits—what game theorists refer to as our *payoffs*.

The zero-sum game is probably the best known game theory concept. In such a contest, each side wants to maximize its own payoff *and* prevent the opponent from achieving anything. Football is a zero-sum game: when the New York Jets win, the New England Patriots lose. But adversaries are not always interested in an all-or-nothing outcome. For example, in a company a zero-sum game approach to career advancement is not rational. Two office workers vying for the same promotion still need to cooperate for the sake of the business, since its success is vital to their own. In these sorts of conflicts, each worker will either focus on a strategy that maximizes the payoffs for them both or one that at least minimizes their losses.

Most game theory scenarios assume that in order for one side to get the greatest payoff it must influence what the other side does. Here's an example, using a couple in a new relationship.

---

housing of both software and computation in a computer's memory. He also designed the trigger for the atomic bomb that the United States dropped on Nagasaki during World War II.

Imagine that Jenny and Al have just moved into a town house and want to figure out the best way to share the hated housework. Game theory takes for granted that, like the United States and the USSR, Jenny and Al don't trust each other. This is not an unrealistic assumption, since some wariness is common among newlyweds and couples in new second marriages. Because these relationships have a limited track record, the trust is often tentative despite their mutual devotion.

As rational "players," Jenny and Al know there are only four ways they can divide the housekeeping. Either neither of them cleans, they both clean, or one cleans and the other doesn't. Both of them want the best deal they can get—what benefits the other is not a priority. Each of them has determined that getting the other to clean will maximize their own payoffs.

This game-theory chart demonstrates how Jenny ranks her choices. She considers the four options open to her and assesses them on a scale of 0 to 10, based on the degree of payoff they offer her.

Jenny's Payoffs

	Jenny Cleans	Jenny Doesn't Clean	Row Totals
Al Cleans	10	4	14
Al Doesn't Clean	2	0	2
Column Totals	12	4	16

Jenny doesn't want to live in a pigsty, so she gets no payoff if neither of them cleans; she gives that option a zero. If only she cleans, she has to spend more time on a task she hates—although she does get something of a payoff (a clean apartment). That option gets a 2. She gives a 4 to having only Al clean. She knows he won't do a good job, since he's often blind to the dust and clutter that stare *her* in the face. Still, she'd rather he wipe down the kitchen counter than she do it. The final option, sharing the workload, offers her the result closest to her housekeeping standards without having to bear the full load. That option gets her top vote: a 10.

From a game theory perspective, there are many interesting calculations you can derive from this chart. But at a basic level, it demonstrates that no matter what rational decision Jenny makes for herself (to clean or not to clean) her highest payoffs require that *Al* do at least some of the work. Look at the Row Totals at the far right of the chart. The combination of Jenny's payoff if Al cleans, whether or not she does as well, is 14. If he never even picks up a broom then no matter what she does, her payoff plummets to 2. In other words, controlling Al's behavior would give Jenny a 12-point gain. That's a huge difference. The bottom line is that for Jenny to get the best deal she can, she *must* get Al to clean.

Here is her husband's chart:

Al's Payoffs

	Jenny Cleans	Jenny Doesn't Clean	Row Totals
Al Cleans	8	2	10
Al Doesn't Clean	7	2	9
Column Totals	15	4	19

Al's payoffs are similar to his wife's, though not identical. Like Jenny, he doesn't want the apartment to be a mess, but he sure doesn't want to clean it himself. He gives that option only 2 points. He gives a higher ranking, 7, to Jenny doing all of the chores—but not too high. He knows that Jenny will be upset if she has to tidy the place solo, which means she'll be grumpy and less interested in having sex (his pay-off). If we look at his payoffs, we see again that his two best outcomes depend on Jenny cleaning. The column totals at the bottom of the chart show the difference in his payoffs depending on whether she cleans, regardless of what he does. When she does clean, he scores a 15. When she doesn't, he's down to a 4. If he changes his own behavior, he gains only one point (10 minus 9), whereas if he changes her behavior, he gains eleven points (15 minus 4). To maximize his payoffs, Al is going to have to convince Jenny to clean.

Al and Jenny might as well be negotiators from hostile countries staring one another down across the table, each believing their side is best off if it can get the other to dismantle *its* missiles. The result of this uncooperative attitude will be endless conflict as they each try to get the other to fold the towels or haul out the garbage. Suffice it to say that either *nobody* is going to be cleaning that town house—or if just one person does, trouble is sure to follow.

The story of Jenny and Al's dirty town house may seem pretty inconsequential, but it demonstrates distrust with great accuracy. If you don't have faith in your partner, you take the stance that he or she should change so that you can maximize *your own payoffs*. Likewise, your partner wants to change *your* behavior for his or her own selfish reasons. When distrust abounds, neither of you includes the other's well-being in your calculations.

Turn this description of distrust around, and you have my definition of its opposite. Trust is not some vague quality that grows between two people. It is the specific state that exists when you are both willing to change *your own* behavior to benefit your partner. The more trust that exists in a relationship, the more you look out for each other. You have your beloved's back, and vice versa. In a trusting relationship you feel pleasure when your partner succeeds and troubled when he or she is upset. You just can't be happy if achieving your payoffs would hurt your significant other.

Once Al and Jenny develop more trust, they will stop playing hot potato with the laundry basket. They will cooperate and clean together because doing so offers their *partner* the highest pay-off. Al's paramount thought won't be, *I better do the vacuuming so Jenny will want to have sex later.* Instead his thoughts will run, *I'm going to vacuum because Jenny worries about turning into a drudge like her mother. I don't want to make her feel that way.* Likewise, Jenny's decisions will take into account her husband's needs and wants. Trusting each other doesn't mean that Al and Jenny will always put the other's needs *ahead* of their own—that is unlikely to be healthy. But it does mean that their happiness will be interconnected. They will each change their own behavior to increase the other's payoffs.

In game theory terms, the couple's decision to clean together is an enactment of the "Nash Equilibrium," first proposed by the Nobel Prize–winning mathematician John Nash (the subject of the Academy Award–winning movie *A Beautiful Mind*). In the Nash Equilibrium, both people end up in a position where they are receiving their maximum payoff and will not benefit more if they try to change the situation by themselves. However, unlike typical players, the now-trusting Jenny and Al have reached this stance in order to increase each other's payoffs, and not just their own.

Of course, it's one thing to use Game Theory to define trust. It's quite another to develop a mathematical formula that can actually calculate its strength in any relationship. I was able to proceed thanks to the Love Lab's massive data bank, which contains voluminous recordings and readouts of couples' interactions. Five of my previous studies readily leant themselves to my current search. Taken together they looked at couples from diverse age ranges, racial backgrounds, and socioeconomic circumstances. One of these studies tracked 131 newlyweds for six years, beginning just a few months after their weddings. My long-time colleague Robert Levenson, Laura Carstensen, and I also followed 160 couples for twenty years, beginning when they were in their forties or sixties. In a third study, I explored the interactions of 100 couples who represented a wide variety of ages and degrees of relationship satisfaction. In yet another, I examined decision making among lower-income couples, and in a fifth I conducted structured interventions with 100 couples in my lab. Follow-ups were done with partners from all of these studies, which meant I could compare their behavior in the lab to their relationship's fate.

In all of these experiments, I recorded the partners' words and body language while they discussed a conflict. This gave me a clear picture of how each acted when they disagreed. I also gathered data on how they *reacted* to each other, thanks mostly to a simple piece of equipment called a video recall dial. This apparatus is similar to the ones that news programs use during presidential debates so their on-air panels of voters can give immediate feedback. Although the device may seem too basic to rely on for complex research, studies confirm that it is quite precise in determining how people feel.

The video recall dial was critical to formulating a trust measurement because it works like a little trust-o-meter. Say I had a video of John promising Mary that (finally!) he would wash the car. I couldn't assume that his announcement increased her trust in him. Maybe she didn't believe him. Maybe she saw this promise as the latest in a long list of empty ones. I couldn't very well stop the clock in the middle of an experiment, stick a microphone in Mary's face, and ask how those payoffs were going. So I used the recall dial instead.

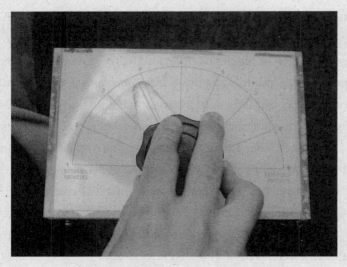

The video recall dial, my "trust-o-meter."

Soon after the videos were filmed, each partner viewed them separately and gave their moment-by-moment feedback by twisting the dial in the positive or negative direction. Going over those readouts, I could tell that Mary *was* happy when John agreed to wash the car, because while watching the video, she turned the dial sharply to "extremely positive."

One challenging aspect of studying relationships this way is that in the course of a single conversation a subject's mood might shift through many gradations of what we'd consider positive and negative. Tapes of the happiest couples still showed moments when they were not in sync—when one of them was upset and the other's recall dial didn't reflect that. Likewise, some couples who didn't make it still displayed moments of empathy and support for each other. To be useful in creating a universal trust measurement, my research needed to cut through this noise and pinpoint the type and frequency of interactions that were most common in a high-trust relationship as well as which were prevalent if the partnership were in danger. Such information would be of enormous use to other couples looking for help in assessing their own relationship. So, to make this huge amount of data manageable, I lumped all of a couple's responses into one of three boxes I called *Nasty, Neutral,* and *Nice.* The Nasty box held all negative behavior including displays of anger, criticism, belligerence, bullying, defensiveness, sadness, disappointment, fear, tension, whining, disgust, stonewalling, and contempt. At the opposite end, the Nice box housed positive emotions and behaviors such as interest, amusement, humor, laughter, excitement, joy, validation, and empathy. The leftovers, those blah reactions that were neither positive nor negative, I put into the Neutral box.

If I gave the couples a say in how I slotted their behavior, they might have disagreed with some of my decisions. But their opinions would not have swayed me, because I classified their words and body language by using what research psychologists call an observational coding system. These "rule books" are part of the canon of psychological research and have been validated a multitude of times over many decades.* So a frown or turned-down lip always codes as negative, a "real" smile as positive, and so on. Once I plot a couple's rections during their conflict discussion, I get a visual representation of their relationship's state. The graph below depicts an unhappy couple's 15-minute conflict conversation. As you can tell from the up-and-down nature of this data, they had wide-ranging responses to each other. We all know that when people argue, their emotions can shift from moment to moment. But the overall trend in this couple was toward the negative.

*The observational coding system my lab uses is called SPAFF (Specific Affect Coding System). Many labs around the world also utilize it because of its high validity and reliability.

The final key to developing a trust metric came when I had each partner view the video of their argument, trust-o-meter in hand. Their ratings let me know how much their partner's well-being influenced their own payoffs.

Imagine that Jean and Phil were subjects in my newlywed study. Although their relationship would end up being long and happy, they weren't always in the same box during their conflict discussion. At times Jean acted Nice while her husband was Nasty, or she was Nasty while he was Neutral. At one point, for example, Jean's body language and words made it clear that she was in her Nice box. She was leaning forward, listening with obvious attention to what Phil was saying. But Phil's words and behavior made it just as obvious that he was unhappy. When Jean watched this part of their interaction, she turned the dial down low. She wasn't getting any payoff from that moment in the Nice box because her husband was upset. Likewise, when Jean was happily relating how proud she felt of her career success, Al later rated the moment high on his payoff scale even though his words and body language on the tape indicated he was in Neutral while she spoke. These responses revealed them to be an in-sync couple with a high-trust relationship. Their payoffs were dependent on what the other was feeling. They ranked low those moments when the other seemed sad or upset, regardless of how they themselves felt.

When couples in my studies had problems trusting each other, the results were much different. I would see frequent instances when one partner remained happy while reviewing segments where the partner was upset, or neutral when the other was happy. Other than frequently being in the Nasty box together, there was little interdependency in their reactions.

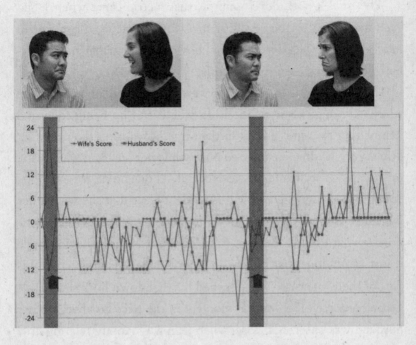

This graph depicts a troubled marriage. The arrow on the left highlights a moment in their interaction when the wife is in her Nice box (her score is above zero) and the husband is in his Nasty one (below zero). The arrow and photo on the right demonstrate a moment when both of their readings are below zero—they are in their Nasty boxes.

The bottom line of all this analysis is that happy couples in my studies spent more time behaving in ways (nice and neutral combinations) that gave them the largest payoffs and the least time in those boxes (Nasty/Nasty, Nasty/Neutral) that offered each of them the smallest. Plus, they were partial to payoffs that were *interdependent*, that maximized their partner's benefits as well their own. In other words, both of them ranked highest those moments when their partner's words or body language indicated a positive emotion.

By comparing the frequency with which couples whose

marriages lasted and those whose did not tended to enter a particular "N" box (Nasty, Neutral, or Nice), and the payoffs they received there, I was finally able to create an equation that could calculate the trust level in any relationship. Today this trust metric allows me to give any couple a trust score from 0 percent to 100 percent after assessing them in the Love Lab.

You don't need to be able to decipher the math to benefit from my findings. Nor do you need to visit the Love Lab. On page 16 you'll find a self-test derived from the trust metric that lets you assess the current trust level of your relationship. Whatever your results, in the chapters ahead you'll find plenty of research-based advice for strengthening your relationship.

After formulating the trust metric, I followed up with two related measurements that also predict a relationship's happiness level. The first quantifies the *trustworthiness* of each partner. Although it may sound like splitting hairs, trustworthiness is different from trust. A couple's mutual trust score indicates how deeply they are in this together and have each other's back. In contrast, trustworthiness indicates a partner's willingness to sacrifice for the relationship, to sometimes put his or her own needs on the back burner because the partnership matters most. Trust and trustworthiness usually go together. If a couple has a strong trust measurement, their trustworthiness usually rates equally high. Likewise, if the trust metric is low, trustworthiness tends to be as well. But this is not always the case. It is not uncommon for a newlywed couple (or a new second marriage) to rate high in trust but low in trustworthiness. When these couples are studied in the Love Lab, we find that almost all of their conflict discussions revolve around issues such as, "Will you choose me over your friends when I need you?" "Will you be here for me when I am upset?" "Are you going to remain sexually faithful?" In time, their trustworthiness score elevates if their relationship is sound.*

When couples are trustworthy they send each other the message that they and the partnership are unique and irreplaceable. During couples' counseling I call this "creating the sacred" because "sacred" and "sacrifice" have the same root—both words originated in early religious practices that involved sacrifice as a form of worship. In a long-term, committed relationship, sacrifice entails both people agreeing to give the romance priority over other goals and dreams. Learning to do this may be difficult for couples who no longer connect emotionally. These "partners" may have coped with years of unhappiness by leading separate, parallel lives. It can be hard to break this habit, but it is certainly possible.

I was also able to compute a betrayal metric that calculates how *un*willing each partner is to sacrifice for the other and the relationship. If a couple's betrayal metric is elevated consistently, they are at dire risk for infidelity or another serious disloyalty. Betrayal is on display when partners turn their rating dials in opposite directions. Her loss is his gain, and vice versa. They often feel happy when the other feels worse. It is as if these couples are always playing a dangerous game of checkers.

I want to make clear what I mean by saying my research can predict divorce, because at times the media have confused my results with other types of findings. Statistics indicate that the divorce rate lies somewhere between 43 percent and 67 percent

---

*In the United States, couples who cohabitate without an engagement (i.e., with no commitment) usually have a low-trust relationship, according to extensive research by Philip Blumstein and Pepper Schwartz, described in their book, *American Couples* (1983). Schwartz expected to find that the longer a couple lived together, the more their trust level would mirror a married couple's, but their research found the opposite. Cohabitating gay and lesbian couples displayed a similar commitment level to married heterosexuals.

(depending on the particular study). These are nationwide figures based on projections of how many couples will split over forty years of marriage. My studies do not relate to these calculations at all. Instead of measuring or predicting long-term divorce rates, I look at what behaviors and attitudes *lead* to couples splitting up. My research focuses on whether the presence of a certain element, such as a low trust level, can foretell a breakup, and if so, with what precision.

Here's how I determine the accuracy of my predictions. Imagine that as part of my newlywed study there are 130 fortune cookies jumbled in a bowl. Six years later we know that 113 of the fortunes read, "This marriage will survive," while the other 17 read, "This marriage is doomed." If you want to identify the 17 cookies that contain this bad news, random guessing is not going to be effective. Your accuracy rate would be only about .0000000000000000003%. But in the lab, if a theory is correct, it will allow me to choose the 17 "bad" cookies a very large percentage of the time. I know my new equations are valid because they have an 85 percent chance of correctly guessing a couple's fate.

You might be thinking that, despite all of the complicated mathematics behind them, my conclusions about trust and betrayal are pretty self-evident. It's true that you don't need an expert's research to inform you that trust is good for a marriage and betrayal is bad. Nor is it necessary to film a couple in a laboratory to determine whether they are living in bliss, or are at war. Sometimes you can just have them over for dinner. But most relationships fall between the extremes. It's common for couples to feel some unease about the future even if they aren't experiencing a noticeable problem in the present. I have worked with many couples who misread their situation, particularly when it comes to understanding the interplay between their payoffs and actions toward each other. This is where the math offers me enormous help. By developing a way to measure trust in any single interaction between a couple, I've gained critical insight into the inner workings of all relationships, including those whose likely future is not so apparent. Based on this research I can offer valid advice to all couples on how to rescue or protect their love.

One of the fascinating aspects of scientific research is that you don't always get what you anticipate. There are always surprises, which is why I think it foolish to offer relationship advice based only on one's own experiences or unproven theories. For example, whatever the quality of your relationship, it's a given that you will each spend time in all three of the "N" boxes. But what does that mean for your future? Is being in Neutral just a step away from being in your Nasty box? Is it a bad omen if you have a hard time staying in Nice when you're arguing? And if you slip into the Nasty box a lot is that a warning sign for your relationship? The answers to these questions might not be what you'd expect. And they matter a great deal to a relationship's future.

What Is Your Trust Metric?

The following quiz will give you a snapshot of your relationship's trust metric. If possible, ask your partner to answer these questions, too. Then compare your scores. Calculating your trust metric will give you ripe ground for talking about your relationship—what's working and areas to improve. (If the results make you anxious, consider discussing them with your partner in the presence of a therapist.) As is the case with many psychological quizzes, some of these questions will seem obvious. But be sure to answer them anyway. You may want to retake this test after you've finished the book and spent time working together on the exercises ahead.

Your Trust Metric

Instructions

For the following items, indicate the extent to which you agree or disagree with each item by circling either SD for *Strongly Disagree*, D for *Disagree*, N for *Neither Agree nor Disagree*, A for *Agree*, and SA for *Strongly Agree*. Note: If you and your partner don't live together or do not have children (separately or together), answer questions about these topics based on how you *think* your partner would react if you did.

1. I feel protected by my partner.   SD D N A SA
2. My partner is faithful to me.   SD D N A SA
3. My partner is there for me financially.   SD D N A SA
4. Sometimes I feel uneasy around my partner.   SD D N A SA
5. I don't think my partner has intimate relationships with
   others.   SD D N A SA
6. From now on, my partner would not have children with
   anyone but me.   SD D N A SA
7. My partner fully loves our children and/or is at least
   respectful of my own children.   SD D N A SA
8. I believe that you can trust most people.   SD D N A SA
9. My partner helps me feel emotionally secure.   SD D N A SA
10. I know my partner will always be a very close friend.   SD D N A SA
11. My partner will commit to help provide for our children.   SD D N A SA
12. When the chips are down, I can count on my partner to
    sacrifice for me and our family.   SD D N A SA
13. My partner does housework.   SD D N A SA
14. My partner will work hard to increase our financial security.   SD D N A SA

15. My partner doesn't respect me.   SD D N A SA

16. My partner makes me feel sexually desirable.   SD D N A SA

17. My partner takes my feelings into account when making decisions.   SD D N A SA

18. I know that my partner will take care of me when I'm sick.   SD D N A SA

19. When we are not getting along, my partner will work with me on our relationship.   SD D N A SA

20. My partner is there for me emotionally.   SD D N A SA

21. My partner does not overuse alcohol and drugs.   SD D N A SA

22. My partner acts romantically toward me.   SD D N A SA

23. My partner is kind to my family.   SD D N A SA

24. I can rely on my partner to talk to me when I'm sad or angry.   SD D N A SA

25. My partner belittles or humiliates me.   SD D N A SA

26. There is at least one person who comes first to my partner rather than me.   SD D N A SA

27. My partner will work with me as part of a financial unit.   SD D N A SA

28. I have power and influence in this relationship.   SD D N A SA

29. My partner shows others how much he or she cherishes me.   SD D N A SA

30. My partner helps carry the load of child care.   SD D N A SA

31. I just can't trust my partner completely.   SD D N A SA

32. My partner keeps his or her promises.   SD D N A SA

33. My partner is a moral person.   SD D N A SA

34. My partner does what he or she agrees to do.   SD D N A SA

35. My partner will betray my confidences.   SD D N A SA

36. My partner is affectionate toward me.   SD D N A SA

37. In arguments I can trust my partner to really listen to me.   SD D N A SA

38. My partner shares in and honors my dreams.   SD D N A SA

39. I fear my partner could stray.   SD D N A SA

40. My partner's words and deeds reflect the values we say we agree on.   SD D N A SA

41. My partner makes love to me often.   SD D N A SA

42. I can count on my partner to build or maintain a sense of
    family and community with me.   SD D N A SA

Scoring

STEP 1

Score your answers to questions 4, 15, 25, 26, 31, 35, and 39 using the following scale. Then add them up:

Strongly Agree: 1

Somewhat Agree: 2

Neither Agree nor Disagree: 3

Somewhat Disagree: 4

Strongly Disagree: 5

Subtotal ___

STEP 2

Score your answers to the remainder of the questions using this scale:

Strongly Agree: 5

Somewhat Agree: 4

Neither Agree nor Disagree: 3

Somewhat Disagree: 2

Strongly Disagree: 1

Subtotal ___

STEP 3

Add your two subtotals to calculate your trust metric.

Total ___

What Does My Score Mean?

0-52

You have a low degree of trust in your partner and your relationship. Not all couples are meant to be together forever, but even matches that struggle with trust issues *can* work things out if both partners make a strong commitment to the process. (Before reading the rest of the book, consider turning to chapter 10. It will help you assess whether your partner is someone you just shouldn't trust.) Reading this book by yourself can clarify your situation and may help you make positive changes in your interactions with your partner. But if he or she will agree, try to work through the exercises together. Some soul searching is in order here: do you both have enough motivation to do this? If so, retake this quiz after you've finished the book and have put its advice into action. If your score remains low, seek more individualized help.

53-105

Your trust level is moderate. You have faith in your partner—but uncertainty as well. You can bolster your relationship by working on the exercises in this book. Although it's best to work together, your relationship can still benefit if you make progress on your own. When one member of a couple becomes clearer about needs and desires, often the relationship comes into sharper focus for both of them, making positive changes easier. If your trust metric does not improve, it's time to decide whether you're both committed to making your relationship your top priority. If your metric is now higher, that's a powerful sign that the more you continue to open up to each other, the happier and more fulfilling your relationship is likely to become.

106-210

You have a deep sense of trust in your partner. Such a sturdy foundation improves the likelihood that your relationship will remain happy over the long term. Still, if you scored in the bottom half of this particular range, it would be worthwhile to have honest conversations about your relationship. If your trust level is very high, this book can still benefit you. Consider reading it together as a romantic experience that will reaffirm just how in love you are—and also give you tools to help you stay that way.

2

The Three Boxes

Jocelyn: Sweetheart, how lovely to surprise me with a vacation
home! Still, I can't help thinking that maybe we should have
discussed such a huge purchase ahead of time. To be honest—
and maybe this is just me—I'm not sure that using all of our
savings for a house with termites and no indoor plumbing was
the best idea.

Miguel: Honey, I appreciate your perspective. Let me hear more.

Do your arguments sound like Jocelyn and Miguel's? I doubt it.
You can't expect anyone to respond so sweetly during a major
disagreement. It wouldn't be real, and neither are Jocelyn and
Miguel. I've never met a couple like them. In my studies, sometimes people "seem" to respond with magnanimity during a

distressing discussion with their mate. But their escalating heart rates and blood pressure tell a different story. In the healthiest relationships, a couple will still feel anger toward each other at times. They will have quarrels, even serious conflicts.

That said, for a relationship to satisfy both partners, you need to spend plenty of time in the Nice box, the home of mutual respect and affection. In game theory parlance, the Nice box offers both of you big payoffs. But no one can stay there forever. When tempers flare, it's easy to lose your ability to respond in a positive and productive manner. In the Love Lab, it doesn't surprise me when neither partner can enter the Nice box during an argument. It is such an obvious observation that one wonders whether *anyone* can enter the Nice box during a fight. Isn't that impossible by definition?

Yes and no. I have yet to encounter couples who can remain "nice" throughout a conflict. But my research shows that in many relationships the box does not remain locked. When I categorize some couples as "nice," I don't mean that they sound like Jocelyn and Miguel. I mean that they are able to enter the Nice box *at all* when tempers flare. In the midst of conflict, these couples find a way to respond, at least for a brief time, in a soothing and loving manner. That's a real achievement. It's not surprising that these couples' trust metrics are high—particularly those who say they appreciate this ability to calm each other. It takes a large measure of trust to do so with success.

When nice couples argue, they are unlikely to use all of the "proper" words or actions that a therapist might suggest for resolving conflict. But they do work it out. Imagine this scenario: Jim is at the wheel as he and longtime girlfriend, Violet, head for a weekend in the mountains. She cries, "Slow down!" as he winds the car around a turn. Jim's driving often makes Violet anxious.

It's a real sore spot in their relationship. As usual, when Violet criticizes his driving, Jim says through gritted teeth: "Stop yelling at me. You're going to *cause* an accident!" But Violet continues to chastise him. If you could mind read, you'd know Jim is thinking: *She's a terrible driver, but I'm the one who gets put down. Nothing I do is ever good enough for her. Why did I agree to come on this stupid vacation anyway?*

By the time they arrive at the mountaintop inn, Jim is so agitated that he almost flings his suitcase out of the trunk. But then, something changes. Violet scans the breathtaking panorama and gasps. "It's like we've died and gone to heaven! Hon, maybe you *did* drive us off a cliff." Despite his agitated state, Jim chuckles. He's always loved Violet's teasing sense of humor. She smiles, gives him a playful nudge, and just like that, their relationship steps back from a real precipice. Violet has employed a common repair technique—humor—to tamp down the tension and soothe her boyfriend.

Repairs are the life jackets of all romantic partnerships. Their effectiveness determines whether a relationship will live or die. Repairs are not complicated. Common ones include jokes, a compliment, a hand squeeze, a question. (On page 105 you'll find a list of common repairs couples in my studies have used.) In a healthy relationship, a repair lowers the recipient's blood pressure and heart rate. The tension level drops enough to allow reason to prevail. If a couple's conflicts always escalate despite repair attempts, this indicates they are trapped in a spiral of misery. Using the "wrong" repair isn't their problem; the couple's history of unproductive, scarring conflict is.

Violet's repair does not resolve the issue between her and Jim, but it allows them to hash it out without sniping and thus save their vacation. Being able to slip into the Nice box during a heated exchange is a promising sign for a couple's future. In the new-lywed study, I found that the capacity to express some positivity while discussing an area of conflict not only predicted whether a couple would be together at the end of the six-year study, but also whether they would still be *happy*. (By the way, conflict over your driving styles is among the most common "unsolvable" relation-ship problems. A sense of humor helps!)

Perhaps my most crucial finding about these couples is the surgical precision with which they time their quick forays into the Nice box. These visits usually occur when one partner's physi-cal state indicates a high stress level. If Violet and Jim had their argument in my lab, you would see that she cracks her joke just when Jim is on the verge of exploding. Of course, she wouldn't have access to our data stream as it records Jim's racing pulse and elevated blood pressure. She doesn't need that information. Her intuition moves her into the Nice box at the right moment. Well-timed repairs are part of the dance between two people who know and trust each other. The power of one partner's positive effect to reduce physiological signs of stress in the other is appar-ent across all of my studies. It has been replicated in my lab and Robert Levenson's.

So that's the truth about the Nice box. It does exist during conflict, although it is elusive. If there is a high level of trust, you can access the Nice box for brief but critical moments during an argument, allowing for repair and thus a constructive (or, at least, less destructive) discussion. You don't need to keep on a happy face for your relationship to flourish. (It's impossible to do that, anyway.) But if you are able to lower the heat when necessary to prevent overload, that's a sign of a high trust metric. Likewise, by working on your ability to make repairs, you can elevate the level of trust between you.

The Boring Neutral Zone

If you're tempted to skip this section because "neutral" sounds boring, you'd be making the same mistake as countless couples and therapists. During conflict, the Neutral box is *not* the Land of Blah. My findings on neutrality are among the most exciting to come out of my research into trust.

Imagine that you're a TV director guiding actors through the following scene:

(A married couple sit on a couch.)

Brianna: I told my mom we'd visit tomorrow.

Lew: We?

Brianna: I promised her.

Lew: There's a play-off game. You should have checked with me.

Brianna: We haven't seen her in a while.

Lew: You were there last week.

Brianna: But you weren't. She gets lonely. Why can't you come?

You could direct Lew and Brianna to spit out these lines while he slams a door and she slams her laptop shut. Or you could have them cuddle while they talk. The one approach you would never take, if you cared about the ratings, would be to have them deliver their lines as if they were discussing the need to restock on paper clips. That approach would make for terrible TV.

But in the lab I don't get to rewrite dialogue or direct its delivery. I just record and analyze it. I've found that some couples do remain neutral during much of their arguments. They don't utilize repair techniques a lot, but they don't seem to need them. Their physiological readouts confirm how unfazed they remain throughout the disagreement. There is no dramatic increase in their pulse rate or blood pressure. And their body language and words don't indicate anything positive or negative. These couples are not bored with each other or apathetic about their relationship. Unlike unhappy couples, neutral ones are engaged and responsive. But they remain calm while expressing disagreement.

In our study of couples in their mid-forties and sixties, I found that happy couples spent about 65 percent of their time in the Neutral box when they disagreed, compared to about 47 percent for unhappy couples. Twelve years later, the happy couples spent about 70 percent of their time being Neutral. So as their anniversaries passed, happy couples shifted even further away from having to soothe each other. And their video dial ratings indicated they received more and more of a payoff from this neutral stance.

If videos of these couples' arguments were posted on the web, they would be the least likely to go viral. People don't want to watch such tame stuff. The popularity of reality TV suggests they are more interested in seeing scenes of ranting, out-of-control couples and tender, weepy moments of reconciliation. Partners who enter therapy are not immune to this bias. None are in search of the humdrum. They want to get past the agony of conflict so that they can reconjure the magic. Their therapist is likely to agree with this goal, thinking something like: *I need to spend our sessions examining why this couple is so negative. When we accomplish this, their relationship will turn around and they will naturally drift away from being nasty to each other and into the Nice box.* There's not a reputable counselor on earth who would turn to a colleague and say, "What a great therapy session I just had with Tammy and Gus. They argued *without emotion* for the entire fifty minutes!" Such an approach would violate the therapist's assumed role, which has been to encourage a positive emotional life between partners.

In a well-known study, Robert Levenson and his student Rachel Ebling created a videotape of the first three minutes of arguments between ten real married couples. Half of them had ended up divorcing; the rest were still together. Bob and Rachel showed the videotape to therapists, researchers, and pastoral counselors and asked them to predict the outcome for each couple. (The tape also became part of an exhibit at the Discovery Museum near San Francisco; visitors made their best guesses and then learned how on-target they were.) On average, the predictions of these professionals were no more accurate than a coin flip. Why were so many of these human-behavior experts unable to identify the doomed relationships? Most of the observers focused on the fireworks when the couples were disagreeing. They didn't consider how much of the time each couple remained calm and unemotional, presumably because they didn't think it was important. But neutrality was indeed key to the relationships' fate. Those couples who spent the most time being unemotional remained married.

It makes sense that the Neutral box would be a great place to sit out a conflict. Think back on a tumultuous disagreement you have had. In retrospect, wouldn't your payoffs have been greater if you had remained unemotional? Most of us would be happy to make that trade—even if the high-drama altercation had ended happily. The deep benefits of neutrality mean that moving toward *less* emotional exchanges, rather than "just" positive ones, is a worthy goal for couples. During conflict, lovers would benefit from spending at least some time in the "valley of peace" rather than remaining always in the "valley of darkness."

The relief of the Neutral box may be the ultimate expression of relationship trust. Don't worry, however, if you and your partner are not yet "ready" to remain neutral. It takes a long time to get there. Couples first need to know that the other will make and respond to repairs at critical times during conflict. But the neutral zone is where a happy relationship often ends up.

Despite their different characteristics, both the Nice and Neutral boxes are great places for partners to spend their time. The ability to access them during arguments bodes well for their future. In game theory terms, it makes sense for couples to spend as much time as possible in these two boxes because they offer the highest payoffs. But unhappy couples seem to defy game theory. They get stuck in the misery of the Nasty box, which is anything but rational.

The Roach Motel for Lovers

All couples fall into the Nasty box on occasion. But only some spend so much time there that they end up in that absorbing state of negativity I call the roach motel. Angel and George, whose disagreement ended with his telling her to "shut up!" are typical of these unfortunate couples. No matter how hard they try or what they say to each other, their efforts to repair their conflicts fall short. Some of these couples torture each other with loud and vocal attacks. Others stew in negative thoughts and feelings. Whatever their style of conflict, these nasty partners all say they hate fighting. They feel sad and bad about it. It gives them no payoff. And yet they can't stop.

By analyzing the interactions of these unhappy partners, I have found two characteristics that help explain the trap. When a couple lands in the Nasty box, at least one of them may become highly sensitive, physically, to the hostility. I have long used the term *flooding* to describe this physical response. When it occurs, a powerful cocktail of hormones (including adrenaline) triggers increased pulse rate, blood pressure, sweat output, and other bodily signs of stress. These hormonal changes, which maximize your physical abilities such as speed and muscle strength, are likely an evolutionary legacy from our prehistoric ancestors who often confronted hostile humans and hungry animals.

Research suggests that because our male forbearers were the hunters and protectors, they became more physically vigilant than females. This evolutionary heritage has left modern men with a more intense fight-or-flight response to perceived danger than their female partners possess. They also experience this arousal for longer after the threat. In my studies, and many others, men are far more likely than a female partner to flood during an argument. When we compare the readouts of a couple's biological responses, men tend to demonstrate more dramatic spikes in physical distress when upset. Because the body does not tailor its reaction to the type of threat, a man may rev up as if he's facing a ferocious beast rather than an angry partner.

Flooding is deadly to relationships. The extreme nature of the body's response makes rational thought almost impossible. In a form of what psychologists call "tunnel vision," the eyes and ears focus only on potential warning signs and escape routes. Nothing else gets through. The sense of humor goes on hiatus, as does the ability to listen, solve problems, or understand another's emotions. Because most therapists are unaware of these findings on flooding, they will ask the afflicted partner to express empathy for the other, which right then he or she is incapable of doing. This just worsens the couple's relationship woes.

Depending on the circumstance, a flooded person may choose to confront his partner (attack!) or refuse to communicate (run!), which I call stonewalling. Both of these responses were apparent in that exchange between George and Angel. When George yelled "Shut up!" his physiological readouts indicated flooding. Although his wife continued to argue, George began to stonewall and refused to respond.

A tendency to flood during arguments prevents repairs from calming things down. If the body and or mind are in overdrive, clarity of thought shuts off. People are not receptive to (nor even aware of) their partner trying to soothe them. My research is chock-full of examples of brilliant but failed repairs in such relationships. If Angel were to crack a joke or offer George encouragement, he would still turn away. No loving message would get through to him. That's why long occupancy in the roach motel kills a couple's trust in each other and faith in their relationship.

Why do only some couples experience this flooding and failure of repairs? It may be that some men are more biologically vulnerable to flooding than others. But in most cases, the underlying culprit is the dynamic between the couple, specifically a deficit in *attunement*. Although psychologists impart various meanings to the word, I define attunement in adult relationships as the desire and the ability to understand and respect your partner's inner world. Attunement offers a blueprint for building and reviving trust in a long-term committed relationship. When this element is in short supply, partners don't demonstrate understanding of each other's inner life or communicate that awareness in a supportive manner. In chapter 6, I will detail how to harness attunement's revelatory benefits to improve or rescue a relationship. But right now I want to focus on what happens when it is *lacking*.

The Five Steps to the Roach Motel

Although "failure to attune" may sound fuzzy and abstract, there is a specific, five-step trajectory that occurs when a relationship has a deficit in this quality.

Step 1: There's a "Sliding Door Moment"

In a committed relationship, partners constantly ask each other in words and deeds for support and understanding. In research parlance, I refer to such requests as "bids." They can be as simple as "Could you get me a beer?" or as profound as "I need you," after a scary medical diagnosis. Not all bids are obvious. Many of them get missed, ignored, or misinterpreted. One partner may say, "I love you," expecting the other to turn around and initiate a hug. But the partner, distracted and just half-listening, says, "I know you do." A husband gets his wife the same book of poster art that he bought her last Valentine's Day. He forgot. She does not.

Every bid made in a relationship initiates what I call a sliding door moment. When one partner expresses a need for connection, the other's response is either to slide open a door and walk through or keep it shut and turn away. Imagine that Henry settles into his favorite chair to watch a movie. His wife, Cindy, wanders over, gazes at the screen, and sighs, "Wow—Paris always looks so gorgeous in movies!" There is a huge catalog of reactions Henry might have to his wife's wistful comment. He could slide the door open by saying something like, "I hope someday we get to go there." I call such a response "turning toward" the partner. Or he could turn away by offering a grouchy grunt or saying, "Shhhh, I'm trying to watch." Any response that doesn't demonstrate interest and connection, slides the door shut.

All long-term relationships are riddled with sliding door moments that end poorly. Even couples who are masters at relationships experience occasions when one partner looks sad or listless or even especially delighted and, for whatever reason, the other isn't tuned in. The partner may be tired or annoyed or just focused elsewhere. Often, we don't think our response, or lack of one, to such a trivial event will matter much.

It's true that turning away from a minor bid is not going to send a relationship hurtling into the abyss. But an abundance of unhappy endings to these interactions without subsequent discussion about what happened does precipitate danger. Over time, one partner or both begin to wonder: *Do I come first, or does someone or something else matter more? Is my partner selfish? Can I risk continuing to trust?*

Step 2: A Regrettable Incident Occurs

As the result of turning away during a sliding door moment, conflict flares. You notice a hurt or accusatory expression on your partner's face and know that somehow you've just made a mess. If you're lucky, your partner will be up-front about what's wrong. "I wanted to tell you what the doctor said, but you couldn't talk about it because you were busy. You knew how nervous I was about getting the test results! I feel you let me down."

If the "offending" partner acknowledges what just happened and accepts responsibility for his or her part in it, the breach can be repaired. If, instead, the partner turns away, the ensuing hurt and anger trigger what I call a *regrettable incident*—an eruption of conflict that becomes an unfortunate part of the relationship's history. Each regrettable incident chisels away a bit at the couple's mutual trust.

Often, the circumstances leading to a regrettable incident are not clear-cut. Relationships are messy. When a door slides shut, both partners might feel injured. Joe becomes upset at a house party when his girlfriend, Maddy, ignores his request that they move to another corner of the room. He thinks she is flirting, which makes him see red. When she doesn't respond to him, he leaves. Maddy doesn't know he is upset or where he has gone. She goes from room to room asking if anyone has seen him. Nobody has. By the time she finds him walking toward his car, she is fuming. "Do you know what you put me through?" she asks. Joe retorts that she has no reason to complain considering that the situation was her doing. She insists that he is being overly sensitive. Joe gets flooded and drives off. The next day they "make up" but resolve nothing. That's how a sliding door moment leads to a regrettable incident.

Again, occasional events like this one will not ruin a relationship. But a pattern of turning away *followed by an inability to acknowledge and repair the breach* brings couples a giant step closer to the roach motel.

Step 3: The Zeigarnik Effect Kicks In

In 1922, an astute twenty-one-year-old psychology student named Bluma Zeigarnik watched as the waiters in a Viennese café handled large, complicated orders without ever writing them down. Intrigued by their remarkable memories, she interviewed them afterward and discovered that none could recall any of the orders they had just filled. Once the waiter delivered the order to the customer's table, he forgot it. Zeigarnik went on to a distinguished career as a psychologist. Her observation in that Viennese café has come to be known as the "Zeigarnik effect:" We have better recall for events that we have not completed than for those we have.

Subsequent studies have shown the power of this effect. We are almost twice as likely to recall "unfinished issues" compared with those we have processed or in some manner put to rest. Between lovers, arguments that end with confessions, amends, and deeper understanding of one another tend to be soon forgotten, although their legacy is a stronger, more enduring relationship. But when a sliding door moment leads to a regrettable incident that goes unaddressed, thanks to the Zeigarnik effect, the hurt remains accessible in our active memory, available to be rehashed again and again. Like a stone in one's shoe, the recollection becomes a constant irritant that leads to an increase in negative attitudes about the partner.

Step 4: Negative Sentiment Override Takes Over

When a pattern of broken trust develops, partners begin to feel like the relationship has emptied out. They no longer feel like friends. With increasing frequency, they see each other in a negative light. University of Oregon emeritus psychologist Robert Weiss coined the term "Negative Sentiment Override" (NSO) for this phenomenon. Under its force, people tend to construe neutral and even positive events as negative. As a result, they enter their Nasty box more frequently. On average, people who suffer from NSO fail to recognize their partner's positive gestures 50 percent of the time. A husband declares one night that he'll cook dinner. His wife, whose major marital complaint is how little work he does at home, reacts with knee-jerk suspicion. Due to NSO, she's convinced he's up to something. Maybe he's trying to show her up as a cook, since his family is joining them. Or he wants to make his parents believe that he's a great husband. She can't accept that he is just being kind.

A common sign of NSO is a tendency to perceive harmless or neutral comments as negative. Nathaniel's wife says, "Oh, look.

The lightbulb blew out again." If he's in the throes of NSO, Nathaniel's inner dialogue will sound something like: *Who died and made me the Official Light Bulb Changer? She can fix it herself!* By contrast, if hurt and suspicion are not tainting his thoughts, Nathaniel is likely to assume that his wife's words mean that, well, the lightbulb blew out. If Nathaniel's wife is also experiencing NSO and sees him frowning out the window, she may read anger, resentment, and contempt into his expression. But if she's satisfied in the relationship, she's more likely to conclude that he's worried about the weather. Happy couples are susceptible to *Positive* Sentiment Override. They perceive each other's neutral acts as positive and don't take personally their partner's negative emotions.

Negative overrides reinforce the belief that the partner is not just thoughtless on occasion, but is a selfish person. If one or both partners end up rewriting their relationship memories with a persistent negative spin, this heralds the death of their love (see chapter 12). It is challenging to switch off NSO once it begins, because circumstances are not black and white. There will be times when suspicion is justified—the partner is being selfish. But there will also be times when the other is falsely accused. The *assumption* and *anticipation* of a partner's negativity harms the relationship, helping to transform the Nasty box into an inescapable prison. Negative Sentiment Override is a litmus test for a troubled relationship.

The following questionnaire will help you determine whether you are experiencing NSO.

Negative Sentiment Override Quiz
Think about an argument, misunderstanding, or discussion of an existing relationship issue that you've had in the last couple of months. Then answer these true-or-false questions.

In the recent past in my relationship, generally I felt:

1. Hurt.   True ❑ False ❑
2. Misunderstood.   True ❑ False ❑
3. Like "I don't have to take this."   True ❑ False ❑
4. Innocent of blame for the problem.   True ❑ False ❑
5. Like getting up and leaving.   True ❑ False ❑
6. Angry.   True ❑ False ❑
7. Disappointed.   True ❑ False ❑
8. Unjustly accused.   True ❑ False ❑
9. "My partner has no right to say those things."   True ❑ False ❑
10. Frustrated.   True ❑ False ❑
11. Personally attacked.   True ❑ False ❑
12. I wanted to strike back.   True ❑ False ❑
13. I was warding off a barrage.   True ❑ False ❑
14. Like getting even.   True ❑ False ❑
15. I wanted to protect myself.   True ❑ False ❑
16. I took my partner's complaints as slights.   True ❑ False ❑
17. My partner was trying to control me.   True ❑ False ❑
18. My partner was very manipulative.   True ❑ False ❑
19. Unjustly criticized.   True ❑ False ❑
20. I wanted the negativity to just stop.   True ❑ False ❑

Scoring

Add all of your "true" responses. Use a calculator to divide the sum by 20. Now, multiply the result by 100 to find your percentage. A score above 40 percent indicates that, right now, you are experiencing Negative Sentiment Override. Working on the excercises in upcoming chapters can help you recover.

Step 5: The Four Horsemen Wreak Havoc

The more negative a couple's interactions become, the less productive their attempts to communicate. The inability to air grievances in a constructive manner heralds the arrival of four negative modes of communication that block the success of repairs. I call these the Four Horsemen of the Apocalypse: Criticism, Contempt, Defensiveness, and Stonewalling. Earlier in my career, I thought that if couples learned to avoid the Four Horsemen, they would automatically communicate in positive ways that would allow love to flourish. This is not the case. Defeating the Four Horsemen will not be enough to resolve all of a couple's problems. That can be achieved only by healing and reestablishing mutual trust. Still, it is critical to avoid letting these horsemen trample you during disagreements because they "egg on" the negativity that keeps you trapped.

First Horseman: Criticism

Although this is the least destructive horseman, it still has devastating effects. If you are unhappy about something in your relationship, by all means express it—but rather than an attack, use what I call a gentle start-up. This approach entails making a straightforward comment about a concern and expressing your need in a positive fashion. It is the opposite of criticism, which assaults the other's character.

> *Criticism:* "You said you'd clean up, but there are still crumbs on the table. You never do what you say you will." (Words like *always* and *never* imply the other has a personality flaw.)
> *Gentle* Start-up: "There are still crumbs on the table. I need them to be cleaned up."

> *Criticism:* "I told you we have to be there by seven. Are you just being deliberately slow?"

Gentle Start-up: "Come on, we're late. I need us to walk out the door right now."

Criticism: "You were supposed to get the *diet* iced tea. You're too self-centered to remember what I asked for."

Gentle Start-up: "Oh, I asked you to get diet iced tea, not regular."

Second Horseman: Contempt

This is verbal abuse that implies the partner is inferior. It includes name-calling, sarcasm, sneering, and belittling.

"*You* call that cleaning? Can't you do anything right? Hand over the sponge."

"*Do* you have some kind of mental problem? Why is this so difficult for you to grasp? We have to be there by seven!"

"*Did* you check the label? Can you read? You show me where it says DIET iced tea."

Third Horseman: Defensiveness

If you're the target of verbal grenades, a desire to defend yourself is understandable. Forms of defensiveness include righteous indignation, launching a counterattack, or acting like an innocent victim (usually by whining). Though you may consider a defensive response justified, it will not end the conflict. Instead, it will raise the tension level. The antidote for defensiveness is to accept responsibility for some of the problem.

Contempt: "You're such a slob—you should've cleaned this up!"

Defensiveness: "I couldn't find the sponge. Where did you stash it this time?"

Contempt: "You're never on time. You're late once again."

Defensiveness: "If I didn't have to wait so long to get into the shower, I'd be ready by now. Quit picking on me."

Contempt: "You didn't get the diet iced tea. What's wrong with you?"

Defensiveness: "Hey, don't blame me. You never told me to."

Fourth Horseman: Stonewalling

When a barrage of tension leads to flooding, the physically compromised partner stops giving out the usual cues that he or she is listening (head nods, eye contact, brief vocalizations). Instead, the listener reacts like a stone wall, blocking all stimuli. We know this is an attempt to recover from flooding, but stonewalling also shuts down any hope of resolving the disagreement.

You can see all of these horsemen at work in the following made-up dialogue. This couple is trying to decide whose parents to visit for Thanksgiving.

He: I think we should spend Thanksgiving with my dad this year.

She: But I already told my parents we were coming!

He: We spent the last two years at your parents'.

She: That's because you don't even bother arranging anything with your side [critical].

He: I was busy [defensive].

She: Well, that's one word for it. Unlike you, I didn't sit around thinking, *Oh, I should make plans*, and then get lazy [contempt]. So don't turn around at the last minute and insist we see your dad. It's really selfish [criticism].

He: You always have to get your way [criticism]. I don't know why I even try to talk to you. You're ridiculous [contempt]!

(He looks down and away and falls silent.)

She: So, what . . . now you're going to ignore me and sulk?

He: (*Silent.*) [stonewalling.]

She: Hello? Anybody home? Figures [contempt].

Last Stop: The Roach Motel for Lovers

What happens when a relationship becomes trapped in back-and-forth negativity? The tragic consequence of the roach motel is, of course, the erosion and eventual death of the couple's trust in each other. She thinks, *He doesn't care how I feel*, and he thinks, *Why can't she be more loving?* They cannot break out of this prison. Each is convinced that the other only cares about his or her own payoffs. If this perception is not altered through skillful intervention that strengthens their ability to attune, they come to believe their once-trustworthy partner is not just ignoring their payoffs, but working against them. In time, the couple transform into adversaries locked in a zero-sum game—it's her payoffs *versus* his in a fight to the finish. The real loser, of course, is their love.

Broken relationships may end in divorce or linger for years, filling the air with shrill confrontations or heavy silences. When such a couple enters therapy, the counselor is likely to focus on improving their communication and negotiation skills. But any form or approach to therapy will be futile without recognition of the fundamental issue: the two no longer trust each other. If these unfortunate couples do not receive guidance in attuning, they become at risk for all kinds of devastating betrayals, including infidelity.

3

"I Didn't Mean for It to Happen" (Why Cheaters Cheat)

I can almost guarantee that whenever you happen to be reading this chapter, the gossip world will be abuzz with lurid details of a celebrity or a politician caught with those proverbial pants down. There are many reasons for our culture's fascination with high-profile strayers. But if your own world has been blown apart by an affair, or you fear that it might be, you are unlikely to care about the latest headline-making scandal or even statistics about how many other people share your misery. Instead, you want to know how and why it happened to you, whether your relationship is salvageable (or *should* be saved), and if future infidelity is preventable.

As painful as the circumstance may be, it is possible for a couple to recover from an affair—though it is not easy. Betrayal can be a red flag that calls attention to deficiencies in a relationship that led at least one partner to feel lonely and devalued. Cheating is a high-risk and, let's face it, stupid approach to fostering change. But it is not impossible for it to lead to a stronger commitment if its causes are understood and addressed.

No repair, however, is possible if the cheater is deemed an immoral monster. It is understandable for the victim to feel devastated and enraged. Yet, despite all of those sensational headlines, people who stray are not evil. When laboratory and clinical research analyze infidelity with dispassion, the relationship itself turns out to be the cause in most cases.

It is rare for a partner to transform into a cheater overnight. He or she heads down the path unwittingly and at a slow, undetected pace. This is why so many affairs seem to come out of nowhere. Consider this couple, a composite of many I have studied at the Love Lab. When James married Marion, he was a successful photographer who supported her while she attended cooking school. When we fast-forward ten years, James's business has been hit hard by the rise of do-it-yourself digital photography, while Marion has just begun a new job as top chef at a highly rated local restaurant. She is excited but worries that she won't measure up. Whenever she confides her anxiety to James, he dismisses her concerns and tells her to be more positive and optimistic. That's the same advice he has always given himself. He thinks he's being supportive, but she perceives his words as dismissive and feels wounded. *But she doesn't tell him.*

Meanwhile, although James acts proud of Marion's success, inside he's feeling great anxiety and self-doubt. The unexpected disparity in their career prospects and incomes triggers memories of his domineering mother, who belittled his father constantly. These fears are heightened because Marion is so busy working that it seems she isn't there for him. Feeling lonely and resentful, he begins to think that his wife is selfish, smug, and superior. He imagines having a partner who would be more loving and supportive of his current struggle. James nurses his resentment and finds himself thinking a lot about one of his old girlfriends who admired him—a stark contrast to how he believes Marion perceives him these days. He shares none of these thoughts or feelings with his wife.

Because they both remain silent about their discontent, James and Marion find themselves fuming inside and keeping their distance from each other. They are on their way toward absorbing negativity and distrust. It might be apparent to us that their relationship is in danger, but couples in this situation often do not perceive and acknowledge that they are in trouble. It's far easier for them to assume that they are going through a "bad patch." At this point, if asked, Marion and James would affirm their mutual love and support and balk at the notion that either of them would ever cheat. And they both would mean it.

One rainy morning at the local coffee bar a redheaded woman drops her umbrella on James's foot. She apologizes, he reassures her, and they commence one of those pleasant, superficial conversations not atypical of people waiting in line for lattes. When she leaves with her coffee, she flashes him a huge smile, which surprises him and also gives him quite a lift. The next day, he runs into her again, and they end up sitting at adjacent tables. They begin to chat, exchanging names (hers is June) and the broad outlines of their lives. She's a computer analyst and lives in a neighboring town. Like him, she is a fan of silent films. Also she is single. James glances around as their conversation continues, but then he relaxes: What could be more innocent than discussing similar interests with a person sitting at the next table in a crowded coffee bar? Okay, he finds June attractive—but it's not the first time he's appreciated a woman other than his wife. But he hasn't come on to her. And besides, he's been sure to mention Marion more than once during their conversation.

As weeks pass, James and June become coffee bar buddies. One morning, after he and Marion squabble, James finds he's less upset than usual because he's thinking of June. Without admitting it to himself, he begins to take extra care while shaving and combing his hair on the days he hopes to run into her. He always feels disappointed when she isn't there. Slowly, June divulges details of her life. She broke up with a guy last year when he got cold feet about marriage. She's been trying out some online dating sites but hasn't met anybody "normal." "I can't believe that someone as gorgeous as you can't get a date!" says James and then blinks in embarrassment.

Their friendship progresses when a Charlie Chaplin film festival opens at a local theater. Isn't it natural for him to suggest they go together? Marion is busy and hates silent movies anyway. So now James and June exchange cell phone numbers and email addresses. Attending films together—and not just silent ones—becomes a frequent event. James still hasn't mentioned his new friend to Marion because she might misinterpret his intentions. That would lead to another big fight. In the interests of being considerate and avoiding conflict, James keeps what he considers a small secret. Besides, he thinks, he gets together with June only when his wife is working late, and June knows he's married. He convinces himself there's no harm in what he's doing.

In time, James confides in June about his marital troubles. She proves an empathetic listener. She advises him to work out his issues with Marion and avoid the misery of divorce (she's been there). He also tells her something even Marion doesn't know: He's on the shortlist for a big job at an advertising agency. June expresses such interest and support that he keeps her informed about his subsequent interviews. When he loses out to another candidate, James is so devastated that even his distracted wife can tell something is wrong. When he confesses his disappointment, Marion says, "If you had told me about it, maybe I could have helped you prepare for the interview and you wouldn't have blown it. Despite what you may think, I do know a thing or two."

"I don't need your help," he retorts. Another regrettable incident goes unrepaired. They both retreat and spend another silent evening in each other's "company."

The next day, when James gives June his bad news, she bolsters him with hugs and sympathy. He can't help but note the disparity between the validation she offers him and the lack of support he perceived from Marion. Unlike his wife, June isn't judgmental. She seems interested in his thoughts and ideas. When he shows her some of his photography, she gushes over his talent. It occurs to him that June offers him the respect and admiration he no longer feels from Marion. He admits what's been hovering on the edge of his consciousness for quite a while: June is a lot prettier and sexier, and nicer to him, than his wife. He fantasizes about how great life would be if he were married to her rather than to Marion. These mutinous thoughts act on his feelings. He senses an increasing emotional gulf with his wife, pushes away his guilt, and replaces that emptiness with thoughts of June.

James and June's relationship doesn't turn sexual until six months after they first meet. But his betrayal started long before then. It began even before he met June, with that first negative comparison he made between Marion and his old, admiring girlfriend. Combined with this couple's tendency to turn away and not express their feelings to each other, that negative comparison began a cascade of events that led to his actual betrayal of his wife.

James is not innocent in this tale, but neither does he sport horns and a tail. It wouldn't be unfair to see him as a well-meaning guy who was oblivious to his own vulnerability. I know that many relationship experts, having heard similar stories time and again, would say that the infidelity occurred because both James and Marion neglected their marriage. They'll say that like automobiles, all relationships need a "tune-up" now and then to keep the engine running smoothly. There is truth to this belief: even if you buy the car of your dreams, in ten years it will be a miserable wreck if you don't maintain it. But people are not cars! Although neglect plays a large role in marital dissatisfaction, it is not enough to land either partner in someone else's arms.

How Cheating Becomes a Possibility

We've already walked through the trajectory that causes a couple's trust metric to plummet. It begins with the tendency to turn away and ignore the partner's emotions. Then there's flooding, a pileup of unresolved regrettable incidents, the Zeigarnik effect, the development of absorbing negativity, and in the end, *distrust*. All of this has begun in James and Marion's marriage. They are dismissive of each other's feelings and don't pick up signs of their partner's distress. Slowly, they begin to keep their dissatisfactions secret. They avoid confiding their needs in order to prevent absorbing conflict. This attempt to "save" the relationship has the opposite effect—it gradually drops the couple's trust metric and brings them ever closer to getting stuck in the roach motel.

This sad trajectory destroys a relationship by turning partners into adversaries, but it does not always position the couple for a betrayal. To my surprise, 30 percent of couples who are locked in miserable, endless battle remain trustworthy. Though their trust metric has plummeted and they are entrenched in a zero-sum game, they still sacrifice for the relationship and put it first. They do not have affairs or otherwise betray each other. In some cases, couples remain loyal because their faith commits them to the sanctity of the family. Depression and low self-esteem can also keep couples from leaving each other. There is much sadness in these relationships.

But in the remaining 70 percent of miserable couples, at least one partner's trustworthiness metric plummets. He or she no longer considers the relationship sacred and is not willing to put it first. Then the betrayal metric increases. When at least one partner rates low in trustworthiness, the relationship stumbles down a trajectory that leads not just to the roach motel, but also to faithlessness.

The Final Poison of Betrayal: The Negative COMP

In the presence of untrustworthiness, negative sliding door moments lead to a poison that I call a negative COMP (or negative comparison). The untrustworthy partner doesn't just turn away. At the same time, he or she compares the partner to someone else, real or imaginary—and the partner loses. For example, Carl hears Priscilla sigh as she looks at his paycheck. Instead of asking her what that sigh meant, he thinks, *My brother's wife, Jeannie, never makes* him *feel bad about his salary.* A tendency to make such negative COMPs—whether the desired "other" is real or imagined— primes the partner for future betrayal.

Although the concept of positive and negative COMPs has long been part of social psychology's research into relationships, for many years it wasn't all that useful because a couple's COMPs could not be measured in a lab. But in a huge contribution to our field, the late, and great, research psychologist Dr. Caryl Rusbult devised a simple self-report questionnaire that assessed each partner's level of devotion. In a series of studies over three decades, she found that commitment is a gradual process in which the partners come to compare the relationship favorably to others with increasing frequency.

For James, the tendency to make negative COMPs begins before he meets June. He finds himself often thinking about his old girlfriend, comparing her admiration of him to the scorn he now perceives from his wife. A game theorist would say that James begins to evaluate the payoffs he receives from his marriage versus what he would get in another relationship, and his wife comes up short. And then along comes June.

It is natural for people in romantic relationships to weigh their current circumstance against other possibilities, real or imagined. If a man smiles at his wife and she returns it, he may think, *Wow, what a beautiful smile. She gets to me like no other woman ever has.* But on another day, her smile may not be so high-wattage, leaving him a bit disappointed. So he thinks, *Darn! I was being flirtatious, and she just didn't get it. I bet that sexy woman over there would have given me a much bigger reaction.* That's a trivial negative COMP and not harmful to a relationship. But over time a succession of such thoughts, made while turning away, can begin the cascade toward betrayal. When Marion pales in comparison to June, James's marriage takes another tumble down the slope toward faithlessness.

Caryl Rusbult found that early in a committed relationship,

positive COMPs reinforce the conviction that "this is the right relationship for me." Partners begin to cherish each other to an increasing degree and feel grateful for their mate's positive qualities. Simultaneously, they minimize their partner's negative traits. When Sharon meets her friend Jodie for lunch, her mind engages in a quick head-to-head between her husband and Jodie's boyfriend. She thinks: *Poor Jodie. Pete is so difficult and has no sense of humor. I'm lucky that Tony is so sweet and funny.* Sharon's fleeting positive COMP increases her gratitude and bolsters her commitment to Tony.

Couples who enjoy an overall positive COMP denigrate alternative matches and develop a sort of "us against the world" attitude. Their number of "pro-relationship" thoughts increases as their dependency on the relationship to meet their emotional needs grows. They come to believe that losing each other would be catastrophic. When times get rough for a couple, the cumulative results of these positive COMPs can help pull them through. Despite increased conflict in her twenty-year marriage, a woman named Shelley says, "Even though Bill gets maddening at times, whenever I look around at my friends' husbands, I feel so lucky. I couldn't imagine being married to anyone else." Although she doesn't realize it, Shelley *had* just imagined alternatives to Bill. He won hands-down.

In contrast, a partner who engages in frequent negative COMPs is feeling buyer's remorse and believes, *I can do better than this.* When I think of the damage wreaked by negative COMPs, I'm often reminded of Abby and Tyler, a young couple who consulted me after five different therapy attempts had failed to bolster their four-year marriage.

Abby works part-time and tends to most of the child care for their school-aged twins, while Tyler is a full-time computer technician. Although his wife handles a disproportionate amount of the child care, Tyler thinks he deserves to spend at least two days a week playing golf with friends after work rather than helping Abby at home. He argues that since he is the primary breadwinner, this "time off" is a fair exchange for the money he earns. He bargains with Abby for the best deal he can get. Not surprisingly, Abby does not agree with his perspective. Over time, in Abby's eyes, Tyler's untrustworthiness increases. He seems to be out only for himself, negotiating with her for the best golfing deal he can get, for example. She is exhausted from the burden of constant child care and resents his absences. By not responding to her needs and by dismissing her requests for child-care relief, Tyler erodes his wife's trust metric. He doesn't consider or act to increase *her* payoffs. He dismisses her complaints, countering with complaints of his own. When she feels down, he tells her that he has it much worse. Tyler and Abby experience many sliding door moments that do not end well. Their sense of disconnection is increasing. Yet so far neither has been unfaithful.

One night at a party, Tyler is engrossed in conversation with an appealing woman named Elise when a tired Abby taps his shoulder, ready to go home. He agrees, but his reluctance is obvious. On the way out the door (he tells me later), he is thinking: *Elise is so much hotter and happier than Abby. My life would be much better if I were married to her instead.* During the car ride home, he complains to Abby that his life has too much drudgery and not enough enjoyment. His wife knows him well enough to understand that she is being compared with Elise, and a nasty argument ensues. Abby lets Tyler know that she wishes she were "married to someone who appreciated me and understood how hard and exhausting my life is." Another negative COMP.

Focusing on "what ifs" is a pattern for Tyler and Abby.

Whenever one of them turns away, thoughts like *Who needs this crap?* are joined by *I'd be happier with someone else.* No wonder those five attempts at therapy were ineffective. The more the inevitable stresses of life rock Abby and Tyler, the more they fantasize about alternatives. Their fundamental problem is not frequent arguments, Tyler's flirtations, or his resistance to fully engaging in life as a father and husband. Their marriage isn't working because, as Rusbult's research shows, they haven't yet committed to each other. Their fantasies of other options show that they both treat their relationship as conditional and marginal. This allows Tyler to be selfish and Abby to feel abandoned—and both to feel justified in turning away. After all, things could be so much better with somebody else.

Abby and Tyler were stunned by the revelation that they were trying to save a marriage that hadn't yet begun. When I last checked in with them, they were again in therapy, making progress by focusing on opening up and turning toward each other during sliding door moments.

Many people in committed relationships make negative COMPs without admitting it to themselves or their spouse. They push those dangerous thoughts away or dismiss them because they assume that "everyone" has them now and then. There is truth to that. But when these musings are *combined with a pattern of turning away and not acknowledging feelings*, as they are with Jim, Tyler, and Abby, they are toxic. By ignoring them, couples miss a major warning that their relationship is heading for trouble.

When couples are stuck in the roach motel and are making negative COMPs, their relationship spirals downward. The more they become trapped in negativity, the more they entertain negative COMPs. These in turn further the unhappiness, triggering more negative thoughts, and down, down, down . . . The roach motel and a preponderance of negative COMPs form what I call the "germ of betrayal." When someone new enters one partner's life, the potential for unfaithfulness is there already. This happens even if, like James, the culprit keeps telling himself, *I'd never let anything happen.*

From Potential to Reality:
The Cheater's Cascade

We now understand *what* it is that primes couples for infidelity: a lack of sharing the true self combined with negative COMPs. But *how* does this "germ of betrayal" lead to behavior that breaks the partner's heart? Why not exercise self-control and act with decency? I believe it's far more fruitful to turn to science for an answer than to focus on human failings. To label perpetrators as evil does not help prevent infidelity nor encourage healing.

From its onset, the march toward infidelity weakens the relationship's "walls" and "windows," as described by the late psychologist Shirley Glass, in her famous book, *Not "Just Friends."* Typically, partners in a long-term, committed relationship keep a window open between each other while erecting walls that protect their privacy from the outside world. This scenario doesn't mean that the two bond only with each other. They both have a life and experiences outside of the relationship—work, family, friends, pursuits. But they each carry within them the safety of this refuge, which is founded on their intimacy and trust in each other. However, once the germ of betrayal invades, toxins assault their refuge without anyone noticing.

First Comes Secret Keeping

The attack forces gear up when partners stop confiding in each other, which leads them to maintain secrets. The silence may descend when a spate of regrettable incidents weakens the couple's commitment. Partners are vulnerable in particular when there are significant life changes such as a new baby or job, or an unforeseen trauma such as a parent's death, illness, a troubled child. Such circumstances can test even the strongest relationship, underlining differences in background, temperament, beliefs. At these times, when one partner reaches out and the other is "missing," disappointment and loneliness will prevail if they don't discuss these regrettable incidents. The avoidance may not be obvious, especially if the couple have vocal fights about the issue. But they are arguing "around" it, leaving the hurt unaddressed and never repaired.

Once there's a history of ignoring and dismissing each other's emotions, and a subsequent decline in each partner's trust metric, the couple may seek to avoid conflict so that the situation doesn't worsen. They steer clear of volatile issues, shoving them under the rug until, as the poet Robert Creely put it, "the rug bunches." They then give wide berth to a now bumpy rug. When couples avoid rocking the boat they may even believe they are *helping* the relationship by having some of their needs met *outside* of it.

When a relationship is so fragile, it can seem counterproductive to confide something that may hurt the partner. What is James supposed to say to Marion when he first meets June? "Guess what, honey, I was at the Cup and Brew today and this amazing woman started talking to me. It felt great!" To put all of that in context for Marion, he would have to let her know that her new job has made him feel vulnerable and "unmanly." No way is he going to confess all of that, maybe not even to himself! Conflict avoiders such as

James equate negative emotions with dynamite. If he told Marion about his inner tumult, he would feel like a marital suicide bomber. So he doesn't mention June or the complex emotions that meeting her has stirred. He ignores it and becomes more likely to "just" make negative COMPs.

But by not confiding in Marion, James deprives her of the opportunity to show support and love. To use Glass's terminology, the lack of disclosure erects a wall *between* the partners that replaces the open window of trust. The result is emotional distance that makes the secret keeper feel lonely.

It doesn't help people like James that our culture so often blames infidelity on a simple lack of discipline or moral character in the face of sexual temptation. In fact, the research evidence suggests that the vast majority of affairs are *not* caused by lust. Fleeting sexual attractions are a part of human biology. Even the most attuned long-term relationship does not blind members to the allure of others. But if the relationship is satisfying both partners' emotional needs, they build a wide fence around these lustful thoughts. Inside a strong relationship, it isn't necessary for partners to divulge their brief attractions to others. But if your trust metric is low, you do need to talk about them, even if it seems that doing so would be destructive. To illustrate the difference, imagine a couple passes a beautiful woman on the street. The husband takes a quick look. His wife notices his wandering eye and asks, "Do you think she's prettier than me?" If the two have a powerful sexual and emotional connection the man can say, "Nah—you're much more beautiful." Perhaps that even qualifies as a white lie. Even if the wife knows he's being untruthful, she'll recognize the love and respect behind the fib. On the other hand, if distrust has poisoned this couple's pleasure in each other, it would be destructive for the husband to avoid the issue by denying the attraction.

I'm not suggesting a cruel response. "Yes—she is much hotter!" is not going to help his relationship. But it would be beneficial if he answered, "I do sometimes notice other women. I think it's because we haven't been talking or having sex much, and it's starting to get to me. I miss you. I miss *us*." I admit that's tough to say, but it's worth it. (You'll find advice on how to have this kind of difficult conversation in chapter 9.)

Next: Walls and Windows Reverse

The greatest danger to the architecture of what I call the "sound relationship house" occurs when unhappiness causes a partner like James to unburden his heart—to the *new* person. He makes his new companion privy to his troubles at home. Now, instead of a wall surrounding the two partners, there's a new wall closing them off from each other and a window has opened between the partner and his or her new friend. This reversal is what James experiences when he starts to confide in June about his life with Marion. But the trouble doesn't stop there. Like James, many "perpetrators" can't bear to lose this new person who offers solace and connection. They build a wall *around the new relationship* to keep it safe from the primary partner.

The Deceiver Trashes the Partner and the Relationship

It is almost inevitable that once you form a coalition with someone other than your mate, your perspective on your long-term relationship changes. A switch is flicked. Negative Sentiment Override kicks in, and you respin the history of your relationship. You focus on your partner's negative qualities and minimize his or her positive traits. Now you see your protective partner as a control freak. His or her deep affection morphs into clinginess. Shyness transforms into snootiness. You used to cherish your partner and denigrate other relationships. Now, you denigrate the relationship and trash your partner. Before, you imagined your future together, dreamed about shared goals, felt fortunate to have found "the one." Now opposite thoughts cloud your mind. This turnaround is going to make you receptive to the sexual overtures of the potential lover.

The Betrayer Considers the *Partner* Untrustworthy

When the windows and walls reverse, making the home unsound, the relationship suffers an ironic tragedy. The potential "cheater" begins to distrust the partner. You would think the opposite would be more likely to occur. But when I analyze the interactions of these partners in the unforgiving light of the laboratory, the results are clear. Keeping a secret creates distance. The more disconnected the future cheater feels, the less he or she believes in the mate. The partner is seen as less trustworthy even though the cheater is responsible for the breach. In the Love Lab, when potential cheaters are asked to talk about their relationship, they will label their spouse as "selfish." The innocent but unhappy partner is seen as only out for himself or herself. The duplicitous partner carries two contrary thoughts: *I'm still married,* and *I'm falling in love with someone else.* To resolve this cognitive dissonance, the disloyal partner often decides that the other is to blame for how vulnerable and alone he or she feels: "It's not my fault," "I haven't done anything wrong," and "I was forced into this out of desperation."

One woman in my studies, Chelsea, was distraught over her mother's recent cancer diagnosis. She asked her husband, Grant, to cancel his rugby game and spend the day with her. But Grant decided to play anyway because without him the team would have to forfeit the game. In Grant's view, showing up for the game was the ethical choice because it disappointed fewer people. Chelsea felt bitter and hurt. But she did not insist that he stay home. By not asserting herself or making her feelings known, she deprived her husband of the opportunity to be there for her, to put her ahead of all others. Instead, as her mother's condition worsened, Chelsea began to turn for solace to her attentive and supportive tennis coach. When their friendship turned sexual, she justified it to herself by perceiving Grant as untrustworthy.

Imagine the sound relationship house being built over time. Then imagine the footage running in reverse at a rapid pace, so the building is thrown apart, brick by brick. This demolition is what a dangerous secret does to a couple. Without intervention, their love is reduced to rubble.

The Line Is Crossed

The betrayer is now primed for a sexual relationship with the new companion. There are probably as many paths to that first physical betrayal as there are affairs. The process tends to be glacial. Over a long period, people give themselves permission to cross small boundaries, to talk about intimate subjects ("I can't believe that someone as gorgeous as you can't get a date!"), confide, look into the other person's eyes, touch briefly, then less briefly, peck a cheek good-bye, then a lingering kiss, fantasize about one another, feel like they are part of a couple, and so on. But even before the new intimacy turns sexual, the cheater's ability to love the primary partner has been crippled. A weakening of the couple's emotional intimacy left the relationship house unprotected.

4

Men, Porn, and Sex Drives

The great comedian Billy Crystal once said that women need a reason to make love, but men just need a place. It would be disingenuous to dissect sexual infidelity without discussing gender differences. Psychological research mostly supports Crystal's line. On average, men are more "sex focused" than women. Whatever the possible biological and cultural causes of this disparity, it would be difficult to argue that it isn't there. Research indicates that men initiate sex far more than women in married and cohabiting heterosexual relationships. Major life events may even heighten this difference. In my research on newlywed couples, three years after the first baby's arrival, men report a desire for sex about three times a week. The women's preference: once every two weeks. That's a ratio of 6 to 1! I also found, through these couples' ongoing responses to a specialized questionnaire, that nearly 70 percent of new parents suffer a decline in the sense of friendship that fuels sexual love. The deterioration of this emotional connection leaves partners vulnerable to making negative COMPs.

A man's relatively heightened sex drive doesn't make him bad, immoral, unethical, or sinful. Still, acknowledging a gender difference does help mitigate its potential harm to a committed relationship. Common wisdom and research indicate that men may at least be more tempted to cheat. But then again, a growing body of research suggests that the female rate of extramarital affairs has been gaining on men's since women entered the work force. And it looks like women cheat sooner in the marriage than do men; for women, the itch starts at two to four years, not six or seven, according to some research.

If men tend to make more negative COMPs than women, it may be because male sexuality is more stimulated by visual input. For most women, emotional connection and touch are what stir sexual feelings. In men, sexual excitement, stimulated by the other's visible characteristics, tends to come first. The man's erotic desire may then develop into a deeper bond. Even loyal men may have a natural tendency to "notice" others. And once you've looked, there's the chance you might imagine having that someone in your life instead of your mate, if negative COMPs abound. But it's important to remember that most affairs are not about sex. They are about coping with a lonely marriage by finding someone interested in you. And that longing for companionship knows no gender.

Are Sex Addicts for Real?

It all sounds too easy—excusing one's infidelity with the claim "Don't blame me; I have a sex addiction." These days there's a perpetual revolving door of celebrity sex addicts. Yet another household name gets caught cheating, claims to be hooked on sex, and rushes to rehab. Once out, the cheating begins again. It's tempting to roll your eyes, but sex addiction does exist and is the root of some adultery.

The technical use of the term *addiction* necessitates the twin criteria of tolerance and withdrawal. The addict requires increasing stimulation to receive the same level of gratification. In time, he needs a fix just to feel "normal." If the addict quits cold turkey, intense psychological and physical pain will follow. It's not known yet whether all cases of high sexual activity meet this definition, but that doesn't prevent them from devastating a relationship.

The kind of therapy that I recommend for couples wounded by adultery (see chapter 10) can assist partners grappling with sexual addiction. But the addict will require additional professional help to overcome his or her obsessions and compulsions. This is true of relationships marred by any sort of dependency—including alcoholism and drug abuse.

Patrick Carnes's book *Out of the Shadows* is probably the most influential work on understanding and treating sexual addiction. Carnes, who treated the golfer Tiger Woods, focuses on the sexual addict's impaired thinking, which entails *rationalization and denial*. Addicts believe their own lies. Carnes posits the following sexual addiction cycle:

1. Preoccupation: every encounter and thought gets processed through the sexually obsessive filter;
2. Ritualization: routines are followed that foster the addiction;
3. Compulsive sexual behavior: engaging in the sexual act(s) at the core of the obsessions and an inability to control this behavior; and
4. Despair: feeling powerless and hopeless about being able to change.

At some point the addict settles on a specific *arousal template*—the object of the addict's obsessions and compulsions, which could be anything from certain lingerie to fantasies of domination and submission. As with other addictions, the obsessive craving overrides everything the sufferer once valued, including family, friends, work, ethics, religion, community. The addict cannot conquer the temptation and salvage the primary relationship without first reversing the impaired thinking, compulsive behavior, and unmanageable urges. To get some idea of how these compulsions lead to stupid risk taking, consider this: male exhibitionists have often been known to display their genitals to women from moving vehicles, thus causing car accidents!

When Porn Begets Betrayal

There are more than 500 million pages of porn on the internet—almost all of it directed at men. Pornography is an industry that generates more than $97 billion a year worldwide. It's no surprise that there is an abiding link between pornography and sex addiction. Even noncompulsive use of these images can damage a committed relationship. Masturbating to an image results in the secretion of oxytocin and vasopressin, hormones linked to attachment. Porn users are in danger of becoming attached to a mere fetish of impersonal sex.

Addiction is not a concern if a couple uses porn to enhance their mutual desire and pleasure during lovemaking. Too often, however, porn is viewed solo and becomes a source of betrayal even if the habit doesn't meet the technical definition of compulsive. Most porn encourages steps that we've already seen can lead to betrayal.

Dismissal of Connection and Emotion

Pornographic scenarios almost always focus on the impersonal and the physical. They depict unromantic, unemotional, and casual sex. Social psychologists Dolf Zillmann and Jennings Bryant analyzed erotica in the book *Pornography*, concluding that in typical pornographic scripts, strangers meet, have sex, and never see each other again. Problems can arise if a regular consumer of porn expects sex in the bedroom to be similar. The porn user may want the partner to act out with him a fantasy that upsets her. He may now "need" this scenario made real in order to become stimulated, because he has so often masturbated while watching or looking at porn that depicts it. Overuse of porn can also lead to an emotional disconnect between a couple. Research by Jennifer Schneider finds that in 70 percent of couples in which one partner has a cybersex addiction, at least one of the couple has lost interest in their sex life.

Secret Keeping

Most porn users feel they must hide this deep fascination from their partner. The secret itself creates distance and diminishes intimacy, which may in turn increase the use of porn.

Negative COMPs

Again, every orgasm results in the secretion of oxytocin and in males, vasopressin, the hormones that fuel emotional connection. The greater the orgasm (as measured in the lab), the more they are secreted. During pornographic activity, orgasms lead to bonding with *images not of the partner*. This lowers the erotic value of the partner by comparison.

Trashing the Partner

As websites continue to push the limits, there is an increase in images that combine sex with degradation and violence, particularly toward women. Most of the fantasies involve power and control over women to satisfy the man. This expectation can traumatize a partner who agrees to act out humiliating fantasies or alienate a disgusted partner who refuses. Either scenario is harmful.

Gateway

Porn serves as a ladder toward actual infidelity, thanks to all of those voyeuristic sites, chat rooms, phone sex come-ons, and opportunities to hook up with professional sex workers or amateurs in one's neighborhood. A "typical" descent from porn to cheating goes as follows: viewing photos, then videos, finding what turns you on fastest and with the most intensity (a particular body type or kind of sexual role play), chatting online with someone with a compatible obsession, fantasizing about meeting in real life, and giving yourself permission to cross boundaries.

If porn is undermining your relationship—or you fear that it might—there is plenty that you can do. The following chapters offer insight and advice to help you open up about personal issues in your life in a way that increases your intimacy. In addition, individual therapy can help the compulsive porn user explore the issues underpinning the problem.

5

Ten Other Ways to Betray a Lover

The devastation of sexual disloyalty is not the only breach of trust that can ruin a relationship. Other forms of betrayal can be just as damaging as an affair, but too often go unrecognized or minimized, including by the victim. When a couple keeps getting stuck in the Nasty box and each feels the other does not put the relationship first, they may not recognize that their trouble is really betrayal. They puzzle over why they are discontented and fighting with no end. They may say their partner has "changed," or they have "grown apart," or are "no longer compatible."

Negative COMPs are at the heart of nonsexual disloyalties just as much as they form the core of affairs. In these cases, when the partner comes up short compared with another, the disgruntled member doesn't cheat but instead expresses disrespect and devalues the relationship in other ways. In some cases, the partner compares the other unfavorably with a *situation* rather than a person. (*If only I had taken that job in New York and not married, everything in my life would be better.*) Although the disrespect may foreshadow infidelity, for many couples these betrayals are themselves the endpoint.

Sometimes both partners are aware that one is making negative COMPs, but neither acknowledges nor recognizes the danger. They figure that no one is ever completely satisfied with their life, right? The disloyalty doesn't seem "as bad as" an affair. But it is. A committed relationship is a contract of mutual trust, respect, nurturance, and protection. *Anything* that violates that contract can become traitorous. True, some betrayal is inevitable between partners. It creeps into even the strongest bond because it's impossible to be in sync all the time. What separates trustworthy couples from others is that they have found a way to correct or get past these missteps so that betrayal does not consume their relationship.

Relationship killers are founded on two building blocks: deception (not revealing your true needs to avoid unpleasant conflict) and a yearning for emotional connection that seems unavailable from the partner. Below are ten common ways I have seen betrayal play itself out in relationships. (It wouldn't surprise me to find new forms of deceit in the future.) Only by confronting any disloyalty present in their relationship can the couple reestablish their trust in each other.

Please note: The worst kind of betrayal—physical or emotional abuse perpetrated to control the victim of the violence—is not on this list. Do not use this book to improve such a relationship. Any kind of unwanted touch signals physical abuse, including forced, unwanted touch in the bedroom. Emotional abuse includes social isolation, sexual coercion, extreme jealousy, public humiliation, belittling, or degrading, threats of violence or other acts that induce fear, or damage to property, pets, or children. If your partner is abusive, acknowledge to yourself that you don't deserve such treatment and enlist help. There are many nonprofit organizations and governmental programs poised to assist people in your situation. You deserve support.

Look over the list below and see if any of these situations feel familiar or trigger uneasiness. If so, you may be facing a betrayal with the potential to be as serious as finding steamy text messages between your partner and someone else. This list isn't about condemning or giving up on your relationship. It isn't about who's right or wrong. As with sexual affairs, these betrayals can be overcome if you recognize the problem and repair the relationship. I've listed them in no particular order—they are all perilous.

1. Conditional Commitment

The underlying attitude is: "I'm here for you . . . until someone better comes along." Tyler and Abby, whom we met in chapter 3, are a classic example of this betrayal. Such partners may flirt, ogle, and send out other signals that they are available, even though they don't follow through. Because they are not fully in the relationship, anything from an argument to the flu to work stress can diminish how much intimacy and support their partner receives. It's not unusual for the betrayed partner to think these triggers are the actual problem ("She's worried about that promotion") when it's the superficiality of the commitment that fuels all those conflicts.

Couples may tumble into a conditional relationship when one pressures the other to marry or cohabitate, thinking the move will deepen their connection. It is almost always an error to marry when you don't want to. It's hard for a marriage to succeed if it is an attempt to *create* a strong bond rather than the *result* of one. The shallowness becomes more apparent as time goes on. Anna recalls her first marriage, which began to unravel when her husband stalled about starting a family. At first she thought he was ambivalent about becoming a father. But when they went to couples' therapy it became clear that his reluctance was about deepening his commitment to her. She responded with a mix of clinginess and desperation, terrified of losing what she had, until she accepted that she never really had it. "Now that I'm remarried, and we have kids, it's easy to look back and realize that my first husband just wasn't really there. He had betrayed me just as much as if he really followed through on his flirtations. Now I realize what a real commitment is from a partner."

In some cases of conditional commitment, one partner isn't comparing the other to someone else, but to *something* else. Deirdre and her longtime boyfriend married so that he could be covered by her health insurance. Still, she considered herself in a "forever" relationship. Then her husband developed a passionate interest in China. He read about the country in his spare time, learned Mandarin, and devoted his vacations to traveling through the country. When he was offered a career-changing job that allowed him to move there, Deirdre didn't want to go. He went anyway, and divorce papers followed. This couple floundered because their shared meaning system decayed. Intimate partners need to open up about what they consider the purpose and significance of their life together. When couples ignore or avoid discussing deep issues, they are left with a shallow commitment. To prevent this, couples can intentionally take time to discuss their goals and dreams, rather than wait for the opportunity to occur.

2. A Nonsexual Affair

It's common for platonic friendships to develop if you are in the trenches with somebody day after day. Some people refer to on-the-job camaraderie as having a "work wife" or "work husband," though you can also forge such connections at the gym, a favorite watering hole or café, or while pursuing a hobby or volunteer work. These relationships are nonsexual by definition, but buddies may get to know intimate details about each other's lives. Having a work wife or work husband is not necessarily a betrayal. Here's the rule: If you think your partner would be uncomfortable watching your interactions with this person, or be upset by the confidences you've shared, the closeness is dangerous. You are reversing the walls and windows of your sound relationship house to hide the new friendship. Should your partner discover a knowing email from this "other," the result can be as devastating as telltale aftershave or perfume on the bedroom sheets.

Margo learns of her husband's sexless affair when they host a backyard picnic for his fellow middle-school teachers. Ken has never mentioned Vicky, the new head of the math department, so imagine Margo's surprise when the woman arrives at the event already knowing the family's cockapoo by name and chiding him for always chewing on Ken's socks. Vicky seems privy to all of Ken's "little ways." She even brings bubble pops for the kids—their favorite treat. Margot raises an eyebrow at Ken. How does this woman know so much? Ken looks sheepish and Margo's stomach falls. Later, when his wife confronts him, Ken argues that his friendship with Vicky is "no big deal" because they are "just friends." He accuses Margo of being irrational and jealous, saying this is why he had kept quiet about Vicky. He knew Margo would go ballistic. Margo is certain there is nothing irrational about her fury and jealousy. Whether or not he can admit it to himself, her husband is cheating. The proof lies in his secrecy.

Jasmine faced a surprisingly common version of this "buddy" problem. Her husband, Charlie, never detached himself from his first wife. Whenever Alice needed help, Charlie galloped in. Jasmine respected her husband for his compassion. He was a "stand-up" guy who knew Alice was struggling with the aftermath of their split. But Jasmine's patience only went so far. One night she arrived home from work to discover Alice sipping peppermint tea on *her* sofa.

"The power went out in her house," Charlie explained.

"Hasn't she ever heard of a *hotel*?" Jasmine hissed. She gave her husband an ultimatum that night: "me or her." Charlie agreed to cut off contact with Alice.

How do you know if your partner's shared connection with someone else is a sexless affair and not an innocent friendship? Is the friendship hidden? Are your questions about the friendship discouraged? Have you asked for it to end and hit a brick wall? Have your boundaries been disrespected ("I asked you not to go to concerts with him")? Is the friend the subject of fantasies during rough patches in the relationship? If the answer to any of these questions is "yes," the friendship is too intimate.

3. Lying

It's easy to see why plain old deceit would damage a relationship. Sometimes both partners are guilty of this behavior. Although Emma and Wayne consider themselves "happily married," frequent, winner-take-all arguments mark their relationship. They start to keep secrets from each other to avoid mounting tension.

Without his wife's knowledge, Wayne doles out money to his jobless, substance-abusing brother. When Emma questions the cash withdrawals from their checking account, Wayne claims he used the money to take clients out to dinner. He knows Emma would be furious if she discovered where the money was really going. Emma only finds out the truth when Wayne's mother calls and begs her to stop Wayne from funding his brother. The ready cash is preventing him from seeking treatment.

Emma is livid. When she confronts Wayne, he shouts out the truth. "I didn't tell you because I knew you'd blow your stack just like you're doing now. You couldn't care less about him. But he's my brother."

Meanwhile, Emma carries on a deceit of her own. She believes that their first-grade son Daniel could use extra help in reading (his teacher agrees), but Wayne is adamant that Daniel is fine and refuses to have a learning specialist evaluate him. An anxious Emma takes Daniel for an assessment without Wayne's knowledge. Daniel is diagnosed with dyslexia. Emma is upset but relieved that the problem has been identified. When she gives Wayne the news, he is furious and hurt that she snuck around him. Her deceit makes it difficult for both of them to focus on their son's problem.

Lies that are uttered to maintain the peace are a breach of trust. Although they are harmful, they do not have to ruin a relationship. Once they are exposed, you can work on the issues that prompted them. But there's another type of lying that should concern you in a partner. There are people who lie all of the time. These chronic fibbers spin out mistruths even when there is no threat to the relationship. The lying is not the other partner's fault, nor due to relationship problems. It is fundamental to the person's character. Chronic lying is a pattern established in childhood if parents are punitive, cold, authoritarian, or dismissive of emotions. The child learns to lie to look good and escape the parent's harsh judgments. In adulthood, this tendency to lie is hard to overcome even when the threat of punishment no longer exists. The help of a psychotherapist may be necessary to break this habit so that an open, honest, and intimate connection with a partner is possible.

4. Forming a Coalition Against the Partner

After five years of marriage, Connie still runs major life decisions by her mother. She asks the older woman's opinions (given with great eagerness) about areas of life that her husband Tom insists should be off-limits, such as how they organize their finances and discipline their children. If Tom and her mother give Connie conflicting advice, she takes her mom's. Worse, the two women have formed what he calls the Let's Criticize Tom Club. They comment on the way he manages his job, the clothes he wears (except the ones that Connie buys him), and even the way he talks. Whenever the couple have an argument, Connie vents to her mother. Connie and her mother are "ganging up" on her husband.

In counseling, Connie blames Tom for his bitterness, insisting that he is overreacting and being unfair. She is close to her mother, what is wrong with that? Through therapy, Connie comes to understand the difference between maintaining a bond with her mother, which is healthy, and forming a coalition against her husband, which is anything but. Tom's anger is understandable because Connie is denying him the emotional support we all expect from our partner. She needs to keep her mother out of her marriage. Only when she acknowledges how betrayed Tom feels and the legitimacy of his complaint, does their relationship improve. (Her mother is hurt by this change and tries to reel Connie back in by increasing her criticisms of Tom, but she is now not successful.)

Another even more common coalition is between the husband and *his* mother. The wife doesn't get along with her mother-in-law, who always seems to butt in. The husband, called on to mediate between the two women, betrays his wife by siding with his mother. ("She's just trying to help," "Don't be so sensitive," "She means well.") This dynamic is the underlying cause of the battle in the first place. The women are vying to come first in this man's life. It is the husband's responsibility to send his mother a clear message that his wife is his priority. He will not tolerate criticism of her. The husband must also keep silent about intimate details of their married life, in particular when he and his wife are having a conflict. He may need to cut back on how much time he spends with his mother or the frequency of phone calls if they are interfering with his relationship.

5. Absenteeism or Coldness

The morning that almost ended Tina's marriage began with her father suffering what would be a fatal coronary. Her husband, Gene, apologized that he couldn't go to the hospital with her because he had a critical meeting. She sat in the waiting room sobbing—and not just over her father's precarious condition. She was in deep emotional pain, but when she called her husband, she got bumped to his voicemail. Tina tried to convince herself that Gene needed to be at that meeting. It was important for their future. She bucked up and didn't let him know how hurt and abandoned she felt. But in a clear example of the Zeigarnik effect, she kept stewing about this unresolved issue, becoming cold and distant from her husband. She turned away during sliding door moments and seemed indifferent to his concerns. "It was like she left the marriage. It felt like she was untouchable by me," said Gene. When he asked Tina what was wrong, she always responded, "Nothing." He attributed the change in his wife to sorrow over losing her dad.

Gene made a critical mistake in not putting his wife first at a time of emotional need. But Tina's subsequent coldness put their marriage in danger. Both reactions contributed to the downward spiral that eventually led them to consider separating. In a long-delayed conversation one evening, Tina bridged the breach when she told him how infuriated and rejected she felt by his absence. Her honesty led him to admit haltingly that he had hidden behind his work that day because he felt inadequate to help her cope with her sorrow. He was afraid that he would say the wrong thing. He expressed genuine surprise over how much his actions had hurt her. Although still wounded by his withdrawal, Tina now considered whether it might have been based on love, not selfishness. She agreed to couples' therapy, where they were able to repair the gulf between them.

Emotional absenteeism doesn't have to be so dramatic. It can be as simple as turning away on a consistent basis when a partner needs emotional support about mundane events, such as a friend standing her up or anxiety over giving a speech. A committed relationship requires being there for each other both through life-changing traumas and everyday stresses. It also means sharing in your partner's joy when good happens. It's true that couples may have different needs for expressiveness. But in a committed relationship a calibration occurs in which each learns what the other requires to feel loved, protected, and supported.

Not all cases of emotional absenteeism are solvable, however. Some people are just unable and unwilling to express warmth and emotional support. When a partner lacks empathy, the relationship will flounder in time, except in rare cases where both people are happiest in an emotionally distant union. Most of us will feel deep rejection if our partner doesn't express affection (and sex doesn't count if it doesn't include an emotional connection).

When you enter a relationship with somebody who lacks empathy, you may assume that your partner is just reserved and will loosen up over time. But he or she does not. Some people have learned to cover up this lack of feeling by imitating the emotions of others. It may take years for the partner to realize the other isn't just the "silent type." But eventually the coldness and pretense of caring come to be recognized as cruelty—a character flaw often intertwined with a need for power and control. Elaine, a stay-at-home mother, said to her husband in therapy, "It would mean so much to me if you said I was doing a great job with the kids, because I *am*." Andrew's answer: "No, I can't do that. I don't like compliments. Don't want 'em. Don't give 'em. That's just who I am. I comment only if something needs fixing. So I'm just not ever going to say that to you." Elaine had to accept that Andrew would never say that he valued her.

6. Withdrawal of Sexual Interest

The standard advice to rev things up with tantalizing lingerie, a weekend away, massage oil, etc., may help if distractions from work, kids, and other stresses or obligations have rendered the bedroom a "no-touch" zone. But a dwindling sexual life cannot be easily jump-started if the problem is related to deeper issues. The inevitable physical changes related to aging could make one or both partners feel insecure and undesirable but too embarrassed to reach out for reassurance. I've seen many cases in which a woman's struggle with weight gain leads a clueless husband to insult her attractiveness. The issue here is usually negative COMPs and disrespect. The partner is not being cherished. There are also many couples with mismatched sexual drives. There is even some evidence that about 15 percent of heterosexual couples over the age of forty-five simply stop having sex. Surprisingly, it is usually the man who loses interest. Many of these couples say this waning does not diminish their relationship satisfaction. But if this withdrawal is not addressed in an honest and loving way, hurt and rejection can consume the relationship. Let's face it: whatever the partner's reason, withdrawal of sexual intimacy is wounding. You'll find specifics about addressing issues of sexual unhappiness in chapter 11.*

7. Disrespect

Bobby's wife was never coy about her contempt. "Why can't you do anything right?" she yelled when he dented the car. She called him a "crazy idiot" when he wanted to change jobs. And yet she was shocked when he walked out the door. Jody's husband was more subtle. Whenever they disagreed, he'd stare at her in disbelief and say, "Any reasonable and intelligent person would see that your way makes no sense." (In other words, you're a crazy idiot!) Todd rolled his eyes when Mindy suggested they cancel the dinner plans with *his* friends in favor of hers when they double-booked.

Whatever your partner's communication style, if he or she

---

*For a game-theory analysis of why some couples stop having sex and the surprising solution, see Appendix 3, p. 257.

implies that you are inferior, you are being treated with disrespect. A loving relationship is not about one person having the upper hand—it's about holding hands. A contemptuous and superior attitude is emotional abuse whether expressed through frequent name calling or subtle slights. One of my favorite examples is people who always respond to a partner's complaint by correcting their grammar or word usage. During one such argument, Paul's wife said, "Why do you always correct me? Just stop it! You know how adverse I am to it." He responded with, "I think you mean *a*verse." Funny, perhaps. But a relationship full of such retorts is not.

8. Unfairness

Most of us accept that life is not fair. Umpires make wrong calls, a lazy coworker gets *your* promotion, the person ahead of you in the supermarket "express" lane has sixty items in her shopping cart—and twenty complicated coupons. But a loving, long-term relationship should be a haven from injustice. This is not a Pollyanna attitude. It's a fundamental of love. There cannot be mutual satisfaction if one member takes advantage of the other. I see this all the time. Money is spent on his big TV but not on an elliptical trainer for her. Or somehow they always end up at *her* favorite restaurant. From such petty power plays, big problems arise.

Perhaps the most common unfairness concerns housework. Despite an agreement to the contrary, someone stops pulling her or, let's be honest here, *his* weight. The laundry lands on the floor, micrometers from the hamper, dirty dishes end up in the kitchen sink rather than the dishwasher, the toilet paper roll isn't replaced. "When we moved in together, we came up with a schedule that had us splitting housework fifty-fifty," says Caitlin. "But soon my boyfriend developed a serious case of hotel-itis. He'd leave the bed unmade, wet towels on the floor, half-finished soda cans on the coffee table." Often, when housework creates tension, the big issue isn't the dust bunnies cavorting under the sofa—it's the unfairness. Nothing puts a damper on romance like arriving home after a long day of work to discover a Mount Rainier of dirty laundry and a note that says, "Went to a poker game."

Another fertile breeding ground for injustice is handling finances. Many couples agree to share this tedious chore, but it ends up falling on one of them. Malcolm recalls, "When I was married, my wife and I decided that we would share the bill paying—which got nerve-wracking when times got tough. Creditors would call and she'd hand me the phone. 'You're better at it,' she'd say. I didn't like it. But it had to be done, so I did it. I wish she had said from the beginning that she wasn't going to. Maybe then I wouldn't have been so pissed off about it."

When a woman decides to stay home after having children, despite an agreement that she'll return to work, the financial burden falls on the partner, who now feels the need to work harder. One person gets to spend the day with their child while the other's family time is reduced. Yes some people revel in being the breadwinner. There's no "right" way to divvy up child-raising responsibilities. Having children is such a transformative experience that you can't know for certain what's going to work for your relationship ahead of time. But if you do want to change a prearranged workload, you need to talk it through. It's unfair to make any major life decision alone and, in essence, say to your mate, "Tough—just deal with it."

9. Selfishness

The interdependency of long-term relationships means that on occasion, partners will need to forfeit their own needs for the common good. Resentment will take hold if one partner refuses to demonstrate this trustworthiness. When his first child is born, Keith throws a tantrum because the infant seat won't fit into his new sports car. His wife, Talia, accuses him of caring more for his new toy than his baby daughter. She knows the charge is unfair. Keith loves their baby. But she is shocked by his resistance to cutting back his work hours, opening a college fund (he wants a motor boat), and understanding that Talia isn't as available for sex. Their daughter's birth uncovers selfishness in Keith she has not seen before. She insists they seek help, and Keith agrees. Together, they learn that Keith's becoming a father has triggered deep-seated needs and fears in him, and these are fueling his self-centered behavior.

10. Breaking Promises

A broken vow is as perilous to love as an intentional lie. Building a life together means agreeing on certain fundamentals and everyday expectations. You dream about your mutual future and make promises to each other, expressed outright or not, that strengthen your bond. But if those promises go unfulfilled or are contradicted, the disappointment jeopardizes a couple's trust in each other and their future.

As newlyweds, Joyce and Kyle agreed to siphon off a certain percentage of their salaries into a savings account that would, someday, allow them to buy a home. But now, Joyce's contributions begin to dwindle. Kyle's controlling approach to their finances has always bothered her. She wants to make her own decisions about whether and when the immediate gratification of a great shoe sale should trump their long-term goal. What is so bad about renting an apartment, anyway? She doesn't warn Kyle about her change in spending habits or its cause. "I don't want to get into it because I know he'll be really angry," she admits. Eventually, of course, Kyle finds out. What ensues is far rawer and uglier than if she had been up-front with him. Kyle feels that Joyce doesn't respect him: "She made a promise and then just decided that it didn't matter anymore. And she didn't tell me. I guess that means that I don't matter much either."

Here's another type of broken promise: When Hillary and Brad marry, they agree that faith will be the cornerstone of their family life. But after their kids are born, Hillary begins to question her commitment to organized religion. By the time the children are in grade school, she resists taking them to Sunday school. Brad always talks about how proud he feels walking into church with their "brood." Religion becomes a hot button for the couple. Their arguments usually turn into theological debates that miss the fundamental issue. Hillary's evolving view of religion has led to a broken pledge. Her new spiritual convictions are not wrong. But the change does leave Brad feeling like a chump. His resentment spreads beyond the issue of churchgoing. He worries that he can no longer trust his wife. It will take counseling for this couple to rework their expectations of each other and find a way to honor both of their convictions.

The most serious issues that lead to broken promises concern addiction. It is almost always impossible to maintain a healthy relationship in the presence of drug abuse, alcoholism, or a dependency on gambling, sex, or pornography. An all-too-common dynamic develops in which the afflicted partner promises to "change" but does not. The other partner wants to believe in the transformation. Each time the addiction reappears, the sense of betrayal deepens. Sometimes the partner enables the addiction, but that doesn't lessen the betrayal. Addiction is a complicated disorder with both emotional and physiological causes. The addicted person must seek professional help if there is to be a chance of salvaging the relationship.

Betrayal vs. Whistle-blowing

A relationship is a commitment, but it shouldn't be a pair of handcuffs or a muzzle. At times, expressing *disapproval* of your partner's deeds can be the most loving and supportive action you can take. Blind acceptance is never a healthy strategy. Alexander Hamilton once said that to mistrust the government to regulate itself is an *obligation* of the citizenry. Likewise, sometimes it's necessary to hold up a mirror for your partner. No one is immune to bouts of narcissism, selfishness, and poor judgment. Calling your partner on such behavior is healthy. In doing so, you are focused on your partner's payoffs, not your own. We need to rely on each other's honesty to challenge our values, even if that means hearing the sting of "What were you thinking?" or "How could you do that?" If you are the recipient of such "corrections," realize that your partner's love is motivating the confrontation. Instead of being defensive, try to focus on what your partner is saying and discuss the issue with openness. Too often, however, a partner's withdrawal of support is not a form of whistle-blowing but a selfish betrayal. When a relationship begins to collapse under the weight of any type of disloyalty, it takes more than apologies, promises, and romantic nights out to strengthen the bond. The couple must first recognize that a form of infidelity is at the heart of the breach. To find their way back to each other, the couple will need to work together on attuning. Only by newly exploring each other's inner world can they succeed at reconnecting.

6

Trust and the Roots of Attunement

Practically every therapist—and self-help book—emphasizes communication and the power of words to resolve differences. Many offer excellent advice. But if the right vocabulary were enough to prevent severed relationships, by now we would have talked our way out of a punishing divorce rate. Too often couples learn to parrot the right words but don't anchor their talks in a profound understanding of each other. It is like learning to memorize French sentences. If you don't understand what they mean, you aren't speaking French.

When couples can understand each other at a deep level and lovingly express that knowledge to each other, real intimacy exists between them. This ability, which we call *attunement*, is second nature to some lucky couples, but many others who are just as devoted find it challenging. Fortunately, attunement is comprised of skills that almost all couples can learn—or learn to strengthen.

The most frequent stumbling block to attunement is a disparity in how each partner "feels about feelings," especially negative ones. Are you comfortable expressing your emotions when angry or sad? If your partner is upset, do you wish you could just escape? Or do you feel like it's your job to "fix it"? Do you want to tell him or her to just "buck up"? Powerful cultural, gender, and individual differences govern the answers to these questions.

The technical term I coined to describe a person's attitude toward feelings is "meta-emotion." "Meta" is a reflexive word that psychologists often use to describe something that folds back on itself. "Meta-communication," for example, refers to how we communicate about communication. Likewise, by "meta-emotion" I mean how we feel about feelings.

Some of us tend to dismiss feelings as unimportant. But emotions are an inherent part of the human experience. They exist no matter how intently one tries to deny them. We know that at least seven of them are universal and hardwired into our brains: anger, sadness, disgust, contempt, fear, interest, and happiness. In the throes of these distinct emotions, people across the globe tend to make the same spontaneous facial expressions (smiles, frowns, furrowed brows, and so on). Some research even suggests that specific emotions trigger the same specific physiological changes in all of us (like an accelerated heartbeat), no matter our background, lifestyle, or cultural origin.

Because most attitudes toward feelings form during childhood, my understanding of attunement's critical role in adult relationships stems from my earlier work on parenting styles. In 1985, I developed a meta-emotion interview that assessed parents' attitudes toward their own emotions and their children's.

The interviews covered the subject's childhood experiences with anger, sadness, fear, affection, pride, and other feelings. The interviewers asked questions such as, "Could you tell growing up when your father was angry?" "What effect did this have on you?" "How did your parents show that they loved you?"

I found great variability in our interviewees' meta-emotion profiles, particularly when it came to negative feelings. One father considered anger insignificant. It was "like clearing your throat, natural, you just get it out and go on." Another man said pretty much the opposite. When someone got angry at him, it felt abusive, as if, "they are relieving themselves in my face."

Data from this study uncovered two distinct approaches to child raising, based on the parents' attitude toward negative emotions and the lessons learned during their own childhoods. When faced with an unhappy, fearful, or angry child, one group of parents (the larger group, unfortunately) tried to change how the child felt through distraction or by admonishing the child to "forget it." These parents, whose approach I call *emotion dismissing*, believed that their children's feelings were a matter of choice. In general, emotion-dismissing parents viewed exploring negative emotions as akin to pouring gasoline on an open fire. They considered anger to be out-of-control aggression, sadness a wallowing in self-pity, and fearfulness a sign of cowardice. Here's how one emotion-dismissing father said he'd react if his son were upset over teasing: "I say, 'Don't worry about it. He didn't mean it . . . Don't dwell on it. Take it lightly. Roll with the punches and get on with life.'"

The other parenting style, which I regret is less common, is *emotion coaching*. Parents who used this approach viewed their child's anger, fear, or sadness as an opportunity to connect and help the child understand feelings. (I am simplifying a bit by divvying parents into two neat categories; in truth, my subjects didn't react uniformly to the full spectrum of their child's negativity.) When I asked a coaching dad the same question about teasing, he said, "If a kid were to be mean to my son, I would try to understand what he's feeling and why. Some kid may have hit him or made fun of him. I stop everything then. My heart just goes out to him, and I feel like a father here and I empathize."

Dismissive parents aren't colder or less loving than coaches. A father means well when he says, "Put a smile on your face, sweetheart. There, that's Daddy's little girl. Isn't that better now?" This sort of parenting offers some benefits. It is action oriented and encourages problem-solving skills. But it's hard for a child (or anyone) to learn or change if he or she doesn't first feel understood and supported. To paraphrase renowned child psychologist Dr. Haim Ginott, guidance is always more effective when *words of understanding precede words of advice.* This is why emotion coaching offers such great benefits to children. In my initial study of three- and four-year-olds, I found that five years later, the coached kids tended to perform more highly in academic subjects, got along better with other children, were physically healthier, and had fewer behavioral problems than the offspring of parents who did not coach. Even when I compared two children with the same IQ, the emotion-coached child displayed greater academic achievement connected to a superior ability to calm himself or herself and to focus attention.

When I talk about attunement between adults in a committed relationship, I am talking about emotion coaching. But I don't apply the word *coaching* to adults. The term suggests a power differential in which the support and understanding flows mostly in one direction, as it does between parent and child. But the skill is the same. Through the use of a new meta-emotion questionnaire that is tailored to adult relationships, my research unit confirmed that partners in happy relationships coach each other. Led by my former graduate student Dr. Dan Yoshimoto, the team interviewed 100 couples, asking partners about the kind of family and culture they came from and what messages they had received about the expression and experience of emotions. We then interviewed the couples together about the history of their relationships. Yoshimoto developed a way to score these interviews so we could analyze the extent to which people felt that they could open up to their partner and vice versa. We discovered a similar proportion of coaches and "dismissers" as in our parenting study. Many of the dismissive partners had the best intentions. Like dismissive parents, they might say things like, "Oh, honey, don't be sad, don't cry, cheer up. Look on the bright side." They thought their words were supportive, but unless their partner had requested this sort of response, the message they were communicating was, "I don't want to hear about it when you feel this way. Go be unhappy somewhere else."

Some emotion dismissers in our study *did* want their partners to take their unhappiness "somewhere else." They reacted with impatience and disapproval and tended to describe their partner as negative or needy. They considered their partner's emotions a burden that worsened their own mood, even when their partner's unhappiness had nothing to do with the relationship. Such couples were facing a serious mismatch in meta-emotion.

What follows are snippets of the meta-emotion interviews with Angel and George, the unhappy couple who couldn't get each other to listen. We've already seen how blunt they could be about their dissatisfaction. During this calmer part of the assessment, they were still not giving or getting the emotional support they both yearned for.

Interviewer: What sorts of things make you sad?

George: I don't feel that I get the respect I need or deserve from my wife. The thing that makes me the saddest is when I feel I'm getting short-changed. I'm not able, you know, to continue to grow, go back to school. My wife, she's quitting her job . . . she doesn't encourage me, "Hey, you know, you're doing a great job." Those types of things they make me sad or angry. I suppose a little bit of both. Where I want to just be away.

Interviewer: How does your wife respond to you when you're sad?

George: Oh, yeah, well, she calls me out, challenges me. "Oh, there you go being moody again. Blah blah blah, yak, yak, yak" (*laughs*). She doesn't really acknowledge it. Therefore, I choose not to share it when I'm sad.

George keeps his sadness to himself for fear that Angel will challenge him. Later in the interview, he acknowledges that he avoids telling his wife when he is mad because then she would get angry, too. And another battle would begin. George feels stuck in a marriage where he cannot express his negative emotions. He sees his wife as dismissive rather than empathetic.

Here's what Angel had to say:

Interviewer: Would your husband know if you were sad, would he pick up on it?

Angel: Yeah, he would pick up on it. Not necessarily know what to do about it.

Interviewer: So, how does he respond to you? What would I see and hear when he responded to your sadness?

Angel: I would say really, probably, he would . . . make himself busy and he would retreat more . . . a lot of times he doesn't *know* what to do. And so he deals with it in a way that he feels he can deal with it. Rarely would he be loving and affectionate. I don't think he would do that . . . if I said to him, "Oh, give me a hug," or, "I need affection," he would, no problem. But he doesn't figure that out on his own.

Interviewer: How do you feel about this response?

Angel: (*Angry facial expression*) I would certainly like for him to be more affectionate. And loving and understanding. And not internalize it. I would certainly like for that to be different. I think I've communicated that to him. But for him that takes a lot of effort. Thinking, *Oh, okay, because she said it's not my fault. It's not like something I've done wrong, or she's not trying to tell me that I need to be doing something different.* That kind of thing.

Unlike her husband, Angel doesn't try to bottle her emotions. From her perspective, getting angry is the only way to get George's attention. Angel wishes that George would be affectionate and loving rather than defensive when she is sad, but she believes it is a lost cause. She doesn't expect her venting to lead to a positive experience, but at least she is putting the issues on the table.

This couple's fundamental problem is an inability to respond to each other's emotions in a way that would deepen their connection rather than drive them further apart. Their mutual lack of empathy, at least in expression, builds up anger and resentment. Trust cannot be maintained under this scenario.

Although it is not a complex skill, attunement requires a shift in meta-emotion away from the dismissing world of Angel and George and toward one where you each accept the others emotions, including anger, sadness, and fear. Attunement is not about memorizing a script. It's about increasing your understanding of your partner and expressing acceptance and support. The easiest way to learn attunement methods is to start small, with nonthreatening conversations that allow plenty of practice in opening up. Based on my work with countless couples, I have found an effective method that will allow most people to do just that.

7

Attunement Made Easy:
The Art of Intimate Conversation

At a dinner party, I listened to a man recount how his four-wheel-drive truck got stuck in a ditch near his house during a snow storm. "I went inside to get something to help improve traction," he began. A woman standing nearby cut him off and said, "Well, while the snow was falling, my family and I were in a head-on collision on Route 5." The man then continued, "So I got an old quilt from the house, and I put it under the rear wheels, and it worked!" I turned to the woman and exclaimed, "My God, you were in a head-on collision? What happened?"

This three-way exchange with its non sequiturs and interruptions is typical of conversations you hear at parties. (By the way, the cars were traveling at a crawl and no one was hurt.) People tend to talk past each other. They don't listen well and rarely ask one another questions, or follow a straight line of thought. The famous Swiss child psychologist Jean Piaget called this phenomenon "collective monologue." He was describing conversations among preschoolers, but his term characterizes many grown-up conversations as well. Superficial chats are the opposite of attuned conversation. At a party, these sorts of interactions are standard and harmless. But talking past each other with frequency is also common in long-term relationships—and between a couple it is damaging. Such cross-talk prevents partners from achieving the kind of closeness that solidifies a bond.

Many people think that effective conversation entails making yourself sound interesting to others, when actually it is all about being *interested in others and listening*. In the chapters ahead, I'll show you how to use attunement skills to avoid counterproductive "collective monologue" during arguments. But don't wait for conflict to arise before you implement this approach. Attuned communication in everyday life is necessary to maintain any relationship.

If you're thinking, *All this talk about opening up sounds great, but my partner is never going to do it!* or, *No way can I do that!*, you may be in for a happy surprise. I have succeeded in teaching many "hopeless cases" to confide in their partners. The key is what I call the art of intimate conversation, which is really a beginner's approach to attunement. Intimate conversation doesn't require that you discuss conflicts or touchy subjects. It is just about *talking*. You can apply these conversational skills without your partner knowing it, though, of course, the more you work together on the process, the better.

This method demystifies the attunement process by breaking it down into four steps. You don't need to be a "people person" to master it. I taught it to Glenn, a middle-aged engineer who was a self-proclaimed curmudgeon. He prided himself on not having any needs. He told me, "People who need people are always disappointed and miserable." Chitchatting was on his "to be avoided" list. He despised work-related banquets and retreats because they required social interaction. And yet he agreed to learn my approach because his emotional distance was frustrating his wife of twenty years. She felt so lonely in the marriage that she was considering leaving him. His two teenaged daughters felt alienated as well. They said living with him was like having a grumpy stranger on the premises who wouldn't care if they ran sobbing from the room. In therapy, Glenn admitted to me that he didn't know how to get closer to them. Acquiring these four skills salvaged his relationship with his family. There were collateral benefits, too. In one session, Glenn reported with amusement that at a recent work event he sat next to a coworker he always tried to avoid because she "talked too much." At the end of the meal, during which he had applied the four skills, the woman exclaimed in surprise that he was such a nice person. With a chuckle, he complained to me that learning to attune was ruining his reputation.

Here are the skills I taught Glenn and countless others. Consider them the ticket to your partner's inner world. To integrate them into daily life, I recommend that couples schedule regular "How was your day?" chats using this method to check in and reconnect. (For many examples of words and phrases you can use during intimate conversations, see appendix 1 on p. 244.)

1. Put Your Feelings into Words

I'm surprised by the number of people I counsel who cannot verbalize their emotions. Because they aren't sure what's going on inside, they are unable to share their feelings with their partner. As you can imagine, this is a huge obstacle when trying to connect. Please don't be dismissive of your emotions or ashamed if you have difficulty articulating them. Instead, let your partner know that identifying your feelings is a challenge. Consider enlisting him or her to assist you in figuring them out.

A great strategy for pinpointing your emotions is to tune into your body as you consider different descriptions of your mood. Distinguished psychologist and philosopher Dr. Eugene Gendlin uses an approach he calls *focusing*. When you're hunting for the right word to describe a feeling, he suggests you "try on" each word while monitoring your physical responses to it. When your body relaxes, you've probably hit on the correct description of your emotions. It's almost as if the body says, "Phew! Yes! That's the right word."

When Gendlin asked one patient how she felt about her job, all she could express was sadness. He then had her close her eyes and channel her feelings into a visual representation. She saw herself standing on a railroad platform as a train pulled away without her. She realized she wasn't just sad about her career, she was also angry and disappointed that she kept getting left behind at work. Often, she helped coworkers with their projects. Then they got the credit and subsequent promotions, not she. The image and words that came to mind expressed just how she felt about the situation. Her body relaxed. Knowing her true feelings (not "sad" but "left behind") led her to change her work goals. Now she understood what she really wanted.

If you use Gendlin's focusing technique, over time you're likely to improve at describing your feelings. My wife, therapist Dr. Julie Gottman, has designed a wonderful approach to help people achieve this focus. After leading them through relaxation exercises, she asks them to say something out loud that is not true, such as, "I don't love my dog Fritz," and notice how their body feels. Next, she has them speak the truth ("I love my dog Fritz") and note the difference in their physical reactions. This exercise shows them how to use their body's responses to determine how the right words fit their real emotions.

A tactic I often use with couples is to hand them a vocabulary list. They scan the words and circle the ones that most describe their current state. Here is an abbreviated version of that list.

I Feel . . .

Positive Emotions

Amused	Lucky	Satisfied
Appreciated	Nostalgic	Sexy
Attractive	Playful	Silly
Excited	Powerful	Smart
Happy	Proud	Turned on
Joyful	Respected	Well liked
Lighthearted	Safe	

Negative Emotions

Alienated	Guilty	Sad
Angry	Ignored	Stubborn
Ashamed	Inferior	Tense
Betrayed	Lonely	Unloved
Criticized	Misunderstood	Unsafe
Defensive	Numb	Upset
Frustrated	Powerless	

2. Ask Open-ended Questions

Avoid queries that your partner can punt with single words such as *yes* or *no*, which kill conversations before they start. Instead, pose questions in ways that require a deeper response. Replace, "Did you have a good day at work?" with "So, what was it like at work today?" Instead of "Did you like the movie?" try "What did you think of the movie?" Or "What was the best part?" And rather than a simple "How's the new mystery you're reading?" ask how it compares to the author's previous work. This technique doesn't apply just to everyday exchanges but also to conversations about significant issues. "Are you upset?" can close off further discussion, but "You seem upset—what's going on?" will encourage it.

3. Follow Up with Statements That Deepen Connection

After your partner answers a question, respond by saying back what you just heard, in your own words. It's okay if your description isn't 100 percent accurate, but don't make assumptions or put words into the other's mouth. When you reflect back your partner's thoughts and feelings in an understanding manner, you encourage him or her to open up more. Tim, the chief financial officer for a small company, comes home one night looking miserable. He tells his wife, Gail, that after poring over the business's latest financial statements, he realizes he might need to recommend layoffs. At first, Gail uses closed questions and makes assumptions about how her husband must be feeling. She gets nowhere. But when she switches strategies, her husband opens up:

Gail: Oh no! Those poor people. You must feel terrible!

Tim: (*Frowning*) Sure.

Gail: You don't feel terrible?

Tim: Of course I do.

Gail [open-ended question]: What are you feeling most of all?

Tim: (*Sigh*) I'm scared out of my mind. It's my job to advise Carl. He's relying on me. But I'm not sure what to tell him, and if I blow it, the company is screwed. What if I say don't lay off anybody and then we go under? Or what if there are layoffs, and they weren't necessary? People will be out of work. It'll be my fault.

Gail [deepening statement]: You're feeling like it's all your responsibility.

Tim: It is! I have to make a decision—but I don't know what's right. I've always believed you just make a decision and move on.

Gail [deepening statement]: But this is a really tough decision for you.

Tim: Yeah, but it shouldn't be. You gotta do what you gotta do. I feel like a failure.

Gail [deepening statement]: It's a really tough position to be in.

Tim: Yeah.

Later, Tim tells his wife how helpful it was to confide his self-doubt to someone he could trust and who understood. (The company does lay off a few people but is able to pull out of the slump before letting others go.)

4. Express Compassion and Empathy

When your partner is upset, be on his or her team whether the issue is trivial or significant. If you think your mate is overreacting or should have a "different" emotional response, stifle the urge to offer your opinion and suggestions. After years of studying couples who have maintained long and happy marriages, I can assure you that being the voice of reason is not always the best approach. Let other people play that role. Yours is to let the person you love know that you're standing with him or her. You get and accept his or her emotions as valid—because *all* feelings are.

Monica is outraged that her older sister sent her kids Christmas gifts that they think are "babyish." She sees this act as one more link in a long chain of evidence that her sister doesn't care about her and her daughters. "We're always just an afterthought," Monica fumes. "It's like she ran into the store at the last minute and grabbed the first things she saw. She just doesn't care."

Monica's boyfriend, Jonathan, is pretty certain that the sister, who is childless, is just clueless that crayons are not de rigueur in middle school. But he doesn't suggest this explanation or recommend that Monica call her sister and talk it out. Instead, he says, "I can understand why you're so upset. She makes you feel like you're unimportant to her. That's awful." Jonathan knows better than to offer unrequested advice or an alternative perspective while she is upset.

Likewise, when Harlan complains that his power-hungry boss is threatening to cut his sales commission, his wife, Judy, doesn't suggest strategies for fighting back. Instead, she shakes her head in commiseration. "I don't know how you can stand working for that man. He's dreadful!" When her husband rants about wanting terrible fates to befall the guy, Judy chimes in with macabre and absurd suggestions that bring a smile to her husband's face. Harlan's boss remains insufferable, but his wife's understanding makes tough times more bearable.

Although you've probably been tempted, don't offer opinions or problem solve until you've gone through all four of these steps. Ready advice sounds glib and insulting to many people. ("Are you saying I can't think of a solution? I am not stupid.") Remember Ginott's motto: understanding must precede advice. I would go even further and warn you not to give advice *at all* unless asked. Just being there and listening is an enormous contribution.

So that's all it takes to draw out your partner. Open up about your own feelings, converse in a style that encourages confidences, and be an ally more than a problem solver. Follow this method in your daily interactions and you'll be amazed by how much you discover about each other. Along with enriching your relationship, learning this approach will improve your skills at turning toward each other during sliding door moments. As a result, you'll prevent a lot of disagreements from ever starting.

8

Turning Toward Each Other

Reporters so often ask me, "What do couples fight about most?" My answer is always the same: "Absolutely nothing. They fight about nothing." A mess just happens and a regrettable incident is born. A couple watches TV. As she tries to follow the program, he grabs the remote and starts scrolling through the listings guide.

"Stop doing that, I can't see," she says.

"Okay, let me just check—"

"No! Leave it. I hate it when you do this."

"Fine!"

"Why did you say it like that?"

"Because you're always going to get your way, so *fine*, have it your way."

No matter how dedicated you are to living happily ever after, small squabbles like the one over that remote are always going to push your buttons. Real life will never be like the pages of a fairy tale (or marriage manual). That's why it's so important to tamp down tension whenever you can by getting into the habit of turning toward each other during sliding door moments. This is an easy skill to master, and there is no exaggerating its benefit. In a telling result from my newlywed study, couples who remained married at the six-year follow-up had turned toward each other 86 percent of the time during their stay at the Love Lab apartment. These couples also expressed humor and affection, and even laughed, during their monitored conflict discussion. None of the other couples did. Those who ended up splitting had interacted in this manner only 33 percent of the time.

These statistics offer fantastic news and a great opportunity. They suggest that you can avoid a lot of misery just by working on responding with interest during trivial incidents. Since these episodes are insignificant and fleeting, repairing them is easy. It's best if you learn how to accomplish this together. But even if just one of you begins to slide the door open with greater frequency, your relationship will improve. In time, your partner is more likely to walk through that door, too.

There is one category of turning away, however, that can demolish a relationship after just one episode and requires serious intervention. In such cases, a devastating interaction causes what my colleague Dr. Susan Johnson calls an attachment injury: a wounding experience that leaves one partner feeling vulnerable and unsafe. An attachment injury destroys the implicit contract between partners to *be there and nurture* each other, to impart the feeling of security that attachment figures (usually parents) often provided during childhood. Johnson treated a grieving woman who suffered an attachment injury when her husband refused to lament and comfort her after a miscarriage. He didn't find such conversations "positive and constructive," so he turned away and left her to recover from the tragedy alone. When the person you have entrusted with your deepest vulnerabilities is unavailable or unresponsive to a deep-seated need, the result is anger, panic, and intense loneliness. The hurt remains a part of your active memory. To quote William Faulkner, "The past is never dead. It's not even past." Without proper intervention, a relationship that suffers this type of damage is likely to shatter.

In most cases, however, it takes an accumulation of turning away and subsequent regrettable incidents before the relationship becomes mired in negativity. So couples have plenty of time to get it right. It's common for a partner to turn away because he or she doesn't realize that the other has made a bid for support and attention. Sometimes the bid is so minor ("Could you see who's at the door?" "Remind me, what time do we have to go?") that it seems immaterial. But it is still important. When little bids go ignored or dismissed, the couple don't move up what I call the "bidding ladder" to more important requests for connection and emotional support. Couples who eat in awkward silence at restaurants are stuck on a very low step of the bidding ladder.

Not all small bids are spoken or obvious. A wife who is making the bed may ask her husband to change the pillowcases, or she may just sigh as he walks by. Attunement means paying attention to your partner's subtle clues. (It also means making your wishes clear, so your partner can read you.) You don't always have to comply with the request, but you should respond with love and sensitivity.

Here is a ranking of minor bids that create sliding door moments, based on statistical analyses of couples observed in the

Love Lab. My team noted how frequently partners made each type of bid and how the other tended to respond. Bids that were made frequently and usually met with a positive response we deemed "easy" and placed near the bottom of the ladder. Those that were asked infrequently and had a relatively low success rate we deemed "difficult," and they earned high rungs on our bidding scale. Keep in mind that this list is just of minor bids—the kind that are easy to handle if you are aware of them.

1. Pay attention to what I say. ("How do I look?" "Wow, did you see that boat?!")
2. Respond to my simple requests. ("While you're up, could you get the salsa?")
3. Help me or work with me. ("Let's get Janey into bed now.")
4. Show interest or active excitement in my accomplishments. ("Do you think I did well?")
5. Answer my questions or requests for information. ("Can you help me fill out this form?")
6. Chat with me. ("Let me tell you what happened when my mom called.")
7. Share the events of your day with me. ("What happened at work?")
8. Respond to my joke. ("Did I tell you the one about . . . ?")
9. Help me destress. ("I think I blew my presentation today.")
10. Help me problem solve. ("What do you think I should do about my boss?")
11. Be affectionate. ("Come here and cuddle with me while I read.")
12. Play with me. ("Hey, let's get out the Monopoly board.")
13. Join me in an adventure or exploration. ("Do you want to hike up Turtleback tomorrow?")
14. Join me in learning something. ("Let's take French lessons!")

Once you recognize when your partner is making a bid, the next step, of course, is to turn toward him or her. This doesn't mean you must say *"oui!"* to learning French or anything else. You just need to respond in a manner that shows you're there. ("You really want to learn French? Wow, where'd that come from?")

How to Repair

There will be many times when you do not respond to sliding door moments with success. But if you are aware of the problem, you can use a repair to prevent the rise of a regrettable incident. Through the years, much of my research has focused on why, when, and how repairs work between partners, and which are the most effective. Repairs don't have to be well spoken or sophisticated to succeed. Although some approaches may be especially effective, any sincere attempt can work if the couple is not stuck in the absorbing negativity of the roach motel.

Here's a very simple repair exchange between partners in my lab. Darice and Reba were a gay couple who were planning their Easter trip to visit Darice's family. Darice had not come out to her extended family. She wanted Reba to help her figure out how to handle the situation—a bid for problem solving. But Reba stunned her by saying she thought Darice should decide for herself what to do. Darice's physiological readings began to show signs of distress, an indication that she felt Reba had turned away from her. Here's what happened next:

> *Reba:* I don't want the responsibility of being part of this decision. I worry that if you decide we made the wrong one, it wouldn't be good for us.

Darice: But you not wanting a say in this makes me feel like it isn't important to you, which is really frustrating. Do you understand?

Reba: Yeah, I do. I do.

That's all it took. With that simple statement from Reba, Darice's heart rate and blood pressure fell back to baseline. (In the end, Darice and Reba decided, together, to come out to Darice's family during their visit, but after Easter dinner.)

What follows is a list of common and effective repairs that couples in my studies used, as detailed by two former students in my lab, Drs. Janice Driver and Amber Tabares. Some of these are likely already part of your repair "vocabulary." Others you'll find easy to add. They are divided into two groups: repairs that appeal to emotions and those that appeal to thought. Emotion-based repairs were far more effective. Both types are most successful if you use them early.

Group One: Cognitive Repairs

These focus on engaging the partner's thought process to defuse tension.

Define the Conflict. "You think it's unfair that I left the car without much gas in it, forcing you to stop at the station. My view is, I don't think that should bother you so much. You have so much more free time than I do these days. So let's talk about it."

Ask for Credit. Point out a recent behavior of yours that was in deference to your partner's wishes. "Just like you asked, I did remember to fill up the car last week."

Compromise. Find middle ground through mutual cooperation. "We could take turns filling it up."

Guard. Warn your partner or request that he or she back off from a specific part of an issue. "I don't think we should drag into this the issue of who does more of the driving because that's a separate problem. It's just going to push my buttons."

Monitor the Conflict. Keep the discussion on track or point out if it's getting too intense. "I'm getting riled up by this." "Whoa, we're letting this get out of hand."

Request Direction. "Tell me what to say now to make this better."

Stop. Try to put an abrupt end to the topic if the discussion has turned destructive.

Group Two: Emotional Repairs

These approaches, which are more effective than cognitive repairs, attempt to lower the tension level by understanding and then acknowledging the partner's feelings, soothing the partner, and disclosing your own feelings.

Agree. Accept that your partner is right to some degree. You can use this repair after you argue your point, or you can make an immediate 180-degree turnaround. "Okay, yeah. I should have stopped for gas on my way home when I saw the tank was almost empty."

Question. Ask something that addresses your partner's feelings or opinions. "Help me understand. Does it seem to you that I didn't fill up the car on purpose?"

Express Affection. Offer a physical and/or verbal expression of caring and appreciation.

Change the Topic. A deliberate shift in subject to something unrelated and minor often works. One couple was discussing the husband's late arrival. His wife suggested that his tendency to be late might stem from childhood because his mother often left him waiting for hours. He became very emotional as he said, "You're probably right. God, I hated her for that." Then he suddenly said, "Say, are those new shoes?" She said, "Yes, but they weren't expensive," and he added, "They're pretty shoes." After this break, his physiology calmed and they returned to the discussion of his lateness.

Make Promises. Agree to a positive change in the future. "From now on I will pay more attention to your feelings about this."

Use Humor. "Wait! I thought the car was a Volt. *Now* you tell me it needs gas?" (Warning: any humor that expresses criticism or contempt toward the partner or belittles the other's point of view is probably not a repair; it will usually backfire.)

Self-disclose. Reveal thoughts or emotions that explain your side of the conflict. "I feel like I do so much of the grunt work around here that I should get a pass on filling up the car. Otherwise I feel really put-upon."

Take Responsibility. Acknowledge your contribution. "I didn't pay attention to how my actions would affect you."

Understand. Communicate empathy. "I can see how you feel. Here you are, already stressed out by your workload, and I just added to your burdens rather than helping."

Reinforce We-ness. Compliment the relationship or emphasize your part-nership by acknowledging how you're similar. "Well, at least we can talk about this stuff rather than just sulking."

We're Okay. This repair affirms that the couple will be okay even if they haven't been good at reaching an agreement during this discussion.

Using these repairs will shut down many confrontations and train you to be more aware of each other's needs. But I don't want to give the impression that repairs will solve all of your relationship woes. They won't for a simple reason: No matter how hard you try, you are going to miss an enormous amount of each other's bids. It's inevitable for conflict to spark on occasion. When it does, working things out will require more intensive attunement tools. These interventions can prevent distrust and betrayal from consuming many relationships. They can also rescue couples who are already trapped.

9

Working Through Your Messes,
Big and Small

If people are honest about how much of the time they pay full attention to their partner's words, 50 percent would be a generous estimate. Based on precise calculations from my study of repairs, it is more realistic to assume that each partner is available around 30 percent of the time. For the other 70 percent, they are distracted thinking about the kids, work, God, gas prices, what's on TV, window treatments, and the NCAA championship. The likelihood that *both* partners will be available at the same time (assuming their availability is independent of each other), is just 9 percent (.3 x .3 = .9). This means that *91 percent of the time* the ground is ripe for miscommunication. Both partners are going to mess up plenty.

One minute everything is fine, the next your brain is shouting "incoming!" When a sliding door moment leads to an unexpected quarrel, it can feel like a mortar attack. How much damage the regrettable incident wreaks depends on whether you and your partner process it afterward, learn from it, and move on. If you are unable to take these steps, the Zeigarnik effect will keep the episode in your active memory and increase negative feelings.

In my clinical practice, I have found that holding weekly State of the Union meetings is the most successful strategy for helping couples who are in conflict. This meeting is a formal encounter in which both people use attunement skills to gain perspective on the argument. Usually, I have couples set aside one hour a week to perform this intervention at home and have them schedule a weekly office appointment to discuss the experience afterward. As couples become more adept at this systematic process, they are able to use attunement skills right away when there is a misunderstanding, rather than waiting for a scheduled meeting.

During their State of the Union meeting, couples make use of what I call the Gottman-Rapoport Blueprint for Constructive Conflict. It is a "couples only" version of the great social psychologist Anatol Rapoport's approach to negotiations between hostile political groups or countries. Rapoport was a twentieth-century game theorist, but with a difference. Unlike most of them, his goal was to reduce the possibility of a nuclear confrontation rather than ensure that the United States would triumph. Therefore, he studied strategies that would increase cooperation between adversaries.

Rapoport is famous among social psychologists for suggesting an extraordinary powerful principle: do not try to persuade, problem solve, or compromise until you can state the other side's position to their satisfaction, and vice versa. In the context of a committed relationship, this tenet means you do not move on to negotiating a compromise until you can say to each other, "Yes! You got it. That's exactly my position and what I'm feeling." To get there, the blueprint has you take turns speaking and listening in a structured manner. First, the speaker shares all his or her thoughts, feelings, and needs on the issue. The listener digests the other's perspective and communicates back a thorough understanding of the partner's position. Then the two switch roles.

This approach may sound familiar because it is similar to a popular method of conflict resolution called active listening. In the latter, you take turns expressing yourself and repeating back what the other has said to confirm that you understand. But there's a critical difference between the two methods. In classic active listening, the sole responsibility for remaining calm and keeping the discussion on track belongs to the listener. After your partner says, "You don't care! You're never home! You're so selfish!" you're supposed to respond with something like "I hear you say that you wish I worked less," and not get defensive. The problem is that you *are* going to get defensive. Everybody does when under attack. The more threatened you become, the more likely you'll flood and lose the ability to respond with understanding and empathy.

The Gottman-Rapoport Blueprint sidesteps this problem by making the speaker as responsible as the listener for success. Both partners have rules they must follow so that neither feels threatened.

In the beginning, following the Blueprint is an admittedly drawn-out approach to conflict resolution. It is faster to say "Get over it!" But that will not work. As with any new skill, implementing attunement will feel strange and awkward at first. When my teenage daughter learned to drive, she sometimes confused the brake and accelerator pedals because they seemed so close together. Now, of course, her foot shifts with precision from one to the other. In much the same way, it takes a while to master advanced attunement skills. But once you do, the process will feel natural.

The Gottman-Rapoport Blueprint for Constructive Conflict

Before you begin, gather clipboards, paper, and pens so you can take notes and jot down your thoughts. I like this low-tech method of keeping track because it slows the conversation, giving you time to concentrate on your partner's words and also to think about how to express yourself. You'll also want to monitor yourselves for signs of flooding. I suggest purchasing a couple of pulse oximeters. These simple, noninvasive devices use readings from your index finger to measure your heart rate and oxygen concentration (which indicates whether you're breathing deeply enough). They cost between $20 and $60 and are easy to find online.

You'll know you're flooded if your heart rate exceeds 100 beats per minute (bpm), or your oxygen concentration falls below 95 percent. (This is standard for almost everybody, regardless of age or gender. For athletes, however, the threshold is 80 bpm.) Stop the discussion and take twenty minutes to calm down. Do not spend the time stewing or otherwise thinking about the conflict. Reengage only when your heart rate is back to baseline. Taking a break can have a dramatic effect. In my therapy work, I find that partners return to the table looking and sounding as if they've had a brain transplant. Once more, they can be logical, neutral, empathic, and attentive. Their good humor also returns.

Always begin the meeting with a review of what's been going right between you lately. Accentuating the positive will defuse some of the tension and render both of you more able to cooperate. Georgia wants to tell her live-in boyfriend, Bobby, how hurt she is that he spent Saturday night with his friends, rather than with her. But she begins the meeting by thanking him for raking the leaves.

As part of these preliminaries, I have couples name five things the other did over the past week that they appreciate. This approach might sound hokey, but to express gratitude for the little kindnesses that too often go ignored is surprisingly powerful. In the midst of the morning rush, you may have the fleeting thought, *Gee, how nice that he made me coffee.* But it's hard to remember or find the time to send even a quick text that says "thx." So if your partner didn't make any grand gestures over the past week, express appreciation for something simple, like not getting impatient when you misplaced the car keys or getting you a snack. When it is your turn to receive appreciations, acknowledge them by expressing gratitude after each one. That might sound obvious, but people often forget this courtesy. Without a thank-you, the partner feels the other took the appreciation for granted.

Next, decide what area of discord you want to focus on for the rest of the discussion. When you first learn this process, it's best to choose a recent disagreement. But once you become more proficient at these meetings, I recommend reviewing an upsetting episode from your mutual past that still feels like a stone in your shoe. By delving into a previous conflict you will gain enormous insight into your relationship. (Directions for that exercise are on page 140.)

Step One: Speaking and Listening

In the course of one meeting, you can expect to trade off the speaker and listener roles multiple times as you work through different dimensions of a disagreement. When it's your turn to speak, you retain the floor for as long as you need to express your feelings and perspective on a particular issue. Your job is not (yet) to persuade your partner about how right you are or to recommend an immediate compromise. I know it is hard to suppress the desire to convince the other, but at this point negotiation would be counterproductive.

Below are the specific bullet points that the speaker and listener must follow (there are three each). I identified them by analyzing the meta-emotion results of high-trust couples in my lab. What these couples do naturally to prevent flooding during disagreements, other couples can learn. In a great bit of luck, I was able to match the six letters in ATTUNE with these six bullet points, making them easier to recall. (Some of this advice will be familiar because it is part of the Art of Intimate Conversation.)

Speaker's Job

A = Awareness

T = Tolerance

T = Transforming criticisms into wishes and positive needs

Listener's Job

U = Understanding

N = Nondefensive listening

E = Empathy

The Speaker's Job

A = Awareness.

Pay attention to your words and manner to avoid making your partner feel cornered and defensive. Remember, the goal is to discuss the problem *without triggering flooding* in your partner.

Accusations and criticism will only backfire. Here are three pointers to help you remain aware of your delivery style.

First, stick to "I" statements. This advice is so common that it's almost a cliché of marriage counseling—but for a good reason. Sometimes during a session with clients, I'll point my finger at each of them and yell, "YOU!" Then I ask how I made them feel. They always report an immediate jump in their heart rate or other negative physical reaction to this experiment. The word *you* is powerful during conflict discussions—and too often its force isn't used for good. Thomas Gordon was the first to make the distinction between complaints that begin with "you" or "I." The chief characteristic of an "I" statement is that it reflects only the speaker's feelings and experience and avoids criticizing the partner. When you say, "I wish you had gotten to the restaurant on time. I felt embarrassed sitting there all alone waiting for you," the focus is on your experience and perception. This gentler approach increases the odds that your partner will respond without being critical or defensive, and perhaps even apologize.

In contrast, a "you" statement points the finger at the partner's motives, feelings, behavior, or personality. "You are so selfish. Obviously you didn't think about how embarrassing it was for me to sit there alone!" isn't a statement. It's an accusation. It will trigger defensiveness and make everything worse. Some "you" statements can be subtle. They may arrive packaged in the form of a question such as, "Why did you do that?" or "Why didn't you do this?" or my favorite, "What is wrong with you?" Does anyone really expect their partner to reply, "What an excellent question! Hold on and I'll go check"?

If you want to change your partner's behavior, don't start by saying, "You always tease me when I eat dessert even though you know I hate that." Try something like, "Could you please praise me when I don't eat dessert rather than tease me when I do? That will make it easier for me to stick to my diet." What matters most is not the pronoun you begin with, but *not to criticize*.

My next suggestion is to specify right away which particular issue or event is under discussion—to stay on-topic. It can be tempting to lay it all out when you have the floor and your partner is "forced" to listen. Resist the temptation to let loose over every irritating or boneheaded move your partner has made since your last meeting (or your first date). Likewise, I hope you realize how counterproductive it would be to offer your expert analysis of your partner's personality disorders or behavior problems. Stay out of your Nasty box and describe the facts of the situation as a journalist would. Here are some examples: "The garbage hasn't been taken out." "The laptop isn't charged." "The kids weren't picked up on time."

Finally, be sensitive to your partner's triggers. No one escapes childhood without some scars, and these can escalate conflict. UCLA psychologist Tom Bradbury coined the term "enduring vulnerabilities" to describe these sensitivities. When you're the speaker, keep your knowledge of your partner's weaknesses in your working memory. I tell couples to imagine that every person (not just their partner) is clad in a T-shirt with their enduring vulnerability emblazoned across the front. Some of my favorites are, "Do NOT try to improve me with constructive criticism," "Wanna see defensiveness? Just try blaming me," "Don't lecture me," and "Don't say 'You should' to me."

If you know your girlfriend is extra sensitive about feeling excluded, be gentle when suggesting that she stay home the night of your high school reunion because you want time alone with your old buddies. You could say something like: "I love going to events like this with you. But this time, I'd like to hang out with my friends. Would that be okay with you?" Likewise, if strict house-keeping evokes unhappy memories of his very rigid upbringing, your husband would probably appreciate a break when it comes to his clutter. This is what I call "preemptive repair." It lets you avoid the friction before it starts.

Your partner's baggage may be a source of great irritation, but it is unrealistic to expect that he or she will ever leave these issues behind. It certainly won't happen at your prodding or insistence on "change." Still, you can prevent a particular vulnerability from causing friction by acknowledging it and working around it with compassion. It helps to remember that your partner is learning to do the same for you.

Like all of the attunement skills in the Gottman-Rapoport Blueprint, awareness is more than a tool for resolving conflict. By weaving it into everyday interactions, you'll be more likely to turn toward each other. Let your partner know you're aware—tuned in—to how he or she is feeling. A simple "What's up, honey?" can clear the air and prevent a major storm. But harsh words and phrases such as, "What is it *now?*" or, "With you it's always some-thing isn't it?" will trigger a torrential downpour.

T = Tolerance.

Even when you're certain that your position is right, acknowledge that your partner's perspective is just as valid. You do not need to agree, but you must accept there can be two different valid *percep-tions* that deserve equal weight. There is something worth learn-ing from your partner's viewpoint.

There's an old Jewish joke about the meaning of tolerance. A rabbi renowned for solving marital problems held separate sessions with an unhappy couple, the Goldsteins, while one of his students observed. For twenty minutes he let Mrs. Goldstein complain with deep bitterness about her husband. Then he said, "You are absolutely right. It's unbelievable how much you have to put up with. I have tremendous admiration for you." She replied, "Thank you, Rabbi! Finally, somebody important understands my viewpoint!" Next, the rabbi met with Mr. Goldstein, who also got twenty minutes for bitter complaints. The rabbi then said to him, "You are absolutely right. It's unbelievable how much you have to put up with. I have tremendous admiration for you." Mr. Goldstein replied, "Thank you, Rabbi! Finally, somebody important understands my viewpoint!"

After the Goldsteins left, the student turned to the rabbi in confusion. "I don't understand—they can't both be completely right!"

"You're absolutely right," said the rabbi. He knew that in any significant disagreement there is more than one reality and they are all "right." To work through a regrettable incident with your partner, you must acknowledge and show respect for opinions you do not share. There is no single view of the facts. Perhaps God possesses the DVD Recording of Ultimate Truth. But, just like the old rabbi, God is probably going to stay out of it.

If you have difficulty respecting your partner's perspective, you could profit from one of Rapoport's insights. He discerned that during conflict, we are inclined to see the other person as dissimilar to us. *We* teem with positive traits and qualities while our adversary is overflowing with negative ones. This tendency is related to what another social psychologist, Fritz Heider, named the Fundamental Attribution Error, which, simply stated is: "I'm okay; you're defective."

With the exception of the guilt-ridden and self-critical among us, we all like to think we are the central character of the Great Play of Life. Everyone else is cast in minor and supporting roles.

As a result, we tend to forgive our own mistakes, but not those of others. This perspective clearly stands in the way of resolving relationship conflict. So when you perceive a positive quality in yourself, turn Fritz Heider's Fundamental Attribution Error on its ear and assume that your partner possesses it too. Likewise, whenever you identify a negative quality in your partner, try to see it in yourself as well. Doing so will generate thoughts such as: "When I was sick, he was nice to me, too," or "Yes, she's being selfish right now, but so am I. Maybe we need to allow each other to be a little selfish at times for this relationship to work."

Even when you're not in a State of the Union meeting, tolerance will keep you respectful of your partner's positions and attuned to his or her feelings. Vince fumes on the ride home from Thanksgiving dinner, convinced that his partner Fred's father was talking politics all day just to make him uncomfortable. Fred is just as certain that Dad was just being himself—the old guy never censors his opinions. He doesn't agree with Vince's view of the facts and doesn't think he should be so upset. But Fred knows that telling Vince to stop steaming and get over himself would not be helpful. We don't choose our emotions. But we can choose to accept our partner's.

T = Transforming Criticism into Wishes

In the midst of an argument, it's far more common to express what we don't want than to ask for what we do. We say, "Stop sulking," instead of "I wish you would tell me what's making you sad." Or "Stop ignoring me!" instead of "I need your attention."

The problem with expressing needs in the negative is that it sounds like criticism and, despite what countless people believe, *there is no such thing as constructive criticism*. Unless it is being sought, criticism triggers defensiveness, which prevents resolution of an argument. No matter how much trust there is in a relationship, no one can listen to personal attacks without becoming defensive. In fact, when we recorded disagreements between partners who measured quite high in happiness, on the rare occasion when the speaker began with an attack, the partner became defensive.

For a conflict discussion to succeed, therefore, you must state your feelings as neutrally as possible and then convert any complaint about your partner into a positive need. Your goal is to give your partner a blueprint for succeeding with you. Think of your negative emotions as a clue to a hidden wish and then express that desire directly. Behind anger you're likely to find frustration that a goal was not realized ("I wanted to get to the party on time"), behind sadness there's usually a longing ("I wish you had gotten home so we could eat dinner together"), and so often hope and expectation are lurking behind disappointment ("If you'd clean the kitchen with me, it would take half the time and I'd get to relax").

During their first State of the Union meeting, Greta and Eddie found it hard to focus on the wishes behind their criticisms. Their main difference of opinion concerned whether to move in together after three years of dating. Greta wanted to make the leap; Eddie was wary. They argued over this difference and also argued about their arguing. ("Meta-arguments" are unfortunately too common in State of the Union meetings.) Greta had a tendency to get teary-eyed and leave the room whenever they had a disagreement. This behavior infuriated Eddie. When it was his turn to be speaker, he had to steel himself not to say, "You act like such a child. You always interrupt me and then just walk out—then I feel like the 'bad guy.' That's why I don't want to live with you!" By taking his time and jotting down notes, he framed his complaint as a wish: "I want to be able to tell you how I feel about living together without you walking out or getting upset before I'm finished."

When it was Greta's turn to speak, she also "edited." She *did not* assert, "You are such a rage-aholic. Whenever we disagree, you get nasty. Anyone would get upset and run away from you." She expressed her wish instead: "I want us to discuss issues calmly without either of us raising our voice. That's what I need to stay in the room and really listen to you." This couple gave each other a description of what would have worked to prevent the regrettable incident.

Please don't wait until a conflict arises to express desires in a positive manner. Think about prevention, too. For example, you are more likely to bypass one of those classic "arguments-while-driving" by saying, "*Please* slow down so I can stay calm and not freak out," rather than "Slow down! You're driving like an insane person!"

The Listener's Job

The State of the Union meeting is a dance. When you're the speaker, you must work to be tolerant, sensitive to your partner's vulnerabilities, and nonjudgmental. These steps will go a long way toward tamping down tension, so anger and anxiety don't overwhelm either of you. When you're the listener, you need to resist the urge to debate or defend yourself. Keeping mum will be easier if you remember that when you speak, you will receive the same courtesy. The listener's goal is to appreciate the partner's emotions—their meaning and history, and whatever events may have escalated the conflict or hurt feelings.

U = Understanding, Not Problem Solving

Follow the example of the emotion-coaching parents in my earlier research and avoid making judgments about your partner's anger, sadness, or fear. Don't say, "lighten up," "you're too sensitive," or "it wasn't that bad!" All emotions and wishes are acceptable (although not all behavior is). Emotions also have their own purpose and logic. Your partner cannot select which feelings to have. If you can't get beyond a belief that negative emotions are a waste of time and even dangerous, you will not be able to attune to your partner enough to succeed. "There's no reason to cry," or "Cheer up" are rarely effective. Instead, try something like "Please help me understand what those tears are all about."

My final advice on understanding each other is to avoid trying to solve your partner's problems or assume responsibility for making him or her feel better during the meeting. I have worked with many couples who struggle with this. Some people consider it part of their job description to rescue their partner. When their noble intentions are resisted, they become hurt and frustrated.

Bill has spent twelve years of marriage walking on eggshells around his wife, Denise. He so dreads her next explosion of anger or sadness that when the couple begin therapy, he wants me to assess whether she has a mental illness. It is clear that she does not. Denise comes from an effusive family, which taught her to be comfortable expressing negative emotions. Bill, raised in a taciturn family, is not. Anything less than cheerfulness and optimism puts him on guard. Sorrow, anger, fear, ambivalence—all of these negative emotions seem the same to him, and they all make him anxious. From Denise's perspective, Bill is always irritable. She tells me that whenever she walks into the room, Bill's impenetrable shields lock into place. She calls him the "Batmobile."

Although Denise insists that Bill never listens to her, he is just as emphatic that he always pays attention. When I analyze their Love Lab data, I conclude that Bill *does* turn toward most of Denise's bids, but not in a way that works for her. His belief that it is his job to rescue her from every bad mood is thwarting their ability to attune. Whenever there is a cloud above her, he recommends a practical strategy based on his experience, or suggests a change of attitude based, again, on what works for him. One of his favorite bits of advice is "When the world deals you a bad hand, you just play the hand you are dealt." He gets ticked off when she responds to such sage wisdom with "Yes, but . . ." (as she almost always does). For all of Bill's good intentions, his suggestions make her feel humiliated for expressing emotion. And that just makes her feel worse.

I helped this couple improve their relationship in part by teaching Bill to "do less" and not problem solve when Denise makes a bid for emotional connection during a State of the Union meeting. Over time, he learns that no harm will befall Denise if he just listens to her instead of giving guidance. He comes to accept that he cannot control what she feels and that it is not his job to get his wife to cheer up, calm down, or develop a sense of humor. All she needs is for him to know her and care.

To ensure that you understand fully your partner's feelings, don't rush through being the listener. Take the time to ask probing questions that encourage your partner to get it all out. ("What else are you feeling?" "Is there more you want to say?") Often, when people are upset, their negative emotions line up like dominoes. The first to topple may be anger, which then exposes fear. When that falls, sadness becomes apparent. If the conversation ends before your partner divulges the full range of feelings, the unexplored negative emotions will fester.

N = Nondefensive Listening

Couples are frequently advised that to resolve differences they must listen to each other's perspective without feeling attacked. But as I've said, when your partner is gunning for you, it's unrealistic to expect yourself to bubble over with tolerance and understanding. Yes, it is the speaker's responsibility to avoid flooding you, but it's also necessary for you to soothe yourself.

For many people, this listening skill is the most difficult to master. Consider Ethan, a guy who dreads confrontations with his wife, Penny, because it is difficult for him to listen to her express anger without flooding. He feels great trepidation at the start of their first State of the Union meeting. Penny wants to discuss the argument that ensued earlier in the week. Ethan forgot they had concert tickets and made plans to go out with friends. His forgetfulness at her expense is an ongoing issue for Penny. She worries that he isn't making their life together a priority. But Ethan insists that he is just absentminded. He was often criticized for this as a child. It is one of his "enduring vulnerabilities." The couple's latest attempt to work out this issue blew up in typical fashion, thanks in large part to Ethan's defensiveness. Their "conversation" went something like:

"Why didn't you remind me about the concert?"

"I'm not your mother!"

"So stop acting like it!"

A couple more rounds of sparring followed. Ethan flooded, and they did not talk to each other for hours, until he ate crow and felt humiliated—again.

Just the thought of Penny bringing up that argument during their State of the Union meeting sends Ethan's pulse racing. To his relief, when Penny is the speaker, she states her complaint without criticizing him: "When I reminded you about the concert, you laughed and shrugged. I felt really hurt because it seems like letting me down wasn't a big deal—you were like, Oops! Sorry! Whatever. And yes, you have agreed to cancel on Neil and go with me. I appreciate that. But it feels to me like you're doing me some big favor." Penny is focusing on her experience. She is concentrating on using "I" sentences. But Ethan still finds it hard to listen. He is almost certain that underneath the "new" Penny, the old one lurks, full of accusatory thoughts.

He wishes he could just say, "Okay, I'm sorry," and put an end to the ordeal. But he knows an apology isn't enough. How can he explain to Penny that he did just forget about the concert? But isn't it also unfair that she always pressures him not to hang out with his friends? And that she is always making plans and being bossy? So isn't part of this her fault? But he isn't supposed to mention any of these feelings until he is the speaker. And then he has to express himself in a way that doesn't make her cry. It seems overwhelming to him to formulate a productive response from such an emotional jumble.

Based on observations of the "master attuners" in my studies, I offer clients like Ethan the following strategies to tamp down defensiveness and keep the meeting constructive.

PAUSE AND BREATHE

If you allow yourself a momentary intermission before reacting to a perceived verbal assault, you will have a better chance of soothing yourself. Take deep breaths, focus on relaxing your muscles, doodle, but don't get distracted or stop listening. Remember what it means to be the listener. You don't react to what you're hearing. Just keep breathing, postpone your own agenda, and concentrate on your partner.

WRITE DOWN WHAT YOUR PARTNER SAYS AND ANY DEFENSIVENESS YOU'RE FEELING

This strategy works well in my own life. When I feel defensive, I try to write down everything my wife says. I remind myself that *I care about her and she's in a lot of discomfort, unhappiness, or pain. I am feeling defensive, but I will get my turn to talk.* Sometimes, just the act of writing down her words verbatim, as well as acknowledging my defensiveness, lets me gather myself before speaking.

REMEMBER YOUR LOVE AND RESPECT

Summon your deep and abiding affection and desire to protect your partner. Say to yourself: "In this relationship we do not ignore one another's pain. I have to understand this hurt." Try to separate your anger and upset over this issue from your over-all view of your relationship. Ethan does this by remembering the day he met Penny in college—he was a work-study student on duty at the cafeteria. He ladled chicken soup into her bowl, looked up into her sparkling eyes, and felt winded. Now, he fills his mind with images of all the ways she demonstrates her love, how she supports him, makes him laugh, and carried him emotionally when his father died. The positives seem so much more important than getting his back up over a couple of concert tickets.

Meanwhile, Penny is looking at him with expectation in those same eyes, waiting for him to let her know he understands, accepts, and respects her feelings. He takes a deep breath. "Okay, when I forgot about the concert, you felt hurt. The way I expressed my-self, laughing and shrugging, made you feel like I didn't care, like it wasn't a big deal that I had disappointed you. It makes sense that you felt that way considering your view of what was going on. Did I get it right?" Penny nods and bursts into tears. Ethan's words are a major breakthrough in their relationship.

E = Empathy

In the original *Star Trek* TV series, Mr. Spock used telepathy to do a Vulcan mind meld with others so he could share their experiences. To succeed, he had to shut off his own consciousness for a while. This is close to what I mean by empathy, particularly when your partner is expressing hurt, anger, or sadness. Attunement requires a mind meld of such intensity that you almost become your partner, experiencing his or her feelings. We all have this ability, but to utilize it we must let go of our own opinions and emotions for a while.

Nothing brings this idea home as clearly as the recent research by Robert Levenson and his former student Anna Ruef. In a series of studies, their subjects watched a video of their conflict discussion twice, both times while turning a video recall dial. During the first viewing, they rated their own payoffs moment-by-moment. The next time around they guessed how their *partner* rated the video. Here's where it gets interesting: The researchers also measured each partner's physiological reactions as they guessed what the other was feeling. They discovered that the subjects who were most accurate in guessing their partner's rating dial reactions displayed physiological readings that nearly matched their partners' during the exercise. They were reliving their partners' physiology as if it were their own. This discovery has profound implications for defining trust. To identify your partner's payoffs requires empathy so deep that it is physical.

This sort of mind-and-body melding is crucial during conflict, when it is also the most difficult. But the more you and your partner work on being nondefensive listeners, the easier it will become. Remember not to get caught up in the facts when your partner is speaking. Instead, concentrate on what he or she is feeling.

When it's time for you to summarize what you heard, be

empathic rather than neutral in your delivery. Instead of saying, "You want me to be on time because if I'm late it makes you feel like you're not important to me," begin with something like "*It makes sense to me* that you would need me to be on time." This approach lets your partner know that you consider his or her perspective and feelings legitimate and justified. Validating your partner's viewpoint does not require you to abandon or ignore your own. It just means that, given your partner's experience, you understand why he or she has these feelings and needs. Validation is such a fundamental component of attunement that summarizing without it is like having sex without love.

Most couples know intuitively that empathy is a mainstay of a loving relationship and not just important during the State of the Union meeting. When Lee's back goes out he becomes grumpy and defiant about his doctor's command that he take things easy and not exercise. His childish attitude annoys and worries his wife, Susan, until she realizes that the injury triggered one of her husband's enduring vulnerabilities: he fears that he is more fragile than other people, because his parents died young. To compensate, he tends to deny there is ever anything wrong with him. Instead of reminding Lee that it is important to do his exercises, Susan says things like "I understand why you wouldn't want to start exercising again. I know you just hate thinking that you might be weak. But, honey, you're not weak. You're a strong, healthy man whose back went out." Susan's ability to attune to her husband and validate his feelings isn't going to solve Lee's back pain, nor necessarily get him to be a "good patient." But it is going to strengthen their attachment because Lee senses that Susan is there for him.

What the First Part of a State of the Union Meeting Sounds Like

When you put these ATTUNE skills to work during a structured meeting, the result is not going to resemble a "normal" conversation. But that won't detract from the benefits. Mercedes and Oscar, a middle-aged couple grappling with serious marital issues, mastered the speaker listener approach as part of my 100-couples study. Their marriage began to fray when Mercedes made a midlife career change and became a lawyer. Now, Oscar feels neglected, and the tension between them has skyrocketed. In the past, the couple's personalities—his calm reserve and her feistiness—complemented each other and made them a strong anchor for their children, a twenty-something daughter, Lydia, and teenaged son with autism, Jack. But their current marital problems threaten to tear the family apart. Mercedes believes that Oscar has encouraged Lydia to reject her by minimizing his contributions to their marital meltdown. She feels that his bad-mouthing also alienated her from his extended family. Oscar insists that the real problem between mother and daughter is Mercedes's lack of support for Lydia, who feels insecure around her successful, vibrant mother.

Their State of the Union meeting focuses on how to heal the family. Oscar wants Mercedes to reach out to their daughter. Mercedes's priority is for Oscar to let Lydia and other family members know that she is not the bad guy. But before they can reach an accord, they need to hear each other out. Here's how they fared as speaker and listener. [My comments are in brackets.]

> *Mercedes:* I'm really sad about Lydia, and I'm also really frustrated. I wish you would help me with this. [Turning criticism into a wish.]

Oscar: (*Long pause.*)

Mercedes: Sad, that's all I feel about this. I'm really almost
done. I've given up a little. It's hard to work on this again.
[Awareness: she's using I statements so she doesn't make Oscar
defensive.]

Oscar: Okay, you feel sad about the kids and you want me to help
out, right?

Mercedes: Yes, my need is for you to talk to Lydia about all this,
and to everyone else in the family.

Oscar: Okay, so it's really your relationship with Lydia you want
my help with, and you need me to talk to everyone in our
family too, right? [Understanding. Oscar doesn't try to solve
the problem yet. He just makes sure he's getting it.]

Mercedes: Right, but do you know about what?

Oscar: No, not really.

Mercedes: I thought so. She's really hurt me, too, the things she
said to me. And nobody knows that part, just the part about
how I hurt *her.*

Oscar: Okay, so you want me to tell everyone your side as well as
Lydia's, right? Both families?

Mercedes: No. Just your family, so they won't think of me as a
monster and will know we are working to patch it up. I don't
want this going on at your dad's seventieth-birthday party,
which is coming up.

Oscar: Okay, I get that. I really do, because Lydia has gone to
Uncle Ted about it, and they all gossip in my family.

Mercedes: Right, so I'm the bad mother right now. In my family
they rarely talk at all. But yours is different.

Oscar: Okay, I get that. I understand your feelings and needs here.
My family tends to gang up on people and hold grudges. It'd

be great if you and Lydia were talking to each other at Dad's birthday party. [Empathy.]

Mercedes: So true about the grudges. I'd like that too if we had a nice birthday party.

Oscar: So, are you done? Do you feel understood?

Mercedes: No, I'm not done. You know the gulf between Lydia and me, well, I'm not supposed to be blaming you, but I think that I need you, really need you, to talk to Lydia and take some responsibility for our conflicts. She's just blaming me, claiming that I neglected you in favor of my law practice. And, while our conflicts are partly my fault, they aren't all my fault. [Starting to accuse her husband.]

Oscar: No, they're not at all. I played a pretty big role in instigating the conflicts because I felt I wasn't getting enough lovemaking. We have been through all that with Dr. G. [Nondefensive.]

Mercedes: Well, yes, we've been through all that. And I know I'm not as affectionate as you'd like, and I'm working on that, right?

Oscar: Right. It's much better now.

Mercedes: And you're working on talking to me about what I need and like in sex, right?

Oscar: Yes. So my responsibility in the rift between you and Lydia was letting her feel sorry for her old man and enjoying her siding with me against you, right? [Understanding.]

Mercedes: Yes, exactly. The word was *triangulating*, remember? I need you to tell her something—not too many details—I still want this therapy to be mostly private. Tell her something about how in our conflicts you had half the responsibility. [Now she's turning the criticism into a wish. She isn't blaming him for bad-mouthing her. Instead, she asks him to help her fix things with her daughter and his family.]

Oscar: Okay, I really get that. Otherwise I keep triangulating you as the bad guy, which you're not at all. I get why that would be real upsetting. I did do that. I'm sorry. [Empathy.]

Mercedes: Okay, apology accepted. Yes, that's it. For now I'd be fine with that. What do *you* want and need?

They switch roles. Oscar is now the speaker.

Oscar: Lydia's been ignored. The whole time you were in school, there was never any time for her. [Not a good start. He is making accusatory "you" statements.]

Mercedes: That's not accurate, really. It's just that Jack got all the attention. Not all, either. I paid a lot of attention to Lydia, too. [Defensiveness. This is going to prevent her from really hearing Oscar.]

Oscar: And she had to take care of Jack. Or felt that she did.

Mercedes: I actually took care of him, mostly, even though I was in school. But the two of them have always been real close. She wanted to take care of him. [More defensiveness.]

Oscar: But she has felt neglected by you especially. I have been able to be close to her. Instead of you. But she needed her mom, still does. [More "you, you, you."]

Mercedes: So let's get to you. I'm feeling a little ganged up on here. You're describing what I did, or didn't do. And you've got it all wrong, I might add. Makes it hard for me to listen and take notes. [Mercedes tries to get them back on track.]

Oscar: Oh, yeah, sorry. I'm describing you instead of me. That's what he said not to do. [Her repair worked.]

Mercedes: Right.

Oscar: I guess I feel angry. Not that I'm angry with you for going to law school or building your practice. I'm real proud of you. I'm real glad I saw you litigate that last case. It was a real treat. You were so hot. The guys on the jury thought so, too.

Mercedes: Thank you. I really did ace that case, at the very last minute.

Oscar: So what am I angry about? I think I'm angry at you for yelling at me in front of Lydia and scaring her. And for the two of you fighting at my mom's funeral, also.

Mercedes: Oh, God, I am feeling so defensive. Oscar, she was upset then because her husband was putting his fist through the wall, and that's what had her upset at the funeral—not me.

Oscar: I didn't know that. She told me she was upset because you and I were fighting.

Mercedes: That too, I guess. Okay, let's get back to what you need.

Oscar: So, I need you to listen to her, a long session of just listening to her. [Transforming a criticism into a wish.]

Mercedes: Okay. You need me to really listen to her and not get defensive like I just did with you. Right? [Understanding.]

Oscar: Right.

Mercedes: Anything else?

Oscar: Well, see she really admires you, and I think she's scared she won't measure up to you. [Awareness. He is using "I" statements rather than accusing Mercedes of intimidating their daughter.]

Mercedes: What? She's an amazing nurse. It's really impressive the way she can think on her feet in emergencies. And I was a lot older than her when I finished law school, so I don't know why she feels like she needs to measure up.

Oscar: Still I know that Lydia doesn't think you're really proud of her.

Mercedes: She doesn't?

Oscar: Have you ever told her?

Mercedes: Not in so many words. You and I have talked about how, growing up no one in my family ever said too much of anything positive or showed any affection for that matter.

Oscar: I know that's an "enduring vulnerability" issue for you. [Tolerance.]

Mercedes: Yeah. Let me see if I got it. So you are mad at me and want me to really listen to Lydia for a really long time, so she gets it all out. Also you need me to directly tell her how proud I am of her. Right? [Understanding]

Oscar: That's it, yes. Maybe you can also tell her how much you appreciate her care of Jack, or really, her sensitivity to him. [Transforming criticism into a wish.]

Mercedes: Okay, I can understand that. She is pretty amazing at being able to communicate with him. In fact, she's taught me a lot. I know, it feels great to me when you tell me that I'm hot when I'm arguing a case I won, so I get it. Tell her directly that I'm proud of her. I will try to do that. Okay. Is there anything else? [Empathy.]

Oscar: No, that's pretty much it.

Despite occasional missteps, Oscar and Mercedes are able to listen, hear, and empathize with each other. They are ready to consider solutions to their conflict.

The Next Step:
Persuasion and Problem Solving

When you both feel heard and understood, you begin to negotiate your differences. Throughout this process, remain open to your partner's influence, but do not overcompromise. When problem solving doesn't work, it is often because at least one partner agrees to give up too much and then reneges. To avoid this mess, start by identifying your core needs to ensure that you—and your partner—are clear on what concessions you *cannot* make. I recommend that couples write down these needs and draw a circle around them. ("I cannot live far from my family," "I have to exercise every day.") Try to keep this list very short by including only needs you know are essential to your happiness and, therefore, the relationship's success. Use "I" sentences to describe these non-negotiables so your partner does not feel criticized or coerced. "I need us to spend more time socializing with others" expresses a core need. "I need you to be more outgoing" is criticism.

Next, draw a much larger circle around the first one. Inside, list any aspect of your position that you can modify. Although you cannot compromise on the need itself, perhaps you can bend on some specifics, such as the timing, location, or methods used to achieve your goal. ("I can live with going out every other weekend," "I can switch to a closer gym so I get home sooner.") The solutions you arrive at won't be as obvious as these examples—if they were, you wouldn't need this process to resolve the conflict! Expect a great deal of struggle and back and forth as you search for ways to weave each other's areas of compromise into an approach that you can both accept. Be open to your partner's creative suggestions. The process can take a long time, but I have seen couples succeed even when their core needs seemed incompatible. After years of living in the suburbs, Pam wanted to spend her retirement years in the city. But her husband, Mike, had long dreamed about them sailing around the world together. By focusing on their areas of compromise, they came up with a solution that both could endorse: they would spend two years sailing and then two years living in New York. After that, they would see where they stood.

There are circumstances that can prevent successful compromise. If it turns out that one person's dream is truly the other's nightmare, there is not a way forward. In a typical case, only one partner wants to have children. Couples usually cannot bridge this difference and sometimes probably should not. But by using the blueprint to sort this out, you can end the relationship with a clear understanding of why you each needed to move on.

In most relationships, though, this process does lead to a compromise. It may take more than one meeting to reach an accord. You'll need time to consider your partner's position and all the options you've discussed. Here's how Mercedes and Oscar use the blueprint to work out their disagreement over their daughter, Lydia.

Mercedes: Okay. Now let's move on to persuasion. I think, let's see, two circles. Okay, in my inner circle, what I can't be flexible about is your talking to Lydia about you having responsibility in part for our conflicts, and that we are working on them in therapy and making progress and, second, is for you to at least talk to Uncle Ted about how Lydia created a lot of this gulf between us by blaming me for our conflicts, taking your side, and you relishing that.

Oscar: Okay, then what are you flexible about?

Mercedes: I am flexible about you not having to talk to everyone in the family about my being a good mom, just Ted, and I am flexible about when you talk to Lydia, as long as it's before the birthday party.

Oscar: Okay, that's totally reasonable. I am inflexible about you and Lydia having a session in which you listen and tell her you're proud of her.

Mercedes: And what are you flexible about?

Oscar: I'm willing to confess to Lydia my responsibility for our fights and to talk about my role in triangulating you as the bad guy. I never saw that before this therapy, and I feel real bad about it. She should hear that.

Mercedes: Okay. I am glad you feel bad about it. And all of this we will try to resolve before the seventieth-birthday party, right?

Oscar: Let's maybe do it this week?

Mercedes: You go first, okay?

Oscar: Yeah, that makes total sense.

Mercedes: Okay, spit shake.

Oscar: Spit shake it is.

Mercedes and Oscar pretty much stick to the rules and move from attuning to compromising with relative ease. Although they are working through a lot of pain, they hear each other's core needs and agree to meet them.

But even with the blueprint as a guide, understanding and compromise can be messy. Couples shouldn't expect to always stay on script or to attune quickly. At their State of the Union meeting, Zach and Judy attempt to reconnect after a mutual meltdown over juggling careers and baby care. The argument occurs when Zach arrives home from a business trip, devastated to hear that their daughter, Carla, took her first steps during his absence. Judy is not sympathetic. She took time off from work to stay home all week with Carla. She is exhausted and furious that Zach only called twice. Neither feels appreciated. At times during their State of the Union meeting, they sound like competitors for the Top Victim Award. But in the end, they move beyond their gripes and work it out. Here are some snippets, with their thoughts in italics and mine in brackets:

Judy [Speaker]: I had it up to here with you being gone all week. I mean life is tough when you're here, but it's an absolute nightmare when you're gone.

Zach [Listener]: But we have a nanny. You have lots of help when I'm gone. [Defensive "you" statement. Not helpful.]

Judy: A nanny whose kids had the flu this week and she herself was running a fever, so I couldn't very well have her around the baby, could I? And getting people to cover for me when I had to be at work was hell . . . On the phone you never once asked about the stress I was under.

Zach: Well, you never asked about how my presentation went either. It went fine, thank you! [More defensiveness.]

Judy: I knew you'd do fine. But I wasn't doing fine, was I? (*I need him to admit that I am suffering while he's off having fun.*)

Zach: But you've cut down on work and I have done exactly the opposite. (*I didn't even want to go to the conference, but the contacts were important for my job, which matters to our future. I could use a little appreciation here.*)

Now Zach and Judy get on track and are able to reconnect.

Judy: Then you come home and want my attention? And sex? What?

Zach: (*Laughs.*) Like having a second baby. [Repair attempt.]

Judy: Exactly. [His repair worked.]

Zach: I can see your point. I remember the time you went to visit your dad when he was sick. I had two days alone with Carla and trying to work, and I just about died from all the added stress.

Judy: I just wish that while you were gone you found the time to call so we could have a real conversation and I could tell you how stressed out I was. [Transforming criticism into a wish.]

Zach: That's true. I was so busy at the conference that I had very little time to even make the phone calls, but I should have talked to you more. I'm *really* sorry. Truth is, all the time I was there I was thinking about you! [Appreciation.]

Judy: I know you were sad because that moment of her walking was really amazing. [Empathy.]

Zach: Hearing about it on the phone was not the same as being there.

Judy: That's for sure. It was the only good part of the week, though.

Zach: I had quite a lot of success at the conference, and I need you to appreciate that I went. [Transforming criticism into a wish.]

Judy: That's a good point. I know you needed to go to do that presentation. I'm really glad you went.

Zach: Thank you. *(She finally gets it! This feels good.)*

Judy: But all I could think about was the nightmare I had on my hands, and I thought here you are, going out for great dinners and grown-up company. All I ate was Lean Cuisine. I only got two showers in a week.

Zach: That truly sucks, and you're right, some of those dinners were really great. I just wished you'd been there. [Empathy.]

Judy: Me too. *(He's getting it!)*

Zach: There was a French meal you'd have loved. With an amazing chocolate dessert.

Judy: Yum!

Zach: Yeah . . . um . . . so, I was thinking about how much I'd like to do an overnight at that B&B on Bainbridge Island.

Judy: I love that place! *(Pause.)* But I don't feel comfortable
leaving Carla yet.

Zach: Even for one night?

Judy: I guess we *could* do that. *(I'm feeling loved and appreciated
again.)*

Zach: You know my main complaint. *(Sex, please!)*

Judy: Yeah, thanks for being patient with me. Let's do it. *(If we
spend a weekend away, it will be nice and lower my guilt over the
whole lovemaking problem.)*

Zach: Great. *(Finally, sex!)*

A major life change—adjusting to parenthood—caused Zach and
Judy to disconnect. But they are finding their way back to each
other. They now see that their relationship can remain a safe haven,
even when they have strong disagreements, if they remember to
express appreciation and support each other. Like all couples, they
can expect to slip into their Nasty boxes on occasion, especially in
times of stress. But because they have mastered critical attunement
skills, they will be able to pull out before lasting harm is done.

The Gottman's Aftermath Kit: Healing Previous Injuries and Hurt Feelings

Once you become familiar with holding State of the Union
meetings, I recommend using the process to revisit regrettable
incidents from the past that still haunt your relationship. Unless
they are confronted and understood, unhappy memories push
couples closer to Negative Sentiment Override. I've developed an
attunement-based approach to help couples shut the door on these
lingering conflicts.

The Aftermath Kit is very similar to the blueprint. Its goal is to increase understanding and empathy. But it is more extensive. The same rules apply: You agree not to argue about "the facts" of the situation. Perception is everything; both points of view are valid. Don't use this recovery kit until you have some emotional distance from the incident and can discuss it *without getting back into it.* Approach your discussion as if you are in a theater's balcony, observing the actors on stage—except the two of you are the actors. If either of you floods, stop the discussion.

After you offer each other appreciations, follow these six steps, taking turns as speaker and listener. (If you need extra help, you'll find suggestions for words and phrases you can use during these steps in appendix 2 on page 250.)

Step One: Recall and Name the Emotions Out Loud.

When you're the speaker, describe *all* of the feelings you experienced during the incident. Do not get into why you reacted a particular way yet. And do not comment on your partner's feelings.

Step Two: Discuss Your Subjective Reality

Acknowledge that your experience did not match your partner's. Don't debate "the facts." Take turns talking about how you each perceived the situation. What did you require from your partner to avoid a regrettable incident? When you're the speaker, remember to describe these needs as positive wishes ("I needed you to . . .") and acknowledge all of them, even if they seem silly or contradictory in retrospect. If you didn't admit to these wishes at the time, mention that as well. The most common needs people express are: wanting to feel listened to, understood, complimented, desired, and comforted. Letting your partner know what was going on inside makes your behavior more understandable. The more specific you make your descriptions, the better. ("I wanted you to stop texting when I was talking," "I needed you to look happy to see me," "I wanted to make love before we went out.") As always, do not criticize or blame your partner and avoid attributing motives, intentions, attitudes, or behavior to him or her. When you're done speaking, your partner summarizes and validates your subjective reality. Once you feel heard, you switch roles.

Step Three: Identify the Deep Triggers

What pushed your buttons when the conflict occurred? Often, triggers are enduring vulnerabilities from childhood. Common ones include feeling excluded, manipulated, vulnerable, falsely accused, judged, disrespected, or unsafe.

Put in your own words *all* of the triggers you experienced.

"It felt like I was being blamed."

"I felt bossed around and disrespected."

"I felt unprotected, like I had to handle everything by myself."

Step Four: Recount the History of These Triggers

Explain where these triggers came from. In your mind, rifle through your autobiography and pause at a page that illustrates the same set of feelings and describe the trigger and its cause—perhaps from your childhood or a previous relationship. Describe what happened and your reaction. You want to share as much as possible so your partner will understand and remember to keep salt away from your old wounds.

"In my first marriage, I always got blamed for everything. My husband would never take responsibility. So when you accused me of making us late to your sister's party, I thought, *Oh no! Here we go again.*"

"As a kid my mother was always telling me what to do. After my dad died, she had complete control. When you told me to clean up, rather than asking, it felt like an order, like I was a little boy again, and it triggered those same resentful feelings."

"My dad always told me, 'Fight your own battles,' even when my much bigger brother was punching me. So when it seemed like you didn't want to hear about my problems with my boss, I felt unsafe again—like I was under attack and all alone with no one to help me."

When you are the listener, realize that your partner's responses to the experience may differ from how you would feel in the same circumstance. Do not criticize or suggest a "better" way.

Step Five: Take Responsibility for Your Contributions and Apologize

It won't fly to make excuses for your part in the current conflict or to shuffle blame based on your history. Own up to the role you played. Some common contributions people acknowledge are being overly sensitive, critical, or defensive; playing the martyr, and not listening. After taking responsibility, apologize to your partner for your specific negative behaviors linked to these contributions. Also, see if you can describe to your partner in a sentence or two the role you played in the regrettable incident. Your partner should do the same.

The couple below is working through a previous argument

about her spending habits that ended in a shouting match. Her deep trigger was feeling devalued when her husband questioned a recent bill, because her tightfisted parents frequently chided her for wanting things, as if it were a character flaw:

> *She:* "I accused you of not loving me, which I know is ridiculous. I'm sorry I overreacted and started yelling when you were speaking."

Her husband's deep trigger was feeling dismissed, a legacy of his first marriage. Whenever he wanted to discuss an area of conflict with his first wife, she would act as if he didn't exist.

> *He:* "I came on much stronger than I needed to out of fear that you would ignore me. That was my fault. I'm sorry. I know it made things a lot worse."

Step Six: Figure Out How to Make It Better Next Time

Use your new understanding of why the unfortunate incident occurred to discuss one way each of you could make it better should there be a repeat. In the example above, the husband could decide to be gentler when questioning her spending habits, and she could agree not to drown out his concerns by raising her voice. Now that they know each other's vulnerabilities, they will respect them—and also help each other detect overreactions. Couples I have worked with who master the technique experience a dramatic rise in their trust metric. When differences spark, they know how to be honest and gentle about their point of view and take a loving step toward each other.

Once you get in the habit of holding weekly attunement

meetings to process past and present differences, the approach will feel less stilted. Your meetings will likely become briefer and more efficient. In time, the need for such meetings will dwindle. Instead, you'll find that you can handle your conflicts with sensitivity as they occur, and thus defuse them before they do significant damage.

Using the State of the Union to handle both current and past grievances bolsters the trust between couples so they can avoid or vanquish betrayal. But there is one exception: This approach alone cannot heal couples reeling from sexual infidelity. Although other forms of betrayal can be as damaging, our culture's misconceptions about the causes of adultery and our general discomfort with issues of sexuality mean that healing from this breach requires special attention and additional, specific treatment. The process is difficult, but it can salvage a relationship if partners are motivated to find their way back to each other and to build a new relationship to replace the one that failed them.

10

Recovering from Infidelity

Comedian Robin Williams once said, "God gave man a penis and
a brain, and only enough blood to run one at a time." With some
alteration that quip could probably be applied to both genders. It
is easy to find opportunities to cheat, but extraordinarily difficult
to recover a relationship afterward. I have often thought that if
people could imagine the arduous steps involved, they would
never consider straying. That they do may prove the process is
not entirely rational.

Recent research shows a relatively good prognosis for couples
determined to recover their love after infidelity. Separate pilot research by Donald Baucom, at the University of North Carolina,
and Andy Christensen, at UCLA, find that at the beginning of
structured marriage therapy, couples who are grappling with an

affair score lower in measures of happiness than do other troubled couples. But they end up with the same level of relationship satisfaction. It's unfortunate, though perhaps not surprising, that the relationship satisfaction level for all of the unhappy couples was still pretty low at the end of both studies. The long-term success rate for typical, nonresearch-based couples therapy tends to be poor, which is why I believe that applying a scientific approach is so critical. These results imply that with an *effective* therapeutic approach, couples recovering from sexual infidelity should have equal potential to overcome the past as others. Although regaining trust offers extreme challenges for both partners, there is reason to be hopeful.

Not every relationship can or should be saved. You need to be honest with yourself and your partner. If you did the cheating, ask yourself if you're ambivalent about leaving your lover. If so, you are probably not ready to rekindle your primary relationship. Likewise, if you were betrayed, you may decide it's best to walk away even if your disloyal partner is begging for a chance to set things right. And, of course, if the disloyal partner is not interested in a rapprochement, trying to convince him or her will just lead to more pain. Instead, use your emotional resources to move on. If you were the victim, don't pressure yourself to heal on any schedule. Respect that you are fragile right now. Discovering that the person you entrusted with your heart betrayed you may lead to questioning everything. You wonder who your partner really is, whether you were ever loved, and even what commitment means. Often you can't help ruminating about the past, going over it in your head, wondering where, why, and how the affair happened. Disturbed sleep, flashbacks, depression, obsessive and intrusive thoughts, emotional numbing, insecurity, self-doubt, and generalized anxiety are common. These are all indicators of the same posttraumatic stress disorder soldiers sometimes experience (although a very different type of trauma is the trigger). Research by Shirley Glass confirms that these symptoms are very common after the discovery or admission of an affair.

Working through all of these issues is complex and almost always requires an experienced therapist. Trying to fix the relationship without skilled professional help is like attempting to perform knee-replacement surgery with a home kit. But before you sign on for extensive, professional intervention, it may be helpful to get some clarity on whether the relationship is worth saving. The old saying "Once a cheater, always a cheater" is unfair to some (but not all) unfaithful spouses. How do you know if you can trust your partner to respect and cherish you moving forward? Can he or she ever become trustworthy—or will your relationship always be at risk?

The questionnaire below can help you begin to find the answers. It will give your relationship a betrayal assessment score—a rough indication of whether treatment would likely be successful. It is based on my analysis of data collected by Dr. Amber Tabares. In her study, couples underwent exercises that shared similarities with the assessment below. By correlating her findings with my own calculations of her subjects' trustworthiness levels, I could identify which unhappy couples were at high risk of future unfaithfulness.

The Gottman Assessment of Future Betrayal

This evaluation consists of two questionnaires. Each of you must complete both. Be honest with each other—and yourself.

Part 1: Characteristics That You Appreciate

Look over the following list of personal qualities and circle all that your partner possesses now that please you even if you are not ready to acknowledge them out loud. Include as many as you wish. If a characteristic was apparent on only one occasion, still circle it.

1. Put a star next to three qualities you circled for which you can recall actual examples and that you are willing to discuss with your partner.
2. Now open up to each other about the positive qualities you starred. Recall the events where these characteristics were apparent and how they made you feel.

A Great Friend	Energetic	Nurturing
A Planner	Exciting	Organized
Active	Expressive	Playful
Adventurous	Fun	Practical
Affectionate	Funny	Receptive
Athletic	Generous	Relaxed
Attractive	Gentle	Reliable
Beautiful	Graceful	Reserved
Brave	Gracious	Resourceful
Calm	Handsome	Responsible
Careful	Imaginative	Rich
Caring	Intellectually stimulating	Sensitive
Cheerful	Intelligent	Sexy
Committed	Interesting	Strong
Considerate	Involved	Thoughtful
Coordinated	Kind	Thrifty
Creative	Lively	Truthful
Dependable	Loving	Virile
Dominant	Loyal	Warm
Elegant	Lusty	Witty

Part 2: Assess Your Reactions.

After you have completed the excercises in Part 1, reflect on how you and your partner reacted during your discussion. Circle your responses to the following statements, using this key.

SD: Strongly Disagree

D: Disagree

N: Neither Agree nor Disagree

A: Agree

SA: Strongly Agree

1. My partner teased me about my personality. SD1 D2 N3 A4 SA5

2. My partner was very complimentary toward me. SD5 D4 N3 A2 SA1

3. My partner made fun of me. SD1 D2 N3 A4 SA5

4. My partner showed me that he or she likes me. SD5 D4 N3 A2 SA1

5. It was hard to come up with anything positive about my partner's character. SD1 D2 N3 A4 SA5

6. My partner was very affectionate. SD5 D4 N3 A2 SA1

7. My partner was sweet toward me. SD5 D4 N3 A2 SA1

8. My partner was vague and unspecific about my good qualities. SD1 D2 N3 A4 SA5

9. I had a good time doing this exercise. SD5 D4 N3 A2 SA1

10. My partner was sarcastic about my personality. SD1 D2 N3 A4 SA5

11. My partner had no trouble coming up with examples of my positive traits. SD5 D4 N3 A2 SA1

12. My partner really listened to me. SD5 D4 N3 A2 SA1

13. My partner was very warm toward me. SD5 D4 N3 A2 SA1

14. My partner had trouble coming up with stories about my good qualities. SD1 D2 N3 A4 SA5

15. My partner was derisive. SD1 D2 N3 A4 SA5

16. We laughed a lot together doing these exercises. SD5 D4 N3 A2 SA1

17. I had trouble coming up with examples of my partner's
    good qualities.   SD1   D2   N3   A4   SA5
18. My partner demonstrated respect toward me.   SD5   D4   N3   A2   SA1
19. My partner had lots of examples of my good
    qualities.   SD5   D4   N3   A2   SA1
20. My partner showed me that he or she admires me.   SD5   D4   N3   A2   SA1
21. My partner mimicked me in a mocking way.   SD1   D2   N3   A4   SA5
22. My partner expressed pride in me.   SD5   D4   N3   A2   SA1
23. My partner used terms like "You always" or "You never"
    to describe negatives about my personality.   SD1   D2   N3   A4   SA5
24. My partner made fun of me.   SD1   D2   N3   A4   SA5
25. Doing these exercises was hard and unpleasant.   SD5   D4   N3   A2   SA1
26. My partner swore a lot.   SD1   D2   N3   A4   SA5
27. My partner belittled me.   SD1   D2   N3   A4   SA5
28. I felt blamed by my partner for what is wrong with
    our relationship.   SD1   D2   N3   A4   SA5
29. These exercises were interesting and fun to do.   SD5   D4   N3   A2   SA1
30. My partner tried to describe nice qualities in
    my personality, but it wasn't sincere.   SD1   D2   N3   A4   SA5

Scoring

1. Count the number of items that you rated either 4 or 5.
2. If the total *number* of items (not their sum) is fewer than 10, you're done with scoring. Your relationship has passed this betrayal detector test. If you are both committed to trying, it is worth the rescue effort.
3. If you rated more than 15 items either a 4 or 5, use a calculator to divide that number by 30. Multiply the result by 100. Put a percentage symbol after this number and you have your Betrayal Assessment Score.
4. A score higher than 70 percent suggests that forgiveness is probably not wise at this time. If you scored below 70 percent, it is worth attempting to forgive.

You may wonder how I know that a high score on this exercise points not just to an unhappy relationship but to a great risk of future unfaithfulness. When a partner shows contempt and disrespect during an exercise meant to generate positive feelings, it means he or she is unlikely to put the partner and their lives together first. This lack of trustworthiness will prevent healing, since making the relationship a priority is mandatory for an intervention to succeed.

Choosing a Therapist

If you conclude that your relationship is worth salvaging, find an experienced counselor or therapist who is effective in working with couples coping with infidelity. Therapists employ all kinds of approaches. In mine, it is the professional's job to "get" the wounded spouse's thoughts and emotions and then describe them to the therapist eloquently and with deep empathy. In effect, the therapist bridges the gap between the partners by articulating with great precision what the hurt spouse is feeling and ensuring that the other fully understands.

You may not be able to find a therapist whose method mirrors what I do, but it is imperative that you find someone qualified who will not subject you to inappropriate or even damaging forms of therapy. Among the "musts to avoid" is any therapist who suggests that you not discuss the betrayal and let bygones be bygones. Just moving on with your relationship is a terrible idea, even if the affair happened twenty years ago. You cannot heal until you have processed the trauma. To offer a grim analogy, this approach is like discovering a malignant tumor during surgery and then stitching the patient back up without removing it. Yet the advice to move on is not uncommon, particularly among pastoral counselors—ministers, priests, rabbis, and imams. Although these advisers are well meaning, this strategy is harmful.

Recently, as part of a segment on Canada TV for a program called *The Science of Sin,* I worked with a couple whose experience illustrates how counterproductive it is to ignore what happened and "get on with it." Here is a partial transcript of my session with them.

John Gottman: Tell me what your own understanding is right now about the affair, why it happened, and where you are now in your relationship.

Laura: We've seen two ministers . . .

Malcolm: They advised us to put all this behind us and move on . . . The affair is over. I have come back to my family. So I am moving forward.

John Gottman: And do you understand his decision to come back to you?

Laura: Not really. No.

John Gottman: Do you want to try to tell her why you're back?

Malcolm: Okay, I'll try again to tell you. I love your family, and our children, and I really value the kind of person you are. I have a lot of respect for you, as a mother. And as a wife.

John Gottman: And how does that sound to you?

Laura: Really how it sounds to me is hollow and empty. I just don't believe you. I don't really know why you're back. I don't know what you saw in her either.

Malcolm: You know she was someone from work. We had that in common. We could talk about work easily.

Laura: I kept asking you to talk to me [about work]. But you were always so quiet.

Malcolm: There wasn't much to say about it. It was stressful. That's it. You had enough to worry about with five kids and all.

Laura: I know it's been very hard for you these past few years . . . But you talked to her instead of me.

John Gottman: There have been some real financial setbacks, I understand.

Malcolm: Yes.

Laura: It's been hard on me, too. But we've done it together, haven't we?

Malcolm: You've been great. You always have been amazing. You handle everything so well.

Laura: So why did you go to her? I saw her picture, and I'm much more attractive than she is.

Malcolm: No, she's not as beautiful as you are.

John Gottman (to Malcolm): Maybe you could explain what happened for you, what you saw in her.

Malcolm: The ministers told us not to talk about it, not to dwell on it.

John Gottman: But it leaves her not understanding why you left, or why you're back, so it might be better to try to explain some of what happened to you.

Malcolm: She was very needy. Not like you at all. She really needed me . . . You [can] handle everything yourself.

Laura: I'm self-sufficient because I had to be. You were always at work. I backed off because you were so stressed these past years. I didn't want to add to your burdens. I hated being so alone.

John Gottman: I recall [as part of my assessment] that your conflict discussion was about you not wanting to be seen as "badgering" him.

Malcolm: Yes, she has been badgering me about the affair. All the details. I haven't wanted to add to her pain. The ministers also said not to dwell on it.

John Gottman (to Laura): I think you haven't badgered him enough. You have both avoided conflict and in our assessments you both scored 100 percent in loneliness. Does that seem right?

Laura: It is for me.

Malcolm: Me, too . . . A lot of times I feel like just a paycheck with a pulse to you. You don't need me for anything. A lot of times I don't even want to come home from work.

Laura: I didn't ever know you felt that way.

John Gottman: But the other woman . . .

Malcolm: I felt she needed me. She had so many problems . . . Her life is a real mess.

Laura: I needed you, too. But you always got so mad when I asked you to talk to me about how you felt, about your work.

John Gottman (to Malcolm): You were silent in this relationship. And you were being strong in the face of all the stresses by being silent?

Malcolm: My whole family growing up, everyone was silent. There was no yelling like in some families. But no one ever said they loved me. I guess they did . . . But I felt I could have walked out and nobody would have noticed. So I am like that. Very, very quiet.

John Gottman: In your marriage you were quiet, like in your family growing up.

Malcolm: She had enough on her hands without me complaining.

John Gottman: So you both coped with enormous hardships, but you did so quietly and alone. Avoiding talking about how alone you both felt left you both vulnerable. To loneliness. And left

Malcolm feeling unneeded. That was the huge attractiveness of the other woman. So, I'd say that your marriage is still in a crisis. Would you agree?

Laura: I would.

Malcolm: I would also.

John Gottman: See, I think those ministers were totally wrong. Research has shown that after an affair, people need to talk about it. Desperately. They need to understand it. They need to build a new relationship. And you don't do that without a lot of pain.

Laura: I am in a lot of pain right now. I don't know what to do to make it better.

Malcolm: I don't know either.

John Gottman: You have to keep talking about it. And the loneliness and conflict avoidance has to change. But you can't do it on your own. You need a competent couples' therapist, not people who keep advising you to avoid talking to one another. Does that make sense?

Laura: It does to me. Now.

Malcolm: To me as well.

It's clear that Laura is still traumatized by her husband's adultery and that they both feel lonely in their relationship. Not talking about it just doesn't work. Without proper intervention, this marriage may continue, but "in name only." In such situations it is common for the couple to lead parallel lives and never connect intimately. They will continue to feel isolated and profoundly lonely.

The advice to "forgive and forget" may be the most prevalent wrongheaded treatment approach out there, but it is not the only one. It's also common for a therapist to instruct the betrayed partner not to be "controlling" once the affair is discovered. The injured party may be told to suppress the desire to check up on the partner or demand accountability, as if ongoing suspicion is a hindrance to healing. It is not! The hurt partner requires confirmation that the future won't hold another devastating blow. That means relentless reassurance for quite some time. For the relationship to survive, the guilty member must tolerate this need, understanding that it is a symptom of the posttraumatic stress that the betrayal created. It will not go away until therapy reestablishes enough trust.

Here is some dialogue between a married couple in my lab who were grappling with this issue of lingering distrust. The husband, who had an affair three years prior, says he wants to have an ex-girlfriend from his college days visit them. Although this woman was not his affair partner, the idea frightens his wife. The husband's response is defensive rather than understanding, which is counterproductive. This couple divorces eventually.

> *Martin:* Okay. I feel, that you're gonna trust me only as long as I am real careful about . . . what I do. I think your jealousy results from lack of trust.
>
> *Maya:* Uh-huh. And a fear. A fear of losing something very precious.
>
> *Martin:* But I've explained to you that my family is the number-one thing in my life and that there's no need to fear. I made that conscious decision, three years ago, and that's not gonna change. I guaranteed you that, right?
>
> *Maya:* And you know, I'm convinced of it? And so it's dissipated the jealousy. But because my feelings of jealousy have been well founded before . . .

Martin: Uh, see, there's where I disagree. I resent the fact, that, in the case of Jillian [the college girlfriend], that I can never see her again. For the rest of my life.

Maya: Do you *want* to see her again?

Martin: Yeah. And I resent the fact that you don't trust me enough. I dated her a year before I even met you. You don't even trust me enough for her to come over and meet you and meet the kids.

Maya: I don't want her to become a part of our lives. I don't want my children befriending her. There's no purpose for it. Unless you're doing like you did a few years ago, where you can kind of gradually get the kids to like her, and then kind of work into a—

Martin: Oh, geez.

Maya: "Bye-bye Maya. The kids like her better than you. Here's your *new* mother."

Martin: No way. I just want to stay in touch. Just to talk over old times.

Maya: She's a big threat to me. If you were really committed like you say you are, you would not do this. You would realize where I'm coming from.

Martin: (Chuckles softly.) You know, probably, if you said it didn't matter to you, then it'd be less important to me.

Maya: Well, I'd be dishonest if I said it didn't matter. Because now you want to see her, but on Sunday we discussed it and you said it was resolved, that it was finished. You lied to me.

Martin: (Chuckling.) I didn't lie to you. Like I said, it's not a pressing need. But I resent the fact that I can't. Whenever you tell somebody "You can never do that"—

Maya: Do you know why I don't think it's a good idea? Because I think you're weak. I think the flesh is weak. And it would not be good for the marriage.

Martin: It would be good from the standpoint that it would be proof that you trusted me, and that would help the marriage.

Maya: No. You resist temptation. You don't go running into its arms. If I wanted you to trust *me*, I wouldn't set up situations that were threatening to you. I don't know why it is that you're not able to see what it's like to be in my shoes.

Martin may be earnest about his unwavering commitment to his marriage. But his past deceit traumatized Maya. Out of respect for her, he should be careful not to do anything that raises alarm. Yet he takes a stand over inviting an old girlfriend into their home. He taunts and tests his wife, insisting that it is her job to prove she is not jealous when instead it is his to prove that he is trustworthy. All he accomplishes is to fill his wife with dread. He needs to respect that he cannot impose an expiration date on her need to be vigilant.

My wife, Dr. Julie Gottman, and I created the following list of counterproductive therapy approaches, based on our knowledge of the therapeutic process and the experiences of couples we've worked with after other therapies failed them. If a therapist communicates any of the following beliefs, find somebody else to work with.

1. It's best not to talk about the affair. Avoid conflict and cool it.
2. Both partners are equally culpable. The more subtle (and common) version of this is: When we examine the psychological dynamics of your relationship, we'll discover that the affair was as much the fault of the betrayed as the betrayer.
3. An affair is much worse when a woman strays.
4. If the cheating was done with a prostitute, it's not as bad.

5. You have to forgive the betrayer before progress can be made.

6. Your shared faith alone is enough to carry you through this.

7. The betrayed partner's anger is bad and will drive the betrayer away.

8. The real goal is to save the marriage at all costs.

9. The real goal is to end the marriage because no relationship can survive such a betrayal.

10. You are not "really" angry about the affair. That's just a cover for being sad, insecure, or afraid for other reasons.

11. You are making too big a deal of this.

12. Women just have to accept that "boys will be boys."

13. There is something wrong with the betrayed person for having explosive feelings.

14. There is a timeline for when you should be over this.

15. If the affair happened years ago, it doesn't matter anymore.

16. If the betrayed person hadn't done X, or had done Y, all this would never have happened. (Example: If she'd put out more.)

17. The way you argued was the ultimate cause of the affair.

18. Affairs are all about biology and gender differences.

19. Marriages are supposed to last only about four years, until the baby can walk and talk well enough, so affairs are inevitable.

20. One-night stands don't count.

21. If the cheater didn't love the sex partner, then it wasn't really an affair.

22. If it involved only sex, it wasn't an affair.

23. If there was no intercourse, it wasn't an affair.

24. If there was no emotional closeness, it wasn't an affair.

25. Your psychological problems caused your partner to stray. For example, if you hadn't been so jealous and overcontrolling, he or she wouldn't have felt the need to cheat.

26. Sexual online chatting doesn't count as an affair. After all, it's just "clicking," not really interacting.

27. Monogamy isn't natural for most species. What did you expect?

Avoiding therapists who espouse these misguided beliefs will not guarantee that you find a therapist who meets your needs. There are so many variables in a good therapeutic experience. But, certainly, knowing who to avoid will improve the odds. What follows is a description of our approach. Even if you can't find a professional trained in it, understanding the process will give you an inside view of how therapy ought to progress and the steps necessary to heal.

The Gottmans' Trust Revival Method: Atone, Attune, Attach

Our system for healing after an affair is founded in my lab results which confirm the effectiveness of the exercises provided in chapters 7, 8, and 9 of this book (the attunement-based art of intimate conversation, the Blueprint, and the Aftermath Kit) as well as my seven principles. It is based, as well, on my clinical experiences and those of my wife, who has worked with me in counseling couples. When it comes to helping couples to recover from infidelity, I describe my evidence as "practice based," because my lab research is not complete. With that caveat, I want to share our approach because most of the couples we counsel experience long-lasting, positive benefits. (In our initial study, which was not controlled, our therapy had a 75 percent success rate.) The method leads couples through three phases of healing. There is no specific time frame for completing the process.

Phase 1: Atone

Rebuilding cannot begin without the cheater's continual expression of remorse, even in the face of the partner's profound skepticism. Throughout this phase, the betrayer must remain patient and nondefensive. Understand that an affair shattered every part of the other's Sound Relationship House and probably triggered a post-traumatic stress response. The result is relentless thoughts like, *Who is this person, really? What are this person's values and morals? I thought I knew but obviously I don't. What can I trust now?* The wounded partner will feel the stirrings of new faith only after multiple proofs of trustworthiness.

Atonement cannot occur if the cheater insists that the victim take partial blame for the affair. Among the accusations I often hear: "You didn't pay any attention to me," "You showed me no respect," "We hadn't had sex in six months!" If a partner strayed in the midst of difficult circumstances, it may seem unfair for him or her to take all of the blame. But he or she must. Healing requires that the cheater listen to and understand the other's pain. Eventually the two will come together to create a new relationship. But that cannot begin until the cheater accepts responsibility without excuse or defensiveness.

At the same time, the betrayed partner needs to work at not shutting the door on forgiveness. If he or she gets stuck in a position of inconsolable hurt and anger, the couple will not be able to resolve conflicts. The wounded partner must agree to cooperate as long as the betrayer is making the same effort. For now, the victim should eschew the Golden Rule in favor of: "Do unto others as they do unto you."

Atonement is a painful process, but the couple emerges with new understanding, acceptance, and budding forgiveness and hope. Here are its components in order:

Confession

Unless there is a thorough airing of misdeeds, mistrust will remain a perpetual issue. The hurt partner is going to need complete honesty before believing the relationship is salvageable. Not knowing is worse than knowing. In the therapist's presence, the cheater must provide candid answers to questions about the lover ("Why him?" "Is she prettier than me?"), how the affair began, why it continued, and how it was carried out, including details of where and when liaisons took place. I know that many couples are uncomfortable with this tell-all approach. Often, the guilty partner wants to spare the other from more hurt. It's true that disclosure will lead to a great deal of pain, but it is necessary.

I recall one wife who learned that, at the lover's request, her husband removed his wedding band during trysts. That detail in particular devastated the wife. Another cheating husband acknowledged that he had seen his affair partner on Mother's Day. Being a loving parent was at the core of his wife's self-identity. For him to disrespect her on that day was almost irreparably damaging. Yet both of these relationships were able to heal in time, in part because the wife could be confident that she knew everything. There were no more secrets, and there would be no surprises.

There is a crucial exception to this tell-all approach. The therapist must guide these discussions so that the cheater does not describe any aspect of the actual sexual activity. Knowing what happened on the other side of the bedroom door can lead the betrayed partner to obsessive rumination that retriggers or exacerbates the posttraumatic stress. My experience in therapeutic work indicates that the therapist must gain the trust of the betrayed partner so that he or she is comfortable with *not* knowing any of those details.

I was fortunate to help in research by Peggy Vaughan that demonstrated the critical role that talking about the affair and offering honest answers plays in healing. In her survey of 1,083 people who were recovering from infidelity, when the cheater agreed to answer questions, the couple stayed together 86 percent of the time. If the betrayer refused to answer questions, the relationship's survival rate was only 59 percent.

Behavior Change, Transparency, and Verification

Confession is not enough. The commitment to honesty must extend into the present. The betrayer can't expect the spouse to accept reassurances that the affair is history. No matter how many times the transgressor says, "I told you, it's over!" the partner needs proof. This means giving the deceived spouse access to the other's daily calendar, the right to probe phone records and credit card receipts, and so on. This invasion of privacy may seem over-the-top and unfair, but it is necessary. Trust won't return without ongoing evidence of fidelity.

Game theory is useful for understanding the critical role that proof plays in reestablishing trust. Much like Rapoport, Robert Axelrod, of the University of Michigan, focused his research on how to ensure that the United States and the Soviet Union played fair when it came to destroying their nuclear weaponry. He ran complex computer programs about trust and deceit to learn the best strategies to move negotiations forward, after brinksmanship had created an atmosphere of deep mutual suspicion. His results emphasized that promises, official accords, and treaties are worthless unless there is *verification* that each side is adhering to every agreement, beginning with the most minor. Only then can both parties negotiate with confidence. In the context of the Cold War, this meant, ideally, inspection of each other's arsenals and proof that some had been destroyed or rendered inoperative. For a relationship reeling from infidelity, verification and transparency include doing as promised, even when it comes to relatively trivial matters such as arriving home at a predetermined time. As part of this verification, the betrayer must constrict activities and relationships that were connected with the affair. In other words, no more unnecessary late-night visits to the library, doctor's office, bar, health club, or any other site where temptation lurked or straying occurred. The guilty partner may have innocent and legitimate reasons for wanting to continue to attend, say, parties or networking seminars. But he or she has to sacrifice such events until trust is rebuilt. The couple must also explore related concerns. Did the betrayer trash the partner to family or friends? Were there people who rooted for the relationship's demise or were complicit? The cheater must sever those friendships forever.

Perhaps the trickiest situations occur when the betrayer's employment requires interaction with the former lover. Leaving the job may not be realistic. But there should be an ironclad commitment to avoid that person as much as possible. If the deceiver is the affair-partner's boss, the spouse sometimes insists that the lover be fired or transferred. But this could be the cause of a legitimate legal suit and just add to the mess.

Understand What Went Wrong

Both partners need to grasp why betrayal occurred in their relationship. It isn't enough to say "I felt lonely" or "I made negative comparisons," or "We spent too much time in the Nasty box." The couple need to fill in the details. Why did the betrayer turn away, engage in negative COMPs, invest less in the relationship, and become less dependent on getting needs met through it? Likewise, why did that partner engage in thoughts unfavorable to the other's character, blame him or her for the unhappiness, stay open to or even encourage flirtation, and give oneself permission to cross that boundary?

Only thorough digging into these questions will prevent future disloyalty. As you review your history of negative patterns, the straying partner must avoid accusing the wounded one. Again, the goal is to understand what went wrong, not to shift the blame. We are the master of our actions. Accepting responsibility is part of healing.

Much of this process requires the cheater to become more aware of enduring vulnerabilities. It's essential to explore what triggered these emotional frailties during conflict or sliding door moments. My session with Laura and Malcolm, who had been counseled by ministers to just move on, demonstrates how the lack of openness about deep-seated needs can lead to disaster. Laura's competence and self-sufficiency made Malcolm feel unneeded and lonely, as if he were nothing but a "paycheck" with a pulse to her. He was susceptible to this intense reaction because his parents' muted expressions of love for him as a child gave him the sense he was unimportant, as if he could disappear without them noticing. This vulnerability led him to turn away during sliding door moments when his wife would ask him about his work stress. Because he felt unneeded by her, he didn't believe she really cared and shut her out.

Explore the Cheater's Reasons for Returning

The betrayed partner needs a clear explanation of why the deceiver wants back in. What is compelling him or her to rebuild the relationship? If the reason isn't made clear, the partner will remain wary that the new commitment is not genuine or will be short-lived. Laura worried that Malcolm would stray again because she didn't understand why he left or why he came back. But during my guided discussion with them, he was finally able to explain it to her. The key was his longing to feel necessary. That unspoken desire drew him away from his wife and toward a woman whose life was a "mess" and who needed his support. But now that he has opened up and shared his "need to be needed" with his wife, they can work together to have Laura fulfill this longing at home. This explanation for Malcolm's return makes sense to Laura. Therefore, it will be possible for her to trust that he's back for good.

Exact a High Cost for Future Betrayals

The deceiver must accept that any future infidelity will mean the permanent end of the relationship. There won't be a second chance. Couples' therapists tend to feel uneasy using the word "punishment." We are far more comfortable with the idea that, as the famed family therapist Salvador Minuchin put it, the betrayer's "sense of moral responsibility" will motivate him or her to recommit. From this perspective, the former betrayer stays true out of a sense of justice, deep empathy, and a desire not to be one of "those" people. However, based on my work with couples, I believe in adding a strong disincentive to straying again. The betrayer needs to know there's a catastrophic cost to any subsequent deceit.

Evidence for the success of this approach comes in large part from research on group behavior by social psychologists. In a compelling study that offers insight into punishment as a deterrent to many forms of betrayal, Vincent Buskens studied the trust relationships between Orthodox Jewish diamond merchants. These businessmen create such high-trust networks that they can exchange million-dollar jewels on only a handshake. To sustain such a high confidence level, this tight-knit community exacts an enormous cost for any betrayal of its code. If you deceive, then your friends, neighbors, and coworkers all shun you. As Buskens explains, those "who are untrustworthy must be expelled or punished severely enough for other actors to see that untrustworthy behavior is only worthwhile in the very short term."

Begin to Forgive

This is the last step in the atonement phase. The hurt partner accepts the other's apology and begins to pardon him or her. But this doesn't mean the erring partner is absolved. In this context, forgiveness means the deceived partner is willing to cooperate and trust, even in the face of uncertainty and the atoning partner's occasional slipups. An "acceptable" slipup is not a return to the affair or a new indiscretion, but an invasion of the past that produces a regrettable incident. A husband might buy his wife flowers from the same store he used for his lover. She knows this because she saw those credit card receipts. Part of forgiveness is to acknowledge that anyone can be untrustworthy on occasion. None of us is perfect. What the betrayer did was shameful, but he or she is changing that behavior.

Game theory can elucidate how forgiveness works under these circumstances. The most well-known mathematical game about trust and betrayal is the "Prisoner's Dilemma," which Axelrod studied in depth. In a typical version, the police subject two suspects to separate interrogations to garner confessions. The prisoners make a pact not to confess—but neither can know whether the other will keep it. If the prisoners stick to their agreement and neither admits guilt, they both go free or receive short sentences. If one prisoner betrays the other and confesses, he or she gets to turn state's evidence and earns minimal jail time, while the other receives the maximum. If they both confess, they each go to jail. Clearly, agreeing not to confess is the best strategy for them both. To achieve the ultimate benefit, they need to abandon pure self-interest in favor of cooperation and trust.

Here's what the game options look like in chart form:

	Davin Cooperates: Does Not Confess	Davin Betrays: Confesses
Ariane Cooperates: Does Not Confess	Davin goes free. Ariane also goes free.	Ariane gets ten years. Davin gets short sentence.
Ariane Betrays: Confesses	Davin gets ten years. Ariane gets short sentence.	Both get eight years.

Countless studies find that if you play the game for just one round, it is rare for the players to stick together and refuse to admit guilt. Time and again, the two choose betrayal (turning state's evidence) as the best alternative. They don't trust that the other will hold out. This result is disappointing—and says a lot about human nature! Axelrod's major question was, If you play the game for multiple rounds, what is the best approach or strategy to maximize the number of times the players cooperate? He developed a sophisticated computer simulation to find the answer. Axelrod's calculations indicate that the most important factor in maximizing cooperation is how a player reacts *after* he undermines it (by deceiving the other one). To recover the other's trust, the erring player needs to cooperate going forward *even if the other player ceases to*. In other words, the atoning player has to rebuff the police even if the other player keeps confessing. Axelrod referred to this as "contrition." The parallels with the process of healing after betrayal are clear: If the cheater is perceived to slip up while the couple is in counseling, he or she must stick with the process and work to win back the other's trust, even if the partner doesn't respond at first. The hurting partner also has a responsibility after a mess-up. He or she must try not to abandon the process of healing if the other continues to atone and work for forgiveness. This means being generous and accepting the partner's apology, for now. Axelrod found that a pardon was most successful in increasing trust if the player offered it just 10 percent of the time. It would be unwise to take this figure literally in the context of an ailing relationship. But it does offer a rough guide to how often to accept apologies and move on. The deceived partner should not tolerate an extensive pattern of missteps, which would constitute a revictimization. But cutting the other a break after an error indicates a willingness to continue to work toward healing. In Phase 1, forgiveness means not walking away if the other "steps in it" from time to time.

Phase 2: Attune

After the couple emerge from the atonement stage with tentative forgiveness, they come together to build a new relationship. First, they acknowledge that the old one didn't meet both of their needs. The victim should not be blamed for this past deficiency, but he or she must cooperate in constructing a new approach.

To reach this challenging goal, the couple use the attunement skills described in chapters 7 through 9. A deep sense of feeling "known" and knowing the partner is the ultimate shield against disloyalty. Giving the partner access to one's sadder, darker, and more vulnerable inner realms requires courage, particularly for those who come from a background where anything but a stiff upper lip is considered unacceptable or even shameful. But sharing enduring vulnerabilities prevents either partner from feeling lonely or invisible, two powerful setting conditions for betrayal.

Couples must also relearn how to handle conflict so that it doesn't overwhelm them and create new distance. For this purpose, I guide them through the Gottman-Rapoport Blueprint and the Aftermath Kit, described in chapter 9. Applying these two methods is a very intense process and therefore requires a therapist who is comfortable with strong emotions and who can build a solid alliance with both partners. All of this work builds a strong foundation of trust and also a high trustworthiness metric. The former cheater is now dedicated to putting the relationship first. As part of this new commitment to cherish each other, the couple goes public with the "new normal" in their relationship. They alert the people closest to them (such as children, in-laws, and close friends) that they have recommitted and are working toward rebuilding trust. Getting the word out helps to establish this new relationship as "real" and garners support from the people who are closest to them.

Phase 3: Attach

Up until now I haven't discussed sex, the topic people often find the most difficult to broach after an affair. In the aftermath of betrayal, the victim often does not want to risk physical intimacy with the straying partner. There is too much fear, anger, and vulnerability. But if the couple is determined to stay together, the ability to attune has to reach the bedroom as well. Without the presence of a sexual intimacy that is pleasurable to both, the relationship can't begin again.

In a long-term love, sexual intimacy is founded on a healthy interdependency that satisfies the longing for connection. This bond serves as a stalwart barrier against "distractions." The keystone to this pleasurable and meaningful sex life is a steady diet of those intimate conversations I walked you through in chapter 7. But now, you include sex as a major topic during these sharing sessions.

Learning to communicate about sex is not just for couples healing from sexual disloyalty. It is crucial for couples recovering from all forms of betrayal.

11

Connecting Through *Intimate* Sex

She: So do you think it's gotten better?

He: Well, sure, it's gotten better, but still a long way to go.

She: You don't like it?

He: Sure, I like it, but there's a lot we can still do.

She: Well, at least we're not like Paul and Lily.

He: I never said we were. I don't know how he puts up with her.

She: He's no picnic either, I can tell you that.

He: I know that; I don't know how they put up with each other.

She: So we're okay?

He: Sure, we're okay. But we could be better, right?

If you didn't know this chapter was about relationship sex, it might not be obvious what subject this couple is circling around.

They could be talking about their style of arguing or their skill at throwing parties. Maybe they want to improve their doubles tennis game? All we can tell for sure is that they do "it" better than Paul and Lily.

This dialogue is a verbatim transcript from one of many studies in which I asked couples to discuss their sex lives. And it is typical. For many partners, frank talks about sexual passion cause enormous discomfort. (In the United States, I find this especially true of heterosexual couples of African, Anglo, and European cultural heritage.) Either these couples don't know how to approach the topic, or it requires many shots of tequila. Shame and fear of rejection are at the heart of this loss for words. Embarrassment about sexual urges or anxiety over performance makes it threatening to trust your partner with your intimate secrets. But for all couples, and especially those recovering from betrayal, openness about sex and eroticism is vital to a deep, loving, and passionate partnership.

Not all relationship experts agree with me that emotional devotion enhances a couple's sex life and vice versa. Some insist that a bright line separates "love," which entails affection and trust, from being "in love," which is about sex, passion, and romance. There are therapists who claim the best sex requires that partners *not* develop a deep bond. Although this approach is hardly common, it does have historical precedent. During the Middle Ages in Europe, the goal of matrimony was purely economic—to support offspring. Marriage was anchored in loyalty and commitment alone, *not* romantic love, which was considered far too unreliable. In fact, medieval puppet shows, a major form of entertainment, often heaped comic scorn on husbands foolish enough to feel passion for their wives. There was even an adjective coined to describe such ridiculous men: uxorious. I've always thought the word sounded like a disease or a white-collar crime.

You can find echoes of this attitude among contemporary sex experts. Perhaps the most prominent is Esther Perel, a couples' and family therapist who made a splash with her book *Mating in Captivity*. In it, she suggests that for many couples the secret to long-term sexual intimacy is emotional distance. She recommends that partners abstain from cuddling or any other contact that mixes affection with eroticism. From her perspective, an element of mystery prevents sexual monotony. The couple's erotic life dies once a woman dons the dreaded flannel nightgown.

I don't doubt that maintaining a distance from your partner can make sex more alluring for some. But "stranger sex" is not what most couples seek. They desire a great erotic life *and* a deep emotional bond—and they want to enjoy both of these pleasures with the same person. It's healthy to have some distance from each other. You don't bring much to a relationship without a strong sense of individuality—your own hobbies, friendships, opinions. But you also need to share for your sex life to thrive. Revealing lingerie may kick-start a romantic evening, but revealing *yourself* is what keeps the passion burning through the years. This process takes more effort to master than a striptease.

In its extreme form, Perel's concept of "impersonal sex" echoes what the great psychiatrist Victor Frankl deemed pornography. This form of erotic activity is not founded on emotional connection and adoration of the partner, but on a specific turn-on, such as voluptuous breasts, "rock-hard abs," or a certain scent. Countless people worldwide find impersonal sex thrilling. If they didn't, there wouldn't be an astounding 500 million or so pornography pages. Likewise, prostitution wouldn't be the oldest profession, and there wouldn't be a fascination with fetishes, kink, and S&M.

As a scientist, I don't judge people for enjoying impersonal sex. But my research convinces me that in a long-term, committed relationship, emotional distance doesn't promote *any* kind of sex. It does the opposite. The experiences of the newlywed couples I tracked for many years make this clear. Once a baby arrives, no couple has to work at being separate. When life turns into an infinite to-do list, it is daunting to find the time for even the most cursory, catch-up conversation. In the typical scenario, the new mother shifts her emotional focus toward the baby while the new dad spends more hours working. Keeping their distance is way too easy.

The impact of this disconnection was apparent at the third-year follow-up of couples in my newlywed study. This time, instead of bringing couples back to the Love Lab apartment, my team hauled our video cameras and instruments into the subjects' homes. Once again, we assessed their words, body language, and physiological reactions as they spoke to and about each other and their marriage. The new data indicated that only 33 percent of couples who were now parents were satisfied with their sex lives. These were also the only couples who carved out alone time and and conversed about deeper matters than emptying the diaper pail. I do not think this is coincidence. What kept these couples satisfied with their sex lives was surmounting distance, not maintaining it. This finding was confirmed in two random, clinical studies I conducted: making time to stay connected emotionally led to more sex between new parents. Contrary to Perel's advice, the lucky 33 percent engaged in a high frequency of cuddling and other nonsexual displays of physical affection. They even had great sex in the presence of the dreaded flannel nightgown! And they were not bored. Some liked to act out fantasies where, for example, they pretended to be strangers who picked up each other at a bar. But such outings were the opposite of impersonal sex. They were erotic fun shared by two people who enjoyed a deep intimacy.

My research findings are not unique. The late sex therapist Bernie Zilbergeld studied 100 US couples aged forty-five and older to learn which sexual techniques best kept the passion going with age. He selected half of the subjects because they reported having a satisfying sex life and the other half because they did not. To Zilbergeld's surprise, his overwhelming finding was the *unim-portance* of technique. What separated the two groups? The sexually active partners had a closer friendship and were committed to making sex a priority.

Defining Romance and Passion

People believe that the feeling of being in love—that mix of thrill and commitment—is beyond description. Not so. Synthesizing my work with previous studies by Caryl Rusbult and Shirley Glass, I think it is possible to articulate a science-based definition of romance. We know that *cherishing the partner* (which positive COMPs encourage) is critical to protecting the relationship from the cascade toward betrayal. I therefore define romance as *the state that occurs when two people both nurture and encourage acts and thoughts that cherish the other as unique and irreplaceable.* Passion is *the state that arises when you nurture a strong and at times almost obsessive interest in your partner that includes desire, curiosity, and attraction.* Put romance and passion together, and you have the opposite of impersonal sex: you have intimate trust.

I'm reminded of legendary actor Paul Newman's famous quip when asked whether he was ever tempted to cheat on his longtime love, actress Joanne Woodward: "Why go out for a hamburger when you have steak at home?" In a less frequently quoted exchange, talk-show host David Letterman asked Newman if he planned to accept a particular Broadway role. He replied that he probably would, since his wife wanted him to. Letterman asked if he always did what his wife requested. Newman answered, "Pretty much. I don't know what that woman puts in my food." These are the sort of jokes a man will make when he cherishes his partner. They reflect his respect and admiration for her, and his willingness to let her influence him.

Talking About Personalized Sex

Considering the profound connection between devotion and desire, why do so many heterosexual couples find giving and receiving sexual pleasure difficult to discuss? Why does what happens in the bed stay in the bed, never to be examined and improved? This discomfort is an artifact of culture. We compartmentalize sex and commitment, as if building a loving relationship and increasing sexual pleasure were separate needs. You can see this segregation in stores and websites that sell books. They tend to keep sex manuals on a separate shelf or web page from relationship guides. The books themselves usually adhere to this split. Most of those that present advice on love and commitment mention sex only in passing. Likewise, it is rare for those concerning sensual pleasure to cover other dimensions of a couple's life.

I'm going to go against this trend by discussing sexual relations in a frank and detailed manner. The physical part of sex is not complicated. The penis, clitoris, and vagina are among the body's least complex organs—their structures are a far cry from the intricate anatomy of, say, the heart or kidney. Likewise, orgasm is one of the simpler bodily functions: engorgement, erection, lubrication, ecstasy—that's pretty much the whole process. What makes sex difficult is that it requires *communication*. There are differences in what turns on individuals. Partners are unlikely to satisfy each other if they're uncomfortable discussing their desires.

Research indicates that broaching this awkward topic often and in a supportive manner correlates strongly with a couple's happiness. The finding is more pronounced when it comes to female satisfaction, at least in heterosexual relationships. In one study, women who discussed their sexual feelings with their husbands were five times more likely to be very satisfied than those who did not. I believe there are two reasons why verbal communication is so important for women. The first is physiological. Men may not need to give their lover instructions to achieve sexual release. As a general rule, they are aroused with great ease and have little difficulty reaching orgasm. Intercourse is often all it takes. But according to pioneering researcher Shere Hite, 70 percent of women cannot regularly achieve orgasm through intercourse.* They require other or additional methods, such as cunnilingus or having their genitals stroked. In addition, it is less common among women than men for orgasm to be the only goal of sex. Research on female sexual response finds that women consider sexual pleasure to be more about intimate touching than orgasm per se. Not all men realize this. (And it is rare for porn to offer a realistic view of what women relish.)

Surveys also find that far more women than men feel inhibited in bed if they don't share an emotional connection with their partner. In my lab, when couples fill out questionnaires about sex, the overwhelming majority of both genders agree with the statement: "Most women want sex when they already feel emotionally close, but for men sex is a way of becoming emotionally close." A classic

---

*By the way, *The Hite Report: A Nationwide Study of Female Sexuality*, published in 1976, remains the bestselling sex book ever, with 48 million copies sold.

example of how this difference fuels conflict between a couple is their contrasting responses to the "end" of a fight. Often, the man wants sex as a way of making up, but the woman doesn't want sex *until* they've made up. This disparity makes it especially important for the woman to feel supported in expressing her sexual needs. Couples run into trouble when the man doesn't listen or becomes defensive.

How can you make talking about lovemaking more comfortable? By applying the intimate communications skills and the Gottman-Rapoport Blueprint to the specific challenge of talking about sex. I teach these methods during the two-day workshops my wife and I hold for couples. Some of our attendees are in new relationships. Others are like Sherry and Hunter, long-term, middle-aged partners with a stagnated sex life. Hunter wishes that his wife were more receptive to his advances. Sherry complains that he is not sensitive enough to her needs. At the end of the two days, my lab tapes them as they apply their newfound communication skills. Keep in mind that their dialogue differs from a typical conversation you'd have at home. They are sitting in front of cameras, implementing skills they just learned. They sound more deliberate and articulate than is common. It takes most people hemming and hawing, and talking around the subject (even in therapy) before they can be clear about what they want. But once lovers begin to open up, confiding becomes far less difficult.

> *Hunter:* Okay, the light is on . . . I'll go first because I'm the one who is mostly complaining here, mostly. So, what do I think? I think we need to spice up our sex life. It's gotten boring. And it needs to happen more often. I get so horny for you sometimes.
> *Sherry:* That's like the old joke about the old age home, the food is awful and the portions are too small *(laughing)*.

Hunter: It's not awful. I never said that. Just always the same, don't you think?

Sherry: What I think doesn't seem to matter much *(angry facial expression)*.

Hunter: Huh?

Sherry: I've told you what I need, but you don't seem to hear me.

Hunter: Okay, don't be defensive. That's what they said at the workshop. Take in information. Okay, my not listening. I know now that that's probably true. Okay, let me do some repair here. Could you try telling me again what you need from me?

Sherry: Not always but mostly I usually need to feel emotionally close to you before I'm in the mood for sex. I have said that again and again.

Hunter: When you say that, I don't know what you mean, or what I'm supposed to do. How do I get you to feel close to me? Isn't that your responsibility? I'm lost here.

Sherry: No, it's not rocket science. Just talk to me, listen to me, hold me, just kiss me, stuff like that.

Hunter: Listen to what? What topic do you want to discuss to feel closer? No . . . I'm really not kidding. I'm asking.

Sherry: Not a topic, just talking.

Hunter: Just talking. Okay, here's where I get lost. How do we just talk about nothing? A no-topic talk?

Sherry: Okay, so I will instruct you. You say, "So how are you doing, honey? How is life treating you?"

Hunter: Okay, I can do that. And then what?

Sherry: Then I say, generally okay, but I had a rough day.

Hunter: Then I say *(smiling)*, "That's too bad about your rough day. I have an idea. Let's fuck"?

Sherry: *(Smiling)* No, then you say, 'That's too bad about your rotten day. What happened to you today, honey?' And I tell

181

you the story of what happened. And you listen, and you get sweet and understanding. And you ask me if you can hold me, and I say, that would be nice, and you hold me, and then you see if I respond to you physically, and then you and I start kissing, and then you caress me slowly, and I respond, stuff like that. And *then* you ask me if I want to fuck *(laughing)*.

Hunter: *(Laughs.)* Okay, that sounds good. But there are times when I approach you and you just say no. I hear that often.

Sherry: When you want sex, what I often say is, "I don't know if I want it."

Hunter: Isn't that a no? That's what I hear.

Sherry: No, it's, "I don't know," as in I don't know, convince me, I'm seduce-able, but I'm not ready for intercourse this very second. But you are, when you ask usually you're already hard and ready to put it into me.

Hunter: Don't get defensive. Yeah, that is often too true. I am ready. But what do I do to seduce you?

Sherry: You could start by asking me what I need.

Hunter: Really? And you'd tell me?

Sherry: Of course, I would. It's not a game. Ask me. I have said that so many times.

Hunter: Ask you. Really? That's seductive?

Sherry: Being asked is a great first step. Yes, it's seductive. Like maybe sometimes I need a hot bath to get relaxed enough, or taking a shower together, soap each other up, or just kissing, or talking for a while and cuddling. It changes depending on I don't know what it depends on. It varies. Rub my back for a start.

Hunter: Okay, those are things I wouldn't have thought of. I can ask you. I'm taking notes. Anything else?

Sherry: You're taking notes? That is so cute. And don't be so disappointed if I do wind up not being in the mood. I'm not rejecting you. I like any kind of connection. Sometimes even when I'm not in the mood and you are, it's okay for us to have sex. We may have to use a lubricant. But it can be like my gift to you.

Hunter: But I want you to come, too.

Sherry: Let me worry about that. Don't make that a demand. I don't always have to.

Hunter: I do.

Sherry: I know that.

Hunter: Sorry.

Sherry: No, that's okay. You're a guy. But, okay let me ask this one. Can I get you off in other ways if I'm just not in the mood?

Hunter: A blow job would be nice.

Sherry: I could have said that. How about a hand job sometimes?

Hunter: Not as nice, but okay sometimes.

Sherry: How can I say no and have it be okay?

Hunter: Just maybe tell me that I am devastatingly attractive to you, but you are totally wiped out or not in the mood at all.

Sherry: I can say that for your ego.

Hunter: The fragile male ego.

Sherry: That's the truth. But what about your "sex is boring" part?

Hunter: I have fantasies.

Sherry: What are they?

Hunter: I can't just come out with them like that on camera here in a lab with wires coming out of my ears. It's real private stuff.

Sherry: Okay. I get that. But can you tell me sometime when we're alone?

Hunter: I'll try. If you don't think they're too weird.

Sherry: No, I won't.

Hunter: You might.

Sherry: Okay, I'll tell you if they turn me off.

Hunter: Okay, I'll tell you one on camera that's more mild. When you wear lingerie it's really sexy, because it's like you are trying to seduce me. You're being aggressive. I like you playing that role sometimes.

Sherry: Okay, I can do that. Surprise you?

Hunter: No, we can plan it for after a date. Then you can feel closer to me.

Sherry: See, that's what I'd like. Take our time with it. Get in the mood.

Hunter: Dinner and a movie?

Sherry: Absolutely.

Hunter: Then we get home and . . .

Sherry: You ask me what I need.

Hunter: You come out in the red lingerie and I ask you what you need?

Sherry: Right.

Hunter: I can do that *(laughs)*.

With humor and open-mindedness, Hunter and Sherry succeed in making plain what they most want from each other sexually. Sherry feels that her husband finally gets it. Before this talk, she had no idea that he didn't comprehend what she meant by "talk to me." He is thrilled that Sherry will join him at spicing up their sex life, as long as they go at her slower pace.

It takes guts to discuss sexual differences and desires with the ease of Sherry and Hunter. The following questionnaire, similar to the one I use in my workshop, will get you started.

Assessing the Sex, Romance, and Passion in Your Relationship

Take this quiz by yourself. For each statement, circle T for True or F for False. Then use the space below to elaborate on your response for later discussion. For example, if you think statement number 1 is true—that your relationship is becoming less passionate—you could explain your answer by writing, "We used to have sex every other night, now we have it once every two weeks."

1. Our relationship is becoming passionless, the fire is going out. T ❑ F ❑
   Explain: _____

2. My partner expresses love, respect, and admiration much
   less frequently now. T ❑ F ❑
   Explain: _____

3. We rarely touch each other. T ❑ F ❑
   Explain: _____

4. We have few tender or passionate moments. T ❑ F ❑
   Explain: _____

5. There are some definite problems with our sex life. T ❑ F ❑
   Explain: _____

6. The frequency of sex is a problem. T ❑ F ❑
   Explain: _____

7. The degree of satisfaction I get from sex in this relationship
   is a problem. T ❑ F ❑
   Explain: _____

8. Being able to just talk to each other about sex, or talk about
   sexual problems, is a serious issue between us. T ❑ F ❑
   Explain: _____

9. We rarely cuddle.   T ❑   F ❑

   Explain: _____

10. The two of us want very different things sexually.   T ❑   F ❑

    Explain: _____

11. My partner does not know what turns me on.   T ❑   F ❑

    Explain: _____

12. Differences in desire are an issue in this relationship.   T ❑   F ❑

    Explain: _____

13. The amount of love in our lovemaking is a problem.   T ❑   F ❑

    Explain: _____

14. The level of satisfaction my partner gets from sex is a problem.   T ❑   F ❑

    Explain: _____

15. My partner does not show that he or she finds me sexually
    attractive.   T ❑   F ❑

    Explain: _____

16. I do not usually demonstrate sexual attraction toward my partner.   T ❑   F ❑

    Explain: _____

17. My partner does not compliment my appearance.   T ❑   F ❑

    Explain: _____

18. I am dissatisfied with the ways we initiate sex.   T ❑   F ❑

    Explain: _____

19. It's not okay with my partner if I refuse sex.   T ❑   F ❑

    Explain: _____

20. It seems as if I often have sex when I don't want to.   T ❑   F ❑

    Explain: _____

21. We have very few ways to satisfy one another sexually.   T ❑   F ❑

    Explain: _____

22. My partner doesn't listen to or doesn't remember how I like to
    be touched during sex.   T ❑   F ❑

    Explain: _____

Scoring

Add up your "False" responses. Use a calculator to divide that number by 22 and multiply by 100. The result is your sexual satisfaction score.

ABOVE 80 PERCENT

Your relationship is strong in affection, sex, romance, and passion. Working through the exercises that follow, particularly the Love Maps, can help maintain your erotic enjoyment of each other.

BETWEEN 80 PERCENT AND 50 PERCENT

You are grappling with some sexual issues. The steps outlined below will help you reverse course and make for clearer communication.

BELOW 50 PERCENT

Your relationship faces serious sexual issues that are probably undermining your bond. The following exercises will aid you in increasing your understanding and support of each other's sexual needs. Doing so will increase your intimacy.

Now that you know your sex score, it's time to start opening up, or divulging more, about what you each want from your sex life. Why not go first? (Somebody has to.)

1. Read at least some of your explanations for your responses out loud. Start with your "False" responses, so the discussion begins on a positive note.
2. Did you agree on each item?

3. Discuss where you disagreed. Take turns being the listener. Pay attention to each other's descriptions of feelings and needs. Turn what you want from your partner into a wish rather than a criticism. (Instead of, "You never pull hard on my penis even though I keep asking you to," say "I love it when you pull harder than usual. I'd love it if you did it a lot more.") Sometimes partners are surprised when one expresses a desire to be touched in a way that contradicts their current mode of lovemaking. Try to avoid being angry, hurt, or judged by what your partner says. Getting it all out there is what this exercise is about. If either of you feels in danger of flooding, let the other know. Use repairs. If these do not soothe the upset partner, take a break. Use the Gottman-Rapoport Blueprint to process what happened. When you're ready, return to this exercise. You may need a day or so to recoup.

4. Talk about what you each find most erotic about your lovemaking. Use the Love Maps questionnaire on p. 189 to trigger discussion. You don't have to divulge everything at first. Baby steps are fine. Don't be shy about taking notes about your partner's turn-ons. Because this new information can be difficult to process, it helps to have a list you can study later.

5. If you want to change your current approach to sex, don't do it all at once. Discuss one thing you could each try next week. Perhaps incorporate massaging each other or experiment with a new position. When you succeed at that, you could add something else the following week and so on.

6. Discuss your progress as part of your weekly State of the Union meetings. Tell each other what has been working well this week.

7. Go to our website Gottsex.com for more ideas.

Here are some suggestions for improving communication about sexual needs.

Suggestion 1: Develop a Ritual for Initiating Sex (and for Saying No)

For many heterosexual couples, a customary procedure, or ritual, for initiating sex helps ensure that lovemaking remains a priority. Noted sex therapist Lonnie Barbach suggests that couples communicate their level of arousal through an "amorous scale" from 1 to 9, with 1 being "no thanks," 5 being "I'm convince-able," and 9 being "oh, yes!" Then one partner can say "Right now, honey, I'm at 8 or 9." And the partner might say "Well, I'm at 5. Why don't we start kissing and see where it goes?" Using Barbach's scale, refusal isn't as personal. It's just saying that right now my body's not feeling it. Therapist Michele Weiner-Davis points out that for men, desire starts the sequence toward wanting sex and touching, whereas for many women, desire comes *after* touching.

Nonverbal forms of initiating sex can also work—as long as you are both clear about what message you're sending or receiving. Some couples signal desire by rubbing the partner's back, or kissing, or giving a foot massage. I once had a couple in my lab who used two small decorative standing porcelain dolls, one male and one female. If he wanted sex, he lay down the male doll, and if she also wanted sex, she lay down the female doll.

Suggestion 2: Chart Your Sexual Love Maps

One significant obstacle for couples wanting to open up about sex is finding the right words to ask how you can best pleasure your partner and express what you want. But doing so is critical to making Love Maps of each other's erotic desires. Below is an exhaustive list of questions you can ask each other during your conversations about sex. Pick and choose among them. You don't need to phrase the questions as written, but I hope they illustrate a way to ask about a subject that many couples find awkward.

Please use this list in whatever manner you find simplest and most comfortable. It may be helpful to begin with the questions that provoke the least anxiety. When you feel more at ease, you can move on to harder ones. Some couples prefer to underline or put a star next to the questions they most want to ask or answer, even though they have a hard time getting the words out. At all costs, avoid judging each other. Express gratitude and understanding when your partner opens up about a particularly uncomfortable topic. If you can talk together about just a few of these questions, that's great. Any honest conversation you can have about sex will likely improve your relationship in bed and out.

Instructions

The following questions can be asked in either a heterosexual or a same-sex relationship. They are not intended to be exhaustive. They are just examples of the kinds of conversations you might wish to have with your lover to increase intimacy.

About Feelings and Intimacy

1. Many people say that their sexual experience is dependent on feelings. Is that true for you? What do you need from me?

2. There is an old saying that some people need sex to feel close, but others only want sex when they already feel close. Do you think that difference exists between us? Is it a problem? If so, how can we make it better?

3. Sometimes one partner may not remember what the other finds exciting and erotic. Are there activities or ways to touch you that I've forgotten? Can you give me a refresher course?

4. What makes sex more romantic and passionate for you?

5. Would you like our sex life to feel more like making love? If so, how could we do that?

6. What do you think were some of the best, most romantic times we've had? What can we do to have more romance?

7. Do you feel that I court you? Or did that stop between us? Is that something you'd like us to work on?

About Libido

1. Do you think we have a similar sex drive? If not, do you think yours is lower or higher than mine? Do you see this difference as a problem?

2. Do you think I can tell when you're in the mood for sex? Am I not reading some of your signals?

3. What would be a good way for us to handle one of us wanting sex and the other not being interested at the moment?

4. Do you ever feel pressured by me to have sex when you don't want to? If so, how do we avoid that? What would be a good way for us to initiate sex? Can we create a ritual or signal to let each other know that we're interested (or not)?

5. How do you usually feel when I'm the one who initiates sex? Does it feel differently when you initiate it?

Your Body Image

1. What do you like about your body?

2. What about your body do you not feel so good about? Do those feelings influence how comfortable you are in bed? Is there something I should do, or not do, to help you feel more comfortable?

3. Tell me honestly, are there things I do that make you not like your body? What could I do differently?

4. What do you like about my body?

Touching and Being Touched

1. There's an old song about liking a lover with "slow hands." Is that so for you? Would you like me to touch you more slowly or faster?

2. Which type of foreplay do you like the best? What doesn't work for you? Is there a part of foreplay you'd like us to work on?

3. Some people say that their partner neglects touching them in some favorite places. Do you feel that's true for us?

4. Are there some ways of caressing that you prefer?

5. Would it help if I asked you, "What do you want and need?"

For Women Only

1. Many women say that they cannot ask for what they want concerning nonsexual physical affection from their partner, such as being cuddled, held, or touched affectionately. How do you feel about that?

2. Many women say that they wish that there would not be the *constant expectation* that all warm touch will lead to sexual encounters. They want more variety and openness. Is that true of us?

3. What are your feelings about my stimulating your clitoris by hand? Does that work for you? How could it be better?

4. How do you feel about my satisfying you by caressing your clitoris?

5. Is manual vaginal penetration also important to you as well as clitoral stimulation?

6. Do you feel embarrassed to ask for clitoral stimulation from me? If so, what can I do to make that better?

For Men Only

1. Many men say that they wish that their partner would pay more attention to their penis. Is that true for you?

2. What are your feelings about me stimulating you by hand? Does that work for you? How could it be better?

3. How do you feel about my satisfying you by caressing your penis?

About Orgasms

1. How important is it to you to have an orgasm when we have sex?
2. Do you feel guilt or shame when you come?
3. Do you feel pressure from me or "society" to have an orgasm?
4. Do you feel judged if you don't come?
5. Are there times when you feel cheated that I have an orgasm and you don't?
6. Are you worried that you take too long or short a time to have an orgasm, or worried about just being different from me?
7. Are you at all embarrassed about how you look or sound when you're coming?
8. Are you very sensitive after orgasm and want to avoid stimulation?

Orgasm Questions for Women Only

1. Some women say that they don't have orgasms. Is that true of you? If so, how do you feel about that? What do you need from me?
2. Is there any relationship between how feminine you feel and whether or not you have an orgasm?
3. Many women say that they hate the fact that their partner expects that all sexual contact will lead to orgasm. Do you feel that way?
4. What about faking an orgasm? Do you ever do that? Maybe to spare my feelings?
5. Do you usually need to come again, after your first orgasm? What can I do to help that happen?
6. Can I tell when you're having an orgasm?
7. Do you usually have multiple orgasms?
8. Do you feel bad having an orgasm during your period?

For Men Only

1. What is the feeling of being erect like for you? Do you feel wanted? Desired? Loved? Urgent?

Oral Sex

For Women Only

1. Many women have said that they enjoy cunnilingus, but say that it rarely lasts long enough. Is that true for you?

2. Many women have said that they enjoy cunnilingus, but that they don't enjoy giving and receiving oral sex at the same time because they cannot just enjoy their own pleasure. Is that true for you?

3. Some women do not like cunnilingus because they worry that they smell bad or are somehow dirty. Some women do not like cunnilingus during their period. Is that true for you?

4. Many women have said that they enjoy performing oral sex, but that there are a few things that are negative about it. Is that true for you?

5. Some women do not like oral sex at all. They have negative feelings about it. Is that true for you?

For Men Only

1. Some women complain that the man uses a short bout of cunnilingus as a quick step to intercourse. Is that true of you?

2. Many men have said that they enjoy performing oral sex, but that they prefer giving and receiving it at the same time because they can then also enjoy their own pleasure. Is that true for you?

3. Some men do not like giving oral sex because they don't like the smell or somehow feel it is dirty. Is that true for you?

4. Many men have said that they enjoy fellatio, but that there are a few things that are negative about it. Is that true for you?

5. Do you like fellatio but have negative feelings about ejaculating in my mouth or my swallowing it?

6. Many men have said that they enjoy fellatio, but that they don't enjoy 69. Is that true for you?

7. Some men do not like fellatio at all, but some men want more of it. What is true for you?

Intercourse

For Women Only

1. How do you feel about penetration?
2. Some women do not want sex during their period. Is that true for you?
3. Some women dislike the expectation that sex will always lead to some kind of penetration. Do you ever feel that way?
4. Do you feel a pressure to have an orgasm during intercourse with me? What can I do to make that better? Do you feel a pressure to have multiple orgasms? Why or why not?
5. Do you feel a pressure to have an orgasm at the same time as me? What can I do to make that better?
6. Have you ever made use of a vibrator or dildo? What was the experience like for you? Is that something you'd be interested in trying?

About Masturbation

1. Many people say that they physically enjoy masturbation, but they feel there is something wrong with it. How do you feel?
2. Some people masturbate to control their own horniness. They feel that they can't talk to their partner about it. How do you feel?
3. Will you show me how you prefer to masturbate?
4. Some people fantasize about erotic situations while they masturbate. Does that describe you? If so, do you feel comfortable talking to me about any of those fantasies?
5. Many women say that they masturbate entirely by clitoral stimulation, but other women say that to come they need to stimulate other erotic zones as well. What is true for you?
6. Many men say that they masturbate entirely by penile stimulation, but other men say that to come they need to stimulate other erotic zones as well. What is true for you?

Suggestion 3: Make Sex More Exciting

Once you feel more comfortable divulging your sexual needs, you might want to try some of these suggestions for enhancing enjoyment. Pick and choose, and come up with your own proposals as well. Select three ideas that you would like to try. Share them with your partner and perhaps plan to incorporate one each week. Continue the process as long as you both enjoy it. For more ideas, see our website, Gottsex.com.

1. Talk to each other about your favorite places to kiss and be kissed.
2. At the beginning and end of the day, kiss for at least six seconds.
3. Buy your partner a surprise present.
4. Put your arms around your partner and tell him or her how sexually irresistible (or handsome, or beautiful) he or she is to you right now.
5. For a day or two, hug, kiss, touch, and caress your partner the way *you* would like to be loved. Then do to your partner what your partner has done to you. Be gentle.
6. Plan a sexual rendezvous in your bedroom. Think about what you will wear, music, lighting. Make sure there is enough time.
7. Use body oil to give your partner a nice, long massage.
8. Buy some sexy lingerie for yourself or your partner.
9. Surprise your partner with your favorite perfume or cologne.
10. Write and read out loud a poem about the wonders of your partner's body.
11. Read an erotic book out loud together.
12. Schedule phone sex with your partner the next time one of you is out of town.
13. Call in late to work one morning after the kids are off to school and have an erotic hour alone together.
14. Have a quickie.

15. Have sex in a new setting.

16. Write your partner a sexy note about where you'd like to lick him or her.

17. Masturbate to orgasm thinking of your partner and write a note about your fantasy.

18. Write your partner about some dirty, naughty sex thoughts that turn you on.

19. Talk dirty to your partner during sex.

20. Try the kitchen counter for oral sex.

21. Take turns being the dominant and the love slave.

22. Play strip poker.

23. Act out a fantasy of your choice. Dress the parts. For example:

    Two strangers on an airplane

    Boss and employee

    Professor and student

    Massage parlor worker and customer

24. Make bets. The winners get exactly what they want sexually from the partner (within reason).

25. Apply whipped cream or chocolate sauce to your partner's favorite body parts—then kiss and lick away.

26. Help your partner masturbate to orgasm while you watch.

27. Have a pillow fight.

28. During foreplay, guide your partner's hand to demonstrate what feels good and respond with sounds of pleasure.

29. Make a rule: no intercourse tonight, just touching.

30. Sit at the back of a movie theater and make out like teenagers.

31. Give your partner a sexy nickname.

32. Give each other a foot massage.

33. Take turns and kiss, lick, or stroke each other's backs or necks.

34. Dress up in period costumes, go out to dinner, then make love.

35. Gently kiss and suck each other's genitals at the same time.

36. Describe out loud what you love about your partner's face.
37. Try a new sexual position and talk about it afterward. Did it work for you both?
38. Dress up and salsa dance or slow dance together at home.
39. Make love while pretending you're animals, like two panthers.
40. Brush and stroke each other's hair.

Suggestion 4: Pillow Talk Ideas

It can help to think ahead of time for romantic phrases you can utter to keep the emotional connection when things get steamy. Here are some ways to express what you might be feeling during lovemaking. Consider this a menu. Choose whichever words ring true. Couples have different styles of expression, so feel free to come up with your own phrases or rewrite these. Don't shy away from naughtier or dirtier words, if it's a turn-on for you and your partner. (For some perspective on this idea, see the book *Talk Dirty to Me* by Sallie Tisdale.) You'll find more suggested phrases on Gottsex.com.

1. I'm all yours.
2. I love cuddling with you.
3. I could kiss you like this for hours.
4. I choose you again and again and again.
5. You are always mine.
6. I am remembering the first time we ever kissed.
7. I remember the first time I saw you.
8. You're so hot!
9. I love the curve of your back.
10. I love touching/kissing your ___.
11. I love how strong you are.

12. I cherish being with you this way.

13. Your eyes are so beautiful.

14. I want to hold you close to me.

15. It makes me so happy to hear your heart beating against mine.

16. I long for moments when we can be together like this.

17. You smell so good here.

18. Yes, do that.

19. You're my closest friend in the world.

20. Something inside me opens when we are together.

21. I love coming with you.

22. I feel so close to you.

23. No one moves me like you do.

24. What would you like me to do to you right now?

25. I want you so much.

26. How does this feel?

27. Don't stop.

28. You're so precious to me.

29. Oh my God.

30. This is so delicious.

31. Thank you for loving me.

32. Put your arms around me now.

33. I love the way you're moving.

34. That was the best.

35. You're such a great lover.

I hope these suggestions help you strengthen your personal sexual bond and enhance your knowledge of each other.

12

How to Know if It's Time to Go

The notion that a relationship may have reached its expiration date is almost antithetical to me. Like many of my colleagues, I believe the death of love is a tragedy. I am a creature of hope and root for couples to prevail. But I have also worked with some for whom love has turned into hate, and hope into bitterness. Sad though it is, sometimes it is the right decision for people to part ways. It is pointless to attempt rescue when a relationship has already expired. In these cases, couples need inner strength and support from others to cope with the heartbreak and move on to happier lives.

Why do relationships fail despite measures to revive them? In some cases, the answer is simple. At least one partner may just want out or be unwilling to acknowledge his or her contribution to the trouble. But there are deeper causes as well. I've had people in failing marriages ask whether their problems were "normal." That's an awkward word to use, but I understand the question. One member may suffer from a mental illness or personality disorder that precludes real intimacy or prevents the other from feeling safe. It's not surprising that such relationships have a high failure rate. A common example is narcissism, a personality disorder that bars authentic connection with another person. In response, the rejected partner can feel anger, fear, or self-doubt. In this brief dialogue, the wife reacts to her husband's narcissism by becoming depressed, which is not uncommon. Her hopelessness prevents her from seeing that her husband's problem is destroying their marriage.

> *Perry (Sobbing):* Nothing matters to me anymore. I don't even care if I die tomorrow. I need help.
>
> *Jake:* Well, as you know, I don't believe in therapy. Can't you at least hold out for a few months till we're on that new health plan? (He's thinking: *Her health problems always cost so much money. She gets those migraines and that stomach thing. Now she needs a shrink. I should have married someone less high maintenance.*)
>
> *Perry:* Oh. (*I'm not worth saving.*)

It is fortunate that Perry's family intervenes and her depression is treated. Once the couple enter marital therapy, she has to accept that her husband lacks empathy and, because he refuses to believe he can be anything less than perfect, is incapable of change. Perceiving no hope for the marriage, she files for divorce.

But in most cases, the decision to save the marriage or let it go isn't so clear. I have counseled many couples where one partner expresses shock that the other wants out. The conversations often go like this:

She: I want a divorce.

He: I had no idea you were that unhappy. Why didn't you tell me?

She: I have tried to tell you for the past nine years!

Or:

He: Why didn't you say anything to me about being upset? We could have gone for therapy sooner.

She: What was the point? It would only have led to more arguing, and it would turn out to be all my fault, as usual.

Such exchanges are so common in a therapist's office that it's been nearly impossible to discern which of these relationships are salvageable. But now I *can* tell whether a partnership has reached its expiration date. I call my gauge the "Story of Us Switch." It detects the *cumulative* trust or distrust and betrayal quotient in a relationship based on how either partner thinks about their shared past. I term this indicator a switch rather than, say, a dial because I rarely see gradations in what people recall about their romantic history. They either have joyful memories or—*click*—bitter ones. There is little middle ground. If the switch is on positive, it acts as a strong buffer against momentary irritability and emotional distance. A negative setting is the end point of Negative Sentiment Override, in which one assumes the worst about the partner. Even if only one partner's switch is "off," it heralds the relationship's death. In psychological research, it is not common to find such a powerful predictor of future disaster. We need to pay close attention to what it is telling us in order to save couples from this fate.

In the lab, I assess each partner's Story of Us through a detailed interview script my team devised, called the Oral History Interview. This list of questions includes the kind of "getting-to-know-you" queries that you might ask a couple you meet at a dinner party, as well as deeper questions that you might employ during a conversation with a close friend. In the interview, we ask couples how they met and their first impressions, details about their dating, how their relationship has changed over time, their philosophy of relationships, and their opinion of other people's.

I base this interview approach on the technique pioneered by Studs Terkel, the renowned radio host whose riveting show featured ordinary people recounting their extraordinary lives. As his guests talked, Terkel avoided the usual neutral responses like "um hmm" that people often use to encourage a storyteller (and that therapists often employ). Such murmurs would sound annoying over the air. Instead, when an interviewee paused, Terkel would exclaim something like, "Wow! That is truly amazing!" Then he'd move on to another question and turn silent again. This approach let him splice himself out of the tape so that only the subject's story remained. His method turned his guests into dramatic narrators of their compelling life stories.

I found that my couples responded to interviews much like Terkel's radio guests. People seemed to *need* to tell their stories. Even the unhappy couples wanted to divulge their past to us. In one study, Robert Levenson and I decided to skip this interview segment in order to save time and money. But our subjects, expecting it to be part of the process, *insisted* on it. Both the happy and unhappy couples wanted to share their memories.

Before any oral history interview, my amazingly capable interviewers make it clear to our subjects that we consider their personal reminiscences unique and can only learn about their relationship through them—*they* are the experts. When the oral history is complete, I analyze each couple's responses and assess how positive or negative their relationship story.

Those with only negative memories have turned their relationship switch to "off." Not all such couples split. Some remain unhappily married, leading parallel lives in which they cohabit but no longer trust each other.

The oral history interview is such a strong measure of relationship satisfaction because the couple's present attitude and concerns color what they recall about the past, shifting both their memories and what they emphasize about their history together. There is a biological basis for this phenomenon. Recent research by neurobiologists into the brain's processes shows that it rewrites and reorganizes memories based on what they mean to us right now. Our identity—how we perceive ourselves, who we think we are, where we come from—depends upon neural networks that continue to develop. For that reason, later experiences influence and even alter what we remember.

In general, the brain stores two kinds of memories, explicit and implicit. The former are conscious remembrances: your grandmother gave you a doll for your sixth birthday, the Red Sox won the World Series (and it wasn't a dream). But implicit memories may not be completely conscious. Instead, the brain responds with a sort of intuition, extracting rules that fit the circumstances. When the traffic light turns red, you remember to brake—you don't need to think it through. But when the brain confronts two opposite realities at the same time—what's called cognitive dissonance—it rewrites your history so that it makes sense and is easier to remember. If you once had fond remembrances of your wedding but now consider your partner a self-centered boor, your implicit memory shifts. The brain spins the past, extracting new rules that fit current circumstances. Now, when you think of your wedding day, what first comes to mind is your new husband's failure to tell you how beautiful you looked.

Whether a relationship is over or just ailing depends on how pervasively negative its history, as the couple tells it. In my lab, therapist Kim Buehlman has developed a way to quantify what people say during their interview and how they say it. We've settled on five basic dimensions that I believe express the richness of the subjects' stories. Called the Buehlman Scoring, this assessment is extraordinarily accurate in predicting the death of a relationship. When applied to couples in another of my studies, which looked at 120 couples with preschool-aged children, the scoring predicted with 94 percent accuracy whether a couple would break up within the next four years.

That sounds impressive, doesn't it? But in truth, such predictions are easy to make because there is little gray area in how partners describe their past. Either they emphasize their good times and make light of the rough spots, or they accentuate their failures and not their successes. Likewise, they either underscore their partner's positive traits in favor of their more annoying characteristics (cherishing), or they do the opposite (trashing).

Here are the five dimensions Buehlman scores during the Oral History Interview. The couples we studied who scored low in all of these areas later divorced.

Dimension #1:
The Fondness and Admiration System

Happy couples tell their tales with warmth, affection, and respect for each other. Here's an amusing exchange from a newlywed couple:

Nancy: He was a straightforward, "not afraid to look at the eyes" kind of person. I just thought finally I met someone that was going to be a real good friend.

Interviewer: Did you have first impressions of her?

Saul: (*Repressing a chuckle*) When we were first introduced, I thought, *Oh, what a sweet smile.* I thought she was kind of cute, and then she walked away, and I tell everybody that my first impression was, *Wow, nice butt!* Real deep.

Nancy: (*Laughing*) It was at the moment that he saw my butt that he fell in love.

Saul: Just kidding. I guess my first impression was just the big smile, and she seemed like a happy person all around, so I guess the attraction was all there.

Interviewer: So, you were interested in her from—

Saul: Immediately.

Spontaneous compliments are common. Here is a typical such exchange from my study of couples in their forties and sixties. They are recounting meeting for the first time at a dance.

Murray: I'll tell my version. I was in the military and got assigned to Baltimore to go to school. And I was down on East Baltimore Street, which is the raunchiest street in town. I was drinking a beer and set my bottle down on the floor. Somebody kicked it over. I looked up, and there she was.

Blanche: My best friend worked at the military base, and she said she had met this very charming soldier. And she was going to meet him at this weekly dance. And she called me at work and said, "I don't want to go by myself, you have to go with me." That's why I went.

Murray: I don't know why . . . but I began to realize that they all
come here because of her, that even though she doesn't talk
very much, she must be the really interesting one in the group.
And so I started to focus in on her. She was the leader of that
group.

Here's another couple high on the love and respect dimension:

Interviewer: Tell me about the first the time you two met and got
together.

Jan: You want to hear it from me because that's my favorite story.
This is true and in a way is rather unusual. I was . . . Ricky
worked at a lady's ready-to-wear store . . . There was a window
trimmer who I dated for a while. His name was Frank. Every
time I went anyplace with Frank, he talked about this fellow
who worked at the store named Ricky. So one time I said,
"Well, Frank, I just don't think anyone can be that great. You
told me he lives downtown. Why don't you call him up and
see if he can join us?" So Frank went to the phone, and he said
Ricky couldn't join us, but why didn't we come over to where
he lived? He lived in a hotel just a couple of blocks away. Frank
reached over me to knock on the door and Ricky opened the
door and he looked at me and he kissed my hand, and I was a
dead duck.

In contrast, couples with a weak fondness and admiration system
tend to recall unfavorable first impressions of their partner. Their
words convey coldness rather than fondness and contempt rather
than admiration. Here is how Cherise describes meeting her husband, Donny.

Interviewer: What was the first thing you noticed about Donny? Is
there anything that made him stand out?

Cherise: The wine was watered down.

Donny: I had a friend with a bottle of wine, that's what she means.

Cherise: Yeah, uh huh. You know, I was late for the ski bus, I was
rushing on, I was the last one, I didn't know a soul. And I just
wanted to go skiing. So he's with this group of people who
were obviously already a group. So I don't really know that I
had an impression of him as much as of the group. The next
evening, we all met and sat in one of the people's rooms and
partied. We were all supposed to go out for dinner together
with him as my date, and he never made it because he and his
buddies drank a little too much, and I ended up having dinner
with one of his friends. We went back to sit in his friend's
room, and of course Donny was there. He had been sent to bed
[by the cops] on his way to the restaurant for being too drunk.
And I woke him up and said, "You know, I just don't think
you're a very nice person."

What a tale of woe! There is nothing positive in Cherise's account: The wine was watered down, she was late, she knew
nobody, her future husband stood her up because he drank too
much. To top it all off, she criticized him to his face.

It's hard to imagine that Cherise would have picked out such
negative details for emphasis as a happy newlywed. If anything,
the couple probably laughed about their first encounter.

Connor and Audrey are another couple whose Fondness and
Admiration System has vanished. When the interviewer asks them
to discuss an event from their dating days, instead of focusing on
a fun time or happy occasion, they recount a major blowup they
had on her birthday. Although they don't express anger at each

other while telling their tale, I could hear the death knell for their relationship in their choice of story.

Connor: There was the one time when I really got mad at you on your birthday.

Audrey: Yeah, that was stupid, that was the most asinine thing.

Connor: I really got mad.

Audrey: Your behavior was just a total doofus.

Connor: I went berserk. I yelled at her because she was—

Audrey: It was *my* birthday.

Connor: I spent, like, two hundred dollars on presents.

Audrey: You know, we'd come back from going out to eat and whatever, and his friend was sitting in the living room with me, talking. And I was having a really heartfelt conversation, and I felt like I couldn't just say, "Well, sorry, Harry, you gotta go home now."

Connor: Meanwhile, I was preparing to go to sleep. I was in my pajamas.

Audrey: He was making this big production, and I felt like, Well. Yeah. I'd like to get Harry out of here, too. But I felt I had to be nice to him. And then Connor just had a complete tirade, and my feeling was, just forget him.

Connor: I just didn't understand that. To me she was just totally being oblivious to the fact that this is supposed to be time for us. It was really a miscommunication. I did kind of go ballistic. I don't get mad very often.

Audrey: He got really angry with me, and I ended up leaving and came back the next day.

If this sort of story springs to mind when a couple is asked about their dating days, their relationship is likely in serious danger.

Dimension #2: Me-ness vs. We-ness

Happy couples tend to relate stories where they worked well as a unit. The sense that they are "in this together" is palpable. Often, their words demonstrate similar beliefs, values, and goals.

Here's an example of a couple with "we-ness" from the twenty-year study I conducted with Robert Levenson.

Interviewer: Can you think of a really good marriage you know?

Diane: We have one.

Adam: I don't know anyone I'd compare to ours. It may sound arrogant, but—

Diane: I agree.

Interviewer: That's actually really nice.

Adam: Oh yeah. We communicate in the same way, have the same goals. Do these things together. I think another thing I'm conscious of, because it doesn't seem to even exist in our kids' marriages as well as it does in ours. Our grandchildren find us fascinating because we laugh a lot together.

Diane: Uh huh. Sharing our weird sense of humor.

Adam: We are more than just tolerating. In a sense, enjoying our differences—the fact that we are exactly opposite.

Diane: We really are different, but we fit together.

Adam: We are more of a whole because of what we have from the other. There is a pride in it, because we are complementary to one another.

Interviewer: How satisfied do you feel with the arrangement of who does what in your marriage?

Diane: Well, I think, generally, it's pretty satisfactory.

Adam: I'm satisfied, yeah.

Diane: When I change the linens on the bed, sometimes we do it together. I help him and he helps me out.

However, when the sense of we-ness is lost, partners often describe their history in a way that emphasizes how it affected them individually rather than as a couple. They focus on getting what they want in a zero-sum game. Warren and Kris could be a "poster couple" for this problem. When the interviewer asks them for a recent example of how they resolved an argument, they describe a conflict over budgeting. Warren's wish list includes a fishing boat, but not the ski boat Krista desires. When the interviewer asks how they reached a decision, they acknowledge that they still have not. They restate their positions without mentioning the other's experience of the disagreement. In the dialogue below I've boldfaced every use of the word *I* or *mine*.

Interviewer: How did you come to some resolution?

Krista: **I** finally said, "Look, **I** don't think it's fair that you get a new fishing boat. You've already got one, so we need to get the ski boat first, and then we'll get the fishing boat next year." And **I** kind of just laid it out like that, and he said, "Well, we could buy both!" But then **I** said, "But that's foolish." And that was the end of it . . . So right now there's just no decision.

Warren: See now, here's a case where it causes some tension, you know. Because this is money that **I've** earned, **I've** saved, so it's **mine**, really.

All relationships have conflicts that are tough to negotiate. The clue to the dead romance in this exchange is not that they aren't able to resolve an argument. It's *why* they are stuck in it: They are focusing on me, not we. They are trapped in the roach motel, each trying to "win."

Dimension #3:
A Love Map of the Partner's Inner World

When my team analyzes a couple's reminiscences, we look to see whether they have vivid and distinct memories of each other. Do they talk about what their partner was like back then? Detailed descriptions indicate that they continue to understand and respect what makes the other tick: what their partner cares about, what makes him or her sad, or happy. We also note whether there is positive energy or a lack of it in their descriptions.

In their sixties, the following couple retain a detailed Love Map of each other:

Interviewer: Were there any adjustments you had to make for each other's personality?

Andy: Oh, yeah. *(Both burst out laughing.)* We were just married, and she decided to make fudge one night. So she makes up this fudge and she's been stirring it with this spoon.

Marcia: (Laughs hysterically.)

Andy: She grew up with a gas stove and this one was electric. She had no idea how to use it.

Marcia: I was trying to light this electric stove with a match. He couldn't stop laughing.

Andy: This is a great story. She opens up the oven and reaches for a match to try and light an electric oven. I knew we were in deep trouble then. She's going to cook the fudge in the oven? But she never had to lift a finger in the kitchen growing up so she didn't know. Later I went out for a while and came back and tried to have some fudge. I tried to lift the spoon from it and the whole pot comes up. It's as solid as concrete.

Marcia: True. I was a young girl who grew up with my older sisters, what were really three mothers in the same house. I never had to cook or do anything. So here was this non-homemaker, and I thought I'd make fudge, and we had company that afternoon, and when he finally came home we had to throw the whole pan away because it was like cement. He loved cooking and knew all about it.

Andy: That's true. I was always really into cooking and baking. So she couldn't cook, but she learned real fast. And she was a real good sport about my teasing. Always has been.

Marcia: (Laughing.) Oh, yeah, he's quite a teaser. But there were no hysterics on my part.

Andy: And the other thing, right away in this apartment, which as a graduate student I didn't pay much for, the damned bed caved down in the middle.

Marcia: Oh, yes.

Andy: And you like to cuddle with your wife, you're just married, you like to have a lot of sex, but by God, you like to be able to roll over, which you couldn't, you'd wind up—

Marcia: . . . Right back in the middle. So there were some fun moments.

Andy: I remember one incident *(pats her leg)*. This is funny. In terms of sex, we enjoyed it thoroughly, right from the beginning.

Marcia: Oh, yeah, we sure did.

Andy: But there was a point where she was acting very upset.

Marcia: (Laughs.) Oh yeah, I remember.

Andy: And she said, "We didn't have sex last night," so sadly.

Marcia: (Laughs harder.) "What's the matter with you?"

Andy: (Laughs.) I said, "There's a certain limit about how much a
    guy can do."
Both: (Laughing hard.)

As you can imagine, couples who lose this connection do not
reminisce with the same contagious humor as Andy and Marcia.
Instead, they remain impersonal and guarded when recounting
their history, mentioning nothing specific about each other. Their
view of their past is "generic" rather than individualized. There is
no longer a Love Map.

Interviewer: So what kinds of things did you do, in those early days,
    when you were dating?
[Long pause.]
Ryan: (Quiet, looks at wife.)
Ashley: Not much of anything to do in a college town. We went to
    the movies, I guess, and . . . *(long pause)*.
Ryan: Um hmm. *(Pause.)* And the film festival was there.
Ashley: (Pause.) We went out to eat, that's about all. It's a small
    college town. You know, rent movies. I guess.
Ryan: Went out to eat. *(Pause.)* Drank a lot of red wine.
Ashley: (Tense laughter.)
Interviewer: You're both wine connoisseurs?
Ryan: Not really. We can't afford to be connoisseurs.
Interviewer: But you enjoy some wine?
Ryan: Occasionally. I guess.

The issue here isn't reticence—not all happy couples are talk-
ative. People have different temperaments and comfort levels
for self-disclosure. But if the relationship is satisfying, even the

quietest couples describe positive memories that are distinctive and special.

Dimension #4:
Glorifying Your Struggles vs. Flailing in Chaos

Couples who describe their relationship history as chaotic are usually unhappy in the present. They don't tell stories of pulling together or learning from their negative experiences. There's no sense in their descriptions that their past troubles and conflicts strengthened their mutual trust. Life, and the relationship, just happened to them. You can see this chaos in the exchange between another newlywed couple whose relationship did not survive.

> *Interviewer:* How did the two of you meet? And what were your
> first impressions of one another?
>
> *Lenny:* We met at a party. She was nice.
>
> *Wendy:* Yeah, we didn't talk much then.
>
> *Interviewer:* And then?
>
> *Lenny:* She moved in with me the next week because there was a
> fire in her apartment.
>
> *Interviewer:* Wow. That was fast. How was that decision made?
>
> *Wendy:* I just had to move somewhere and, he said, well, okay, you
> can stay here for a while.
>
> *Interviewer:* And your impressions of him?
>
> *Wendy:* He was okay. Nice, I guess.
>
> *Interviewer:* Then what happened?
>
> *Lenny:* Her mom got cancer and we decided to move up there to
> Wisconsin to take care of her.

Interviewer: That's amazing that you both did that. How long had
   you been together at that point?

Wendy: About a year.

Interviewer: How did you decide to do that together?

Lenny: I don't remember.

Wendy: It just kind of happened. Like the fire.

Lenny: Yeah, just like that.

Here's another couple who derived no insight or meaning from
the hardship of being separated geographically. It created distance
between them, but they didn't work to counter that.

Travis: I think it was easier for me than it was for you.

Rona: Yeah. You know, suddenly I'm at a new job, a lot of
   pressure. I'd better be good.

Travis: It just happened, and I have to adjust to it, she's not
   around, so in order to, like, sort of not feel so bad about the
   relationship, her not being there, basically you try to minimize
   the relationship to where you don't even think about it. You
   have to almost bring yourself to a point of ambivalence about
   the relationship.

Rona: Your relationship is completely stagnated when you're
   separated like that. There is no movement forward. There's no
   change, there's no growth, there's nothing.

Interviewer: How did you make such a hard decision to be
   apart?

Rona: It just sort of happened. And then you're in this holding
   pattern, and you talk once a week, and you do these emails—

Travis: And you have to adjust, you know . . . You start to
   emphasize, you start thinking about the more negative things.

Rona: That's what happened, all right.

In contrast, happy couples express pride over having survived difficult times. They glorify the struggle by emphasizing how it strengthened their commitment. They believe they steered their own course together, based on their common goals, aspirations, and values. They have built a system of shared meaning and purpose. Whether couples display this positive energy when recalling past hardships is not at all dependent on the depth of the difficulties they faced. How they *interpret* the negative and positive events is the key. Here's a happy couple who married at eighteen because she got pregnant. The pregnancy was a crisis for both of them, yet they stuck together. It wouldn't be surprising if such a life-changing event and the hardships that followed led to a lot of unhappy memories. But because their marriage satisfies them both, their "Story of Us" switch rests firmly in the "on" position. They express pride in their tenacity.

> *Randy:* Jonine was four months' pregnant when we got married.
> *Interviewer:* So did you think you "had to" get married?
> *Jonine:* No, not at all.
> *Randy:* I think it was more of me respecting Jonine. I don't
> think it was a "Well, you guys have to get married now." [He
> emphasizes his respect for his wife at the time.]
> *Jonine:* And I think it was kind of protective, right? [She remembers
> him protecting her rather than resenting the burden.]

They talk with great enthusiasm about their "shotgun" wedding, even though their families both decided not to attend.

> *Randy:* It was an awesome wedding.
> *Jonine:* Yeah, we had a beautiful wedding . . . We got married in a
> gazebo.
> *Randy:* There was a boat, all decorated.

But once the baby was born, life got tough.

> *Jonine:* I think it was probably a lot harder for Randy because he'd
> been used to kind of being such a free spirit and doing so many
> things on his own, and having the responsibility of a family was
> just a humongous change for him.   .
> *Randy:* Yeah. I accepted my responsibilities at home, but I don't
> think I was there a lot. *(Looks at Jonine.)*
> *Jonine:* He accepted them . . . he never had a bad temper, he'd
> never, you know, done anything really, really bad, but he'd
> come home drunk almost every night.

If their life together were not happy in the present, it is unlikely
that Jonine would remember Randy's behavior at the time as not
"really bad." Jonine recounts that they fought so much early on
that she wanted a divorce. But the couple don't spend much time
recalling that possibility. Instead, they focus on how they worked
it out. They decided to move to Utah, where they knew no one.

> *Randy:* We really needed to get out of there, away from my
> friends, and that's what we did. And that changed things a
> lot . . . We were *forced* to be together.
> *Jonine:* And we had to kind of rely on each other a lot.
> *Randy:* Pull each other to make it through.
> *[The* couple talk with pride about how they worked together to
> save their relationship.]
> *Interviewer:* So tell me about becoming parents. Apart from
> everything else, what was that like, having your son?
> *Randy:* It was awesome. It was awesome.
> *Jonine:* I think that that's probably about the only thing that we
> agreed on in the beginning of our relationship.

Randy: Yeah, how we would do things and what he needed and didn't need.

Jonine: I don't think that we ever fought over issues of raising our son.

Interviewer: So your values were very similar.

Randy: Yeah.

Jonine: And despite Randy's partying and stuff, he was a wonderful father. It was certainly a good experience having the baby.

A happy couple's tendency to glorify past struggles is most obvious during their Oral History, but you can find it in subtle form in other discussions that are not focused on the past. These gay partners, part of another study, are in conflict about their work schedules. One is a harried architect, the other a graduate student. Although this issue challenges their relationship, they talk with ease about their history together and how they handled this situation with more success in the past. Even though this is a "negative" conversation, their positive history is still evident and bodes well for their future.

Darrel: Seven years ago, although we battled over your working Friday nights, it was like the roof came down and everybody understood that this was a calamity if our weekends got interfered with. And then slowly over the years, that's gotten eroded, and then you went to school.

Jeff: What do you mean, it got eroded?

Darrel: Well, all of a sudden we just kind of got used to the fact that sometimes those weekends are going to get eaten, and it was no longer the crisis that it once was.

Jeff: Right, and then the issue came up when I started practicing, because that ate into the hours that were available for us.

Darrel: Yeah. I remember having conversations when you started where we agreed that you were going to keep your nighttime commitments to one night, maybe two a week absolute max. The first year we figured out how to make it work. The second year it was two nights a week, and then by the fourth year it was like, if you happened to be free one night during the week, that was my lucky week.

Dimension #5:
Disappointment vs. Satisfaction

When couples are at risk for splitting, at least one of them will express disappointment that the relationship isn't what it promised to be. Often, when reviewing the choices they made in the past, they express cynicism about long-term commitment. This exchange is short and to the point.

Interviewer: What advice would you give to young couples who are thinking about getting married?
Husband: Wait!
Wife: Just don't do it.

Here's a snippet from another couple. The wife is upset that the husband isn't including her in discussions about his will. She feels that after all of this time, he still doesn't see them as a "we."

Stefan: She thinks very much she has a right to be involved with how I structure my will. Is that reasonably close to true?
Bridget: Yes. See, to *me*, writing wills is this thing you do together. And even though it's *his* will and *her* will, you sit down and you talk about taking care of each other, and, like, that's one of

those areas where in my view there should be this totally open thing, and that's a total together thing.

Stefan: (Nods.) That's what she thinks. I think different.

Bridget: I'd say that's a pretty accurate description. Our friends were having a disagreement the other night, and I said, "This marriage thing isn't all I thought it would be. What it really turns out to be is a big game of control."

In stark contrast, satisfied partners believe their relationship has met their expectations. This couple describes knowing right away that their partner was right for them. It's clear from their description that they still do.

Interviewer: How did you decide that this was the person that you really wanted to marry?

Steve: I can't think of when the decision came, it was just kind of a general feeling.

Interviewer: What was that feeling like?

Steve: I just loved being with her.

Interviewer: How about for you, Gail?

Gail: Well, it was after being in a car with him for three weeks. We had a great time, and I saw parts of the country that I have never seen before. It was amazing to me that two people could spend that much time together in that close of a proximity and not fight. We had fun and compromised about how far we wanted to go each day and what we wanted to see and when we wanted to stop, and I had never in my life experienced that. I was, like, "Wow."

Steve: (Laughing.) True enough.

Gail: I called my mom from the road and I'm going, "Wow, this is so much fun," and she said, "I don't know *why* you're doing this, you don't even know this person," *(she laughs)*, and I mean, this was true, he could have been a—murderer or something. *I just knew it was easy and right and it has been.*

When I compare the stories these couples tell about their lives together, the contrast between those who will remain married and those who will split is apparent. But there is help for many couples who are headed for a Negative "Story of Us." A relationship is salvageable if not all five dimensions are negative. The complete loss of a positive history doesn't happen quickly. Often, there is time to rescue the relationship.

But once the Negative "Story of Us" switch is thrown, it is very hard to reverse. Any intervention is almost certainly too little, too late. Even if there's a positive change in one partner's behavior, the other remains suspicious, thinking something like, *Well, the demon finally did something nice, but this relationship is still hell.* At this point, I believe it is usually best for the partners to acknowledge the death, mourn the loss, and move on.

Self-Test: When to Bail

This assessment will help you determine if the Negative "Story of Us" switch is close to being thrown in your relationship—or already has been. This is not a brief quiz for good reason: making the decision to leave is significant and requires much thought.

My Story of Us
Please answer each item, circling SA if you Strongly Agree with it, A if you Agree with, N if you Neither Agree nor Disagree, D if you Disagree, and SD if you Strongly Disagree with the item.

1. I am disappointed in this relationship.   SA5   A4   N3   D2   SD1
2. I love a lot of my partner's personality traits.   SA1   A2   N3   D4   SD5
3. I love talking about the history of our relationship.   SA1   A2   N3   D4   SD5
4. I love telling stories about how the two of us met.   SA1   A2   N3   D4   SD5
5. Our lives are very chaotic.   SA5   A4   N3   D2   SD1
6. My partner can be extremely selfish.   SA5   A4   N3   D2   SD1
7. I love to plan things in our life with my partner.   SA1   A2   N3   D4   SD5
8. My partner doesn't empathize with me when I get angry.   SA5   A4   N3   D2   SD1
9. I think we can get through any adversity together.   SA1   A2   N3   D4   SD5
10. My partner belittles me.   SA5   A4   N3   D2   SD1
11. My partner is always thinking of my needs.   SA1   A2   N3   D4   SD5
12. I often get mocked by my partner in public.   SA5   A4   N3   D2   SD1
13. My partner expresses a lot of pride in my accomplishments.   SA1   A2   N3   D4   SD5
14. My partner might very well betray me.   SA5   A4   N3   D2   SD1
15. We are a great team.   SA1   A2   N3   D4   SD5
16. After an argument I think, *Who needs this?*   SA5   A4   N3   D2   SD1
17. The two of us think the same positive way about our history.   SA1   A2   N3   D4   SD5
18. This relationship is not up to what I expected.   SA5   A4   N3   D2   SD1
19. We definitely think of ourselves as "we," not as completely separate.   SA1   A2   N3   D4   SD5
20. I'm sure that my partner gives me high blood pressure.   SA5   A4   N3   D2   SD1
21. Sometimes my partner makes fun of me.   SA5   A4   N3   D2   SD1
22. We often get so excited talking that we finish each other's sentences.   SA1   A2   N3   D4   SD5
23. I don't think the struggle in this relationship is worth it.   SA5   A4   N3   D2   SD1
24. My partner understands me.   SA1   A2   N3   D4   SD5

25. We argue about the same things over and over again. SA5 A4 N3 D2 SD1
26. My partner does not accept my sadness. SA5 A4 N3 D2 SD1
27. There is a lot of fondness and affection between us. SA1 A2 N3 D4 SD5
28. We argue a lot, but we don't get anywhere. SA5 A4 N3 D2 SD1
29. My partner compliments me often. SA1 A2 N3 D4 SD5
30. My partner often spontaneously tells me how much he or she loves me. SA1 A2 N3 D4 SD5
31. My partner will probably cheat on me. SA5 A4 N3 D2 SD1
32. We love talking with one another. SA1 A2 N3 D4 SD5
33. My partner is glad to see me at the end of a day. SA1 A2 N3 D4 SD5
34. I have talked to my partner about separation or divorce. SA5 A4 N3 D2 SD1
35. I am fully committed to this relationship. SA1 A2 N3 D4 SD5
36. My partner tells other people how much he or she cherishes me. SA1 A2 N3 D4 SD5
37. My partner has told me that I am sexually unattractive. SA5 A4 N3 D2 SD1
38. Sometimes my partner threatens me. SA5 A4 N3 D2 SD1
39. We have built a great life together. SA1 A2 N3 D4 SD5
40. My partner is proud of me. SA1 A2 N3 D4 SD5
41. My partner shows me a lot of respect. SA1 A2 N3 D4 SD5
42. My partner can get extremely negative. SA5 A4 N3 D2 SD1
43. My partner yells at me a lot. SA5 A4 N3 D2 SD1
44. Our values are very similar. SA1 A2 N3 D4 SD5
45. My partner is very affectionate. SA1 A2 N3 D4 SD5
46. My partner is very sexually attracted to me. SA1 A2 N3 D4 SD5
47. My partner says things to hurt me out of spite. SA5 A4 N3 D2 SD1
48. My partner tries to convince other people that I'm crazy. SA5 A4 N3 D2 SD1
49. My partner insults my family. SA5 A4 N3 D2 SD1

50. My partner tells me that I am sexually inadequate.	SA5 A4 N3 D2 SD1
51. My partner tries to catch me in inconsistencies to show that I'm lying.	SA5 A4 N3 D2 SD1
52. My partner expresses disappointment in me.	SA5 A4 N3 D2 SD1
53. My partner's negativity just goes on and on.	SA5 A4 N3 D2 SD1
54. I am angry at home a lot.	SA5 A4 N3 D2 SD1
55. I feel very close to my partner.	SA1 A2 N3 D4 SD5

Scoring

1. Add up the number of items that you scored as a 1 or 2.
2. Use a calculator (if necessary) to divide that number by 55.
3. Multiply by 100. The result is your "Story of Us" percentage.

75 percent or above. You have a very positive "Story of Us." This score is a strong indication that your relationship is solid. That is a real accomplishment.

74 to 46 percent. Warning bells are ringing, especially if you scored near the lower end of the range. Now is the time to subject your relationship to serious assessment. Have there been new tensions or conflicts? Life changes? Simmering discontents? If you haven't already, work through the book's exercises and see if they bolster your faith in each other. If not, consider seeking professional help together.

45 percent or below: Your score indicates your relationship is in grave danger and may not be salvegeable. However, a passing circumstance, such as a recent regrettable incident that you haven't worked through yet, can cause a score to drop temporarily. So if you do rate low, implement the suggestions I've offered on coping with conflict. Retake the test when you feel "back to normal." If you continue to receive a low number, but you and your partner are committed to saving your relationship, seek help from a well-qualified therapist as soon as possible.

If there is clear, compelling evidence that your relationship is already over or unsalvageable, and you want to move on, I believe it's okay to let it go. But if you do, please don't retreat from the possibility of a relationship in the future. Losing at love puts you at a critical crossroads. The decisions you make now will have profound implications for your future.

13

Learning to Trust Again:
A Life-Saving Skill

Which do you think is worse, a miserable marriage or an isolated, lonely life? It may sound like a ridiculous question—like asking which type of torture you prefer. I pose it because I've found it's not uncommon for people to stay in a bad marriage or relationship to avoid being alone. There are others who respond to betrayal by leaving their partner and vowing never to get close to someone again. As one woman said, "I prefer living with goldfish—they don't cheat on you." The problem is that both of these reactions to betrayal are unhealthy. And by that I don't "just" mean that they are emotionally and psychologically destructive. I mean they can kill you.

The evidence is devastating and clear. Couples in low-trust relationships have a higher death rate than others. This correlation became apparent to me, thanks to additional analysis of the twenty-year study of older couples I ran with Robert Levenson and Laura Carstensen. We noted that more of the couples in zero-sum relationships dropped out of the study than did others. These were the partners who, when the tapes were rolling during their conflict conversation, treated each other like adversaries. Their relatively high dropout rate didn't surprise me. I figured they found participation too unpleasant to continue—or had split up and didn't want to look back. This sort of attrition is why, like most scientists engaged in long-term studies, I begin with more subjects than necessary for accurate results.

But recently, Dr. Tara Madhyastha conducted additional research and uncovered a grimmer explanation for the absent subjects. When she categorized the couples based solely on their conflict discussions, she discovered that a shocking number of zero-sum husbands were dead. Over the twenty years, their mortality rate was 58 percent, compared with 23 percent for men in cooperative marriages. Here's another way to look at it: If the couple had a zero-sum conflict conversation at the start of the study, then even when we account for age and other factors that affect health, the husband's odds of dying over those twenty years were *eleven times higher* than men in mutually cooperative relationships. They were also seven times higher compared to couples with a mixed style (meaning one partner displayed a cooperative style and the other was zero-sum). These results are consistent with a number of studies that find men who believe their wives love them are likely to have significantly lower severity of ulcers and lower rates of coronary artery blockages and angina.

We don't know why the husbands died in disproportion to the wives. Perhaps it's because a man's blood pressure, pulse, and other physiological measures of distress are more reactive to conflict. But being in a miserable marriage takes a toll on women, too. The wives who engaged in zero-sum conflict reported more psychological and physical health symptoms than the other women. There's a fascinating study that underlines the benefit of a high-trust relationship to a woman's health. The researcher, Dr. James Coan, had female volunteers undergo MRI scans while their ankle received mild shocks. Before the test, each subject filled out a questionnaire that indicated whether she was happy in her marriage. Coan tracked the difference in each woman's response to the stress, depending on whether a stranger or her husband clasped her hand during the experiment. In the stranger's presence, the parts of her brain that signal danger and alarm were activated completely. But if the wife had described her marriage as high-trust, the fear response shut off almost entirely when her husband held her hand. Women who felt insecure in their marriages saw much more activity in these brain centers than did the happy ones. (Coan found the same results among gay men and lesbians who said they felt married to their partner.)

How did the husband's presence bring down his wife's fear response? A growing body of research suggests that a high-trust relationship stimulates a woman's production of oxytocin, often called the "cuddle hormone" because it is associated with couple-bonding, maternal attachment, and has a calming effect on our physiology.* The hormone therefore guards against stress reactions that compromise health. The role of oxytocin (and

---

*We have a very picky little rodent to thank for much of our understanding of oxytocin's significance in couple bonding. Because she mates for life, the female prairie vole plays very hard to get. She will spurn male after male if he isn't up to her exacting standards. But when pioneering researcher Dr. Sue Carter injected oxytocin into female prairie voles, they tore up their "lists," and pretty much accepted the first experienced male who came along.

vasopressin, its male counterpart) is just further evidence of how our relationships influence our physiology and vice versa.

Coan theorizes that partners benefit each other by "co-regulating" their physiologies. Put simply, they calm each other when they are unable to soothe themselves. We know from our studies of couple conflict that once flooding kicks in it is very hard for our own brain to deactivate the fear response. But high-trust partners do this for each other all of the time. In their book, *A General Theory of Love*, doctors Thomas Lewis, Fari Amini, and Richard Lannon describe this in the context of the parent-child relationship. They write that the two simultaneously transmit information to each other that can "alter hormone levels, cardiovascular function, sleep rhythms, immune function, and more."

In my study of 100 diverse couples, I found that when the wife's trust metric was high (even if the husband's was not) both partners had lower baseline blood velocities. This is good news because low blood velocity is a check against developing high blood pressure. We can't yet say whether the wife's high trust level caused this mutual, lower blood velocity, but there was an association between the two. It's interesting that the husband's trust level was less of a factor in blood velocity. I've come to believe that, in general, a wife's sense of security tends to influence the relationship dynamics more than does her husband's. When a man realizes how critical it is that he make his wife feel secure, the relationship reaps enormous benefits, and so does their health. Of course, the need to earn the partner's trust knows no gender. For everybody, a stable, trusting relationship is linked to relatively high survival rates from cardiovascular disease, cancer, surgery, and other illnesses.

The message is clear: a happy relationship is good for your health. A low-trust one can be deadly. If yours is broken beyond repair, moving on can improve your odds of good health. But what you do *after* you leave (or are left) may be most important of all. Here's the answer to that question I posed at the beginning of this chapter: What is worse for your health, marital misery or being alone? A wretched relationship is devastating to one's health, but statistcs show that unremitting loneliness is even deadlier.

The high mortality rate of isolated people has been well documented. A classic epidemiological study of 9,000 people by Drs. Lisa Berkman and Len Syme, of the University of California at Berkeley, found that close friendships and marriage granted people about an extra decade of life. (Follow-up research by Dr. Lois Verbrugge determined the effect is even greater when married couples are actually happy!) In other words, after six years the survival probability of people who were married or had confidants (meaning a close, trusting relationship with somebody) was approximately 80 percent, while for those without these social connections, it was 50 percent. Even an unhappy marriage offered benefits, especially to men. All of this research suggests that lifelong isolation shortens life expectancy more than a bad marriage.

Scientists do not yet know the biological basis of the link between loneliness and early death. But the leading theory, based on work by University of Chicago social psychologist and psychophysiologist Dr. John Cacioppo, points at higher blood pressure due to arterial vasoconstriction (the narrowing of blood vessels).

I'm not advising that people remain in unsalvageable marriages to "protect" their health. The solution to this statistical bad news is not to endure an agonizing relationship. It is to avoid moving on to a lonely and isolated life. You want to enter a new loving relationship or establish or strengthen bonds with friends, not shut the door on the world. Below is a table that shows the different potential health outcomes for a woman who has extricated herself from a bad marriage. Should she trust a new man who is available for romance? She is facing *the most important social decision she will make in her life*. What she chooses is likely to affect her future health and her longevity.

	Tomas Is Trustworthy	Tomas Is Untrustworthy
Cynthia trusts Tomas and enters into a committed relationship.	Gains in health, recovery from illness, increasing personal wealth, happiness, well-being, longevity, and raising secure, strong children. Payoff = +15 years of life.	Relationship ends or continues as a low-trust relationship. Chronic physical stress reaction including high blood pressure. Negative payoff = between -4 and -8 years of life even if she gets out.
Cynthia doesn't trust Tomas and decides not to enter into a committed relationship.	Large cost of lifelong loneliness, including increases in physical stress reactions such as high blood pressure. Negative payoff = -10 years of life.	Her savvy in detecting treachery bodes well for her ability to commit to a trustworthy person. Payoff = +15 years of life (same as the high-trust couples I've studied).

There are no reliable statistics on the percentage of people who describe themselves as lonely, nor why so many of these people do seem resistant to ending their isolation. But we know that people who remain lonely for a long period have common characteristics. Although they crave attention and connection, they have a poor ability to detect deceit. In some cases, they accept unfair treatment in order to be liked; in others, they react with extreme suspicion to people who are, in fact, trustworthy. Since they expect to be betrayed, they reject potential partners before any real connection can occur. Isolation is the result.

When Cacioppo used MRIs to trace glucose metabolism in the brain, he found that lonely people experience less of a pleasure boost when viewing happy faces than do others. When they are asked to imagine a social event, the parts of their brain associated with fear light up.

It is understandable to feel wary of relationships if you aren't confident that you can tell whom to trust, especially if you have at least one toxic relationships in your past as "proof." If you are grappling with this issue, I want to bring home the importance of working to improve your ability to recognize when another person *is* trustworthy. Research indicates that without intervention, loneliness doesn't lessen over time. And as we've seen, it is likely to harm your health.

Trust always comes down to risk. If you make yourself vulnerable to another person, there is never a guarantee that you won't be hurt. But more often than not, it's worth it. This is not a platitude but a fact. It is the consistent finding of research into what's often called the Trust Game. Though these studies have not focused on intimate relationships per se, their findings are applicable to romance. The game works in this fashion: Anonymous person number one, whom we'll call Mary, is given $10. She can choose to keep the money or send all or part of it to anonymous person number two, whom we'll call Bruce. Mary knows that based on the game rules, any money she sends to Bruce will triple in value. If she sends him $1, he receives $3. If she sends $5, he gets $15. Any money that Bruce then decides to send back to her will triple in value again, but only for Mary. When this game is played for only one round, Mary knows that Bruce has no stake in sending her back any money. His notions of altruism and, perhaps, fair play will guide his choice. So how much money should she risk giving him? He might return nothing or quite a lot. Her decision will reflect her fundamental trust level, because she knows nothing at all about Bruce.

Studies show that almost all Marys send at least some money to Bruce during a one-round trust game. Usually she sends him about $5. She is willing to risk half of her treasure based on trust that he will respond in an honorable manner and share the profit with her. Bruce has now received $15. He knows any money he doesn't keep but sends back to Mary will triple for her. In one typical study, out of 30 Bruces, 18 returned an average of $5, which was then tripled, so Mary ended up receiving $15 for the $5 she had shared. Eleven of the Bruces sent Mary back the original amount she sent him. So, if she trusted him with $8, in effect he returned $24, giving her a $16 profit. These studies show again and again that the more Mary trusts Bruce, the more money she gains. Individuals who risk trusting others benefit more than those who are suspicious.

Life tends to go better for people who have the courage to trust others. But, of course, it's imperative to recognize when suspicion is appropriate. To hone your trust radar, follow the example of people who have an excellent track record in assessing others. These savvy people tend to score high on measures of social intelligence, which means the ability to interact well with people, individually and in group settings. Their "default" position when they meet someone is to be trusting. But they are not gullible. If there is reason for skepticism, they become wary.

Lesson Number One about detecting deceit: untrustworthy people think only of their own payoffs. If someone treats you unfairly and does not reciprocate kindness, do not trust him or her, no matter how charming. Tricksters and selfish con artists often *are* incredibly charming and reassuring (think Bernie Madoff), so we tend to dismiss evidence that we otherwise would not.

Based on my exhaustive research on trust and betrayal, I believe there are five detectable criteria for separating the trustworthy from the shysters. If you meet someone who possesses the following qualities, I think it worth the risk to open yourself up, perhaps little by little. There is no guarantee. But if you learn to assess others with fairness and objectivity, in time you are likely to encounter someone with whom you can connect in a deep and loving way. The opposite is also true: If someone fails any part of the following smell test, walk away.

Honesty

Do not trust someone who lies to you. Too often we come up with excuses for the other person. It was a misunderstanding. She had her reasons. It wasn't that bad. It was only one time. Take a clear-eyed look: Has this potential lover ever deceived you? Have you witnessed him or her lying to others? Do you find yourself questioning the veracity of what he or she says and then talking yourself out of your doubts? If so, move on.

Transparency

A partner's life should be an open book, without secrets. Make sure this new person invites you to meet friends, family, colleagues, and also confides in you about major stresses, ambitions, goals. When you ask, "Where have you been?" he or she should answer without hesitation.

Accountability

Is there proof that this potential partner keeps promises? Are you able to check the details of any significant transactions with others, financial or otherwise? Do not trust someone who remains vague or unreachable about these issues. It's best to be suspicious of people who say "Just trust me" in response to a specific question. Trustworthy people don't feel the need to tell you what to think!

Ethical Actions

Does this person display just and fair conduct with consistency? Does he or she express and demonstrate values in tune with your own? If you're not comfortable with someone's morals, do not continue the relationship.

Proof of Alliance

Any potential mate should demonstrate being on your side and having your back—even in small ways. You want evidence that he or she does not operate out of sheer self-interest nor form coalitions against you. You want proof that he or she takes your interests to heart. It is a wonderful sign if someone demonstrates selflessness toward you.

If you subject the people you meet to this clear-eyed assessment, you will gain confidence in your ability to size up others. I'm not suggesting that becoming more discerning is effortless, but I am certain that learning to trust again is worth it.

14

What Is True Love?

Often interviewers ask me to define love and to impart a few words of wisdom gleaned from my studies. Yet the best advice I can offer any couple isn't about the science of making successful repair attempts and avoiding the roach motel. It is to revere each other and be grateful that you are in each other's life. I know that exposing your relationship to the unyielding light of science can be intimidating, so I hope many of you find reassurance in the book's last quiz, below. Consider it a final check on the state of your union. It is a long questionnaire, but like love itself, well worth the effort. You may discover that despite setbacks, troubles, or grievances, you share a solid trust that keeps your love strong. And if not . . . I hope you've gained a deeper understanding of trust's fundamental role in happiness—and a map for finding more of it in your life.

Quiz: Is This the Real Thing?

Instructions

For the following items, circle either SD for *Strongly Disagree*, D for *Disagree*, N for *Neither Agree nor Disagree*, A for *Agree*, and SA for *Strongly Agree*.

1. I fully trust my partner.   SD D N A SA

2. My partner fully trusts me.   SD D N A SA

3. I trust my partner during lovemaking.   SD D N A SA

4. I feel safe with my partner.   SD D N A SA

5. My partner feels safe with me.   SD D N A SA

6. I am strongly attached to my partner.   SD D N A SA

7. My partner has a strong sense of attachment to me.   SD D N A SA

8. I have no secrets from my partner.   SD D N A SA

9. My partner has no secrets from me.   SD D N A SA

10. We comfort one another well.   SD D N A SA

11. I feel loved by my partner.   SD D N A SA

12. My partner makes me happy.   SD D N A SA

13. I make my partner happy.   SD D N A SA

14. I would say that I love my partner.   SD D N A SA

15. I am currently "in love" with my partner.   SD D N A SA

16. My partner is currently "in love" with me.   SD D N A SA

17. My cost-benefit analysis of this relationship is mostly benefit, not cost.   SD D N A SA

18. I am fully committed to my partner.   SD D N A SA

19. My partner is fully committed to me.   SD D N A SA

20. I have forsaken all others sexually.   SD D N A SA

21. My partner has forsaken all others sexually.   SD D N A SA

22. My love is not conditional (dependent on anything).   SD D N A SA

23. My partner's love is not conditional (dependent on anything).   SD D N A SA

24. My partner makes me laugh.   SD   D   N   A   SA

25. I make my partner laugh.   SD   D   N   A   SA

26. We don't make each other jealous.   SD   D   N   A   SA

27. We love kissing one another.   SD   D   N   A   SA

28. We have a sense of moral responsibility for one another.   SD   D   N   A   SA

29. We love a lot of the same things.   SD   D   N   A   SA

30. I love the way my partner's mind works.   SD   D   N   A   SA

31. My partner loves the way my mind works.   SD   D   N   A   SA

32. I love the way my partner smells and tastes.   SD   D   N   A   SA

33. My partner loves the way I smell and taste.   SD   D   N   A   SA

34. We support one another's work.   SD   D   N   A   SA

35. It's easy for us to be together.   SD   D   N   A   SA

36. We are there for one another financially.   SD   D   N   A   SA

37. We often share excitement and joy.   SD   D   N   A   SA

38. I love the way my partner treats other people.   SD   D   N   A   SA

39. We often soothe one another.   SD   D   N   A   SA

40. We help one another with life's stresses and pains.   SD   D   N   A   SA

41. We help one another to be the person we each want to be.   SD   D   N   A   SA

42. We see, acknowledge, and enhance one another's
goodness.   SD   D   N   A   SA

43. We love giving presents to one another.   SD   D   N   A   SA

44. We have built a life together we both highly value.   SD   D   N   A   SA

45. My partner turns toward me when I am in need.   SD   D   N   A   SA

46. I can turn toward my partner when I am in need.   SD   D   N   A   SA

47. I can depend on my partner.   SD   D   N   A   SA

48. I am sexually attracted to my partner.   SD   D   N   A   SA

49. I feel desired by my partner.   SD   D   N   A   SA

50. I am sexually satisfied in this relationship.   SD   D   N   A   SA

51. We are concerned about one another's health.   SD   D   N   A   SA

52. If I do something nice for my partner, I can count on
my partner doing something nice for me.   SD   D   N   A   SA

53. We have built a life together with purpose and meaning. SD D N A SA
54. We have a history together we both value. SD D N A SA
55. We have built a group of friends we both care about. SD D N A SA
56. We know and have the same understandings about our
    kin (primary families). SD D N A SA
57. My partner knows and respects my dreams. SD D N A SA
58. I know and respect my partner's dreams. SD D N A SA
59. My partner knows and accepts my preferences. SD D N A SA
60. My partner understands me. SD D N A SA
61. There are no unfair power imbalances in our relationship. SD D N A SA
62. We help heal one another's past wounds. SD D N A SA
63. We know and respect one another's enduring
    vulnerabilities. SD D N A SA
64. I can keep anger in control and not hurt my partner
    very much. SD D N A SA
65. My partner can keep anger in control and not hurt me
    very much. SD D N A SA
66. My partner is not very defensive. SD D N A SA
67. We accept one another's personalities, faults and all. SD D N A SA
68. My partner accepts influence from me. SD D N A SA
69. We share power fairly. SD D N A SA
70. I can be myself with my partner. SD D N A SA
71. I like who I am when with my partner. SD D N A SA
72. My partner can admit being wrong. SD D N A SA
73. We can easily talk about anything. SD D N A SA
74. It's easy to be together. SD D N A SA
75. We often have intimate conversations. SD D N A SA
76. I love to touch my partner. SD D N A SA
77. My partner loves touching me. SD D N A SA
78. My partner is my close friend. SD D N A SA
79. We know and support one another's dreams in life. SD D N A SA

80. We have a lot of fun together.   SD D N A SA

81. We are very sensual with one another.   SD D N A SA

82. We love to learn together.   SD D N A SA

83. We help renew each other when we are burned out.   SD D N A SA

84. I love our vacations.   SD D N A SA

85. We are very emotionally in tune with one another.   SD D N A SA

86. There is lots of fondness and affection between us.   SD D N A SA

87. My partner admires and respects me.   SD D N A SA

88. We respect each other's separateness.   SD D N A SA

89. We enjoy food together.   SD D N A SA

90. We forgive one another.   SD D N A SA

91. I feel confident we can work out our differences.   SD D N A SA

92. We fight together constructively.   SD D N A SA

93. We can compromise and solve problems together.   SD D N A SA

94. We can cope with life's stresses together.   SD D N A SA

95. We continue to court one another.   SD D N A SA

96. We love to plan and dream together.   SD D N A SA

97. I think we can get through any adversity.   SD D N A SA

98. We are definitely a "we," rather than two "me"s.   SD D N A SA

99. My partner thinks about what I need.   SD D N A SA

100. I miss my partner when we are apart.   SD D N A SA

101. I am usually delighted to see my partner upon reunion.   SD D N A SA

102. I want to meet my partner's needs.   SD D N A SA

103. My partner wants to meet my needs.   SD D N A SA

104. We operate with a sense of fairness.   SD D N A SA

105. We are a real team.   SD D N A SA

106. I can name a lot of my partner's positive qualities.   SD D N A SA

107. My partner's irritability is usually temporary.   SD D N A SA

108. My partner is not very distant emotionally.   SD D N A SA

109. I have empathy for my partner's pain.   SD D N A SA

110. My partner has empathy for my pain.   SD D N A SA

111. We each believe we are better than anything else out
there.   SD D N A SA

112. We have similar values, and my partner respects my
beliefs.   SD D N A SA

113. We share a sense of meaning and life dreams.   SD D N A SA

114. We intensely love many of the same things.   SD D N A SA

115. My partner takes care of me when I am sick.   SD D N A SA

116. I take care of my partner when my partner is sick. SD D N A SA

117. We have a holiday cycle we value and support.   SD D N A SA

118. We agree on what a home is.   SD D N A SA

119. We support each other's cultural and religious values. SD D N A SA

120. Our relationship keeps getting better over time.   SD D N A SA

Scoring

SA number of answers___.   Multiply by 5 _____

A number of answers___.   Multiply by 4 _____

N number of answers___.   Multiply by 3 _____

D number of answers___.   Multiply by 2 _____

SD number of answers___.   Multiply by 1 _____

Total: _____

If you and your partner both score 450 or more, your relationship is a keeper.

Whatever your score, I hope that the research and advice in these pages have illuminated for you what it takes to create a relationship that is mutually satisfying and adds profound meaning to your life. The first step toward nurturing true love is to recognize what it looks like, with all of its imperfections and complications. The second is to honor it. Over the years I have seen too many people turn away from their partner and toss out a good relationship. I have come to believe that the greatest obstacle to love may be a sense of entitlement that leads people to exit a marriage because they "deserve" the "perfect" one. It's got to be out there, somewhere. Right? To be blunt: it is not. No long-term love affair can be a photocopy of an idealized one—whether our image of perfection is our parents' marriage, a celebrity's, or one we conjure.

Consider it excellent news that someone else's love story is never going to be yours. True love is woven out of honoring and understanding each other's unique gifts, vulnerabilities, and eccentricities. Your journey is not going to be like any other couple's, and that's how it should be.

Being in love isn't static. It deepens over time. Louise Erdrich wrote in her novel *Shadow Tag*, "Why can't I recover the feelings I had at the beginning? Infatuation, sudden attraction, is partly a fever of surfaces, and absence of knowledge. Falling in love is also falling into knowledge. *Enduring love comes when we love most of what we learn about the other person and can tolerate the faults they cannot change.*" [Emphasis mine.]

A long-term, committed relationship will hit bad patches. We are going to have to accept the detritus of mistakes and regrettable incidents we create. But a loving partnership gives us wonderful gifts that make life worth living: a sense of purpose, greater health and wealth, and, of course, loving care and nurturance. Learning to cherish another person and allowing that person to cherish you is the greatest blessing of life. Love is the most sacred experience we can have. Remember that you build trust by being there for one another, and strengthen loyalty through gratitude, cherishing and honoring what you create together. To paraphrase Proverbs 31, an excellent partner is a jewel more precious than rubies. With a love that you can believe in, you will experience good and not evil all the days of your life.

Appendix 1
Extra Help with the Four Skills of Intimate Conversations

If you're feeling tongue-tied, try the following suggestions.

Skill #1. Putting Your Feelings into Words

A lot of mixed emotions	Angry	Beautiful
Abandoned	Anguished	Belittled
Accepted	Annoyed	Betrayed
Affectionate	Apathetic	Bitter
Afraid	Appreciated	Boastful
Agitated	Appreciative of you	Calm
Alarmed	Apprehensive	Close to you
Alienated	Astounded	Clumsy, awkward
Alone	Baffled	Comfortable
Ambivalent	Bashful	Concerned
Amused	Battered	Connected

Appendix 1

Contemplative	Joyful	Resentful
Critical	Like a failure	Restless
Depressed	Like an innocent victim	Righteously indignant
Disgusted	Like apologizing	Romantic
Disliked	Like arguing	Sexy
Distant	Like everything is falling	Shameful
Exhausted	apart	Shocked
Exhilarated	Like hitting something	Shy
Free	Like I have no energy	Successful
Handsome	Like I want to be	Surprised
Happy	belligerent	Tense
Horny	Like kicking something	Tired
Hungry	Liked	Tolerant
I am not sure how I feel	Lonely	Tranquil
I want to assert my rights	Loved	Unaccepted
In awe	Misunderstood	Unappreciated
In disbelief	Neglected	Unattractive
Inspired	Regretful	Uncomfortable
Insulted	Rejected	Understood
Irritable	Relaxed	Upset
Irritated	Relieved	

Skill #2: Asking Questions

1. What are you feeling?
2. What else are you feeling?
3. What do you need most here?
4. What do you really wish for?
5. How did this all evolve?
6. Who are the main characters in these feelings you're talking about?
7. What would you really like to say here, and to whom?
8. What are the feelings here you are afraid to even think about?

9. Do you have any mixed feelings? What are they?

10. What do you see as your choices?

11. What are the positive and negative aspects of each of your choices?

12. Do you think this has affected our relationship (or another relationship). If so, how?

13. Do you wish you could have done things differently? How so?

14. What are your obligations (or duties) here?

15. Do you have a choice to make? What is it?

16. What would you really like to ask of me?

17. What do your values tell you about all this?

18. Think of someone you really admire. What would he or she do and how would he or she view this situation?

19. Do these feelings and needs have any spiritual, moral, ethical, or religious meaning for you? What are they?

20. Is there anyone or anything you disapprove of here? Who or what?

21. Is there anything or anyone you admire here? Who or what?

22. Is there anything you've learned from this? What?

23. Who is going to be most affected here? How will they be affected? Why?

24. Does this remind you of anything else in your personal history? What?

25. What meaning does it have for you to bring this up now?

26. How does this affect your identity, your idea of yourself?

27. How does this situation touch you?

28. How does this situation change you?

29. How have you changed or how are you changing, and how has that affected this situation?

30. How did this all begin, what was the very start?

31. What's your major reaction or complaint here?

32. Who do you think is most at fault here?

33. How do you think things will be resolved in the next five years?

34. How do you *wish* things would be resolved in the next five years?

35. Pretend that you only had six months to live. What would be most important to you?
36. What are your goals here?
37. How are you thinking about how all of this fits into your life as a whole?
38. What, if anything, makes you angry here?
39. What are the "shoulds" here? (Like what should you take responsibility for?)
40. What is your biggest "turn off" here?
41. Are there parts of yourself that are in conflict? Which?

Skill #3: Probing Further

1. Tell me the story of that.
2. I want to know everything you're feeling.
3. Talk to me; I am listening.
4. Nothing is more important to me right now than listening to you.
5. We have lots of time to talk.
6. Tell me your major priorities here.
7. Tell me what you need right now.
8. Tell me what you think your choices are.
9. It's okay not to know what to do here, but what's your guess?
10. I think you're being very clear. Go on.
11. Tell me all of your feelings here.
12. Help me understand your feelings a little better here. Say more.
13. I think that you have already thought of some solutions. Tell me what they are.
14. Help me understand this situation from your point of view. What is most important to you?
15. Tell me what you're most concerned about.
16. Tell me more about how you are seeing this situation.
17. Talk about what the decision is that you think you have to make.
18. If you could change the attitude of one of the key people in this situation, talk about what you would do.

Skill #4: Expressing Empathy

1. You're making total sense.

2. I understand how you feel.

3. You must feel so hopeless.

4. I just feel such despair in you when you talk about this.

5. You're in a tough spot here.

6. I can see how painful this is.

7. The world needs to stop when you're in this much pain.

8. I wish you didn't have to go through this.

9. I'm on your side.

10. I wish I could have been with you.

11. Oh, wow, that sounds terrible.

12. You must feel so helpless.

13. It hurts me to hear that.

14. I support your position.

15. I totally agree with you.

16. You are feeling so trapped!

17. You are making total sense.

18. It sounds like you were really disgusted!

19. No wonder you're upset.

20. I'd feel the same way.

21. I think you're right.

22. You are in a lot of pain. I can feel it.

23. It would be great to be free of this.

24. That must have annoyed you.

25. That would make me mad, too.

26. That sounds infuriating.

27. That sounds very frustrating.

28. That is very scary.

29. Well, I agree with most of what you're saying.

30. I would have been disappointed by that, too.

31. That would have hurt my feelings, too.

32. That would make me sad, too.

33. POOR BABY!!!

34. Wow! That must have hurt.

35. Okay, I think I get it. So what you're feeling/thinking is . . .

36. So what you're saying is . . .

37. I would have trouble coping with that.

38. What I admire most about what you're doing is . . .

39. That would make me feel insecure.

40. That sounds a little frightening.

Appendix 2
Suggestions for Working Through the Gottman's Aftermath Kit: Healing Previous Injuries and Hurt Feelings (Chapter 9)

Below are some ideas for putting your thoughts and feelings into words for each step of the kit.

Step One: What I Felt at the Time

1. Defensive.
2. Not listened to.
3. Hurt.
4. Totally flooded.
5. Angry.
6. Sad.
7. Unloved.
8. Misunderstood.

9. Criticized.

10. Insulted by your complaint.

11. Like you didn't even like me.

12. Not cared about.

13. Worried.

14. Afraid.

15. Unsafe.

16. Tense.

17. I was right and you were wrong.

18. Both of us were partly right.

19. Out of control.

20. Frustrated.

21. Righteously indignant.

22. Morally justified.

23. Unfairly picked on.

24. Unappreciated.

25. Disliked.

26. Unattractive.

27. Stupid.

28. Morally outraged.

29. Taken for granted.

30. Like leaving.

31. Like staying and talking this through.

32. Overwhelmed with emotion.

33. Not calm.

33. Stubborn.

36. Powerless.

37. I had no influence.

38. I wanted to win this one.

39. My opinions didn't matter.

40. I had no feelings at all.

41. I had no idea what I was feeling.

42. Lonely.

43. Alienated.

44. Inflexible.

45. Guilty.

Step Two: My Needs

Here are some common needs people express during Step Two. Acknowledge all that you were feeling at the time. Listen with empathy to your partner's descriptions.

1. To be listened to.

2. To be held.

3. To be offered help.

4. To feel understood.

5. To have you validate my feelings.

6. For you to initiate sex.

7. To cuddle more.

8. To know when you find me irresistible.

9. To talk more about our kids.

10. For you to ask me about my hopes and aspirations.

11. To have a conversation with you.

12. To talk to you about my day.

13. For our reunion to be warm and affectionate.

14. For you to be more affectionate with me, to touch me more.

15. For you to look happy when you first see me at the end of the day.

16. For you to ask me about my work.

17. For you to put down the paper, look up from your computer or mute the TV when I want to talk.

18. A foot rub, back rub, or a massage.

19. For you to offer to do a household chore so I can get some relief.

20. For you to tell me I look nice.

21. For you to answer when I call your name.

22. A romantic drive or getaway.

23. To go out to dinner and a movie.

24. To take a long bath together.

25. For you to cook a meal or order food in for one night a week.

26. To see my friends.

27. For us to have an adventure.

28. Some time alone.

29. To feel you appreciate what I do.

30. To feel you value me.

Step Three: Triggers

What pushed your buttons and escalated the interaction? Here are some categories:

I felt:

1. Excluded.

2. Powerless.

3. Not listened to.

4. I couldn't ask for what I needed.

5. Scolded.

6. Judged.

7. Blamed.

8. Disrespected.

9. No affection from you.

10. Unsafe, scared.

11. I didn't trust you.

12. Uncared for.

13. You weren't there for me when I was vulnerable and needed you.

14. I couldn't just talk about my feelings without you going ballistic.

15. Once again I was the bad guy and you were innocent.

16. I was not getting taken care of.

17. Unloved.

18. It was so unfair to me.

19. I had trouble with your anger or yelling.

20. I had trouble with your sadness or despair.

21. Trapped.

22. You had no passion for me.

23. I couldn't ask for what I needed.

24. All alone.

25. Controlled.

26. Manipulated.

Step Four: Taking Responsibility

Express your role in the fight or miscommunication.

1. Very irritable.

2. Not expressive of my appreciation toward you.

3. Taking you for granted.

4. Overly sensitive.

5. Overly critical.

6. Not sharing very much of my inner world.

7. Emotionally unavailable.

8. Turning away more than typical.

9. Easily upset.

10. Feeling depressed.

11. Feeling like I had a chip on my shoulder.

12. Not very affectionate.

13. Not making time for good things between us.

14. Not a very good listener.

15. Not asking for what I needed.

16. Feeling a bit like a martyr.
17. Feeling like I needed to be alone.
18. Not interested in taking care of anybody.
19. Very preoccupied.
20. Very stressed.
21. Feeling a lack of confidence in myself.
22. Running on empty.

Apologies: I'm Sorry I:

Overreacted.

Was irritable and grumpy.

Said mean things.

Hurt your feelings.

Was so insensitive.

Was so selfish.

Didn't calm down.

Escalated things.

Yelled.

Kept interrupting you.

Was impatient.

Didn't listen to you.

Summary:
My *specific* contributions to this incident were . . .

Step Five: How to Make It Better

Write down one way you think that *your partner* could make it better the next time this kind of incident occurs? Write down one way that *you* could.

Appendix 3
Why Some Couples Stop Having Sex: A Game Theory Analysis

What is happening in the American bedroom? Not very much, according to a growing body of research. For some reason, a dwindling sex life is quite common in long-term relationships. Although the cause is unknown, experts often blame the dearth of passion on the woman, either claiming her libido has declined or she is focused on her kids, not her relationship. Drug companies have taken notice of this desire gap and are vying to be the first to close it with a Viagra-like pill for females. But do women really need a medication to put them in the mood? I don't think so. There is a solution to the problem that is amazingly simple. I discovered it by applying the mathematics of game theory to the problem—just like I did with issues of trust and betrayal. This approach yielded results that can help every couple rekindle the flame—and no one needs to decipher algebraic equations in order to benefit.

Below, I'll show you exactly how I used game theory to solve this common dilemma. Here's the punch line: For a couple to have sex often, neither can meet the other's rebuff with anger, rejection, or any punishing behavior. There must not be a negative payoff for the partner saying "no." In fact, the declining partner must even receive a bit of a positive payoff.

Consider these two scenarios: Ian is in the mood, but Amy is not. He understands that he has to accept Amy turning him down, but that doesn't make it okay to him. He believes that she is denying him something he has a right to. If he can't convince her to change her mind, he will sulk, sigh, argue, accuse, criticize, or ignore her. Whatever the specifics of his negative reaction, he is punishing Amy and sending the message: It isn't okay for you to say no. Of course, none of this is going to put Amy in the mood. It will do the opposite and just ratchet up the tension and resentment between them, probably making her less interested in having sex the next time.

The second scenario: When Amy turns down sex, Ian accepts it. Just like that. He doesn't hold a grudge, doesn't see sex as a right or expectation. Amy even gets a little positive payoff for saying no. Here's an example, using a time-worn scenario:

Amy: Not tonight. I have a headache.
Ian: Poor baby. I understand completely. I love you.

Ian's caring response is a far cry from the traditional: "But you always have a headache." And it is far more effective. Receiving a positive payoff for turning down sex does not lead Amy to say "no" more often in the future. Instead, the payoff reinforces that

Ian loves her, that at its core their sex life really is about making love, not just increasing the frequency of sexual release. In essence, Amy just said "no" to sex, and Ian's response was to make her feel loved. And, as we know, in an atmosphere of loving payoffs, sex becomes more frequent. In a trusting relationship, sex won't be just erotic. A fairly large portion of the time it will also be passionate lovemaking.

But don't take my word for it. Let's look at the numbers.

We know that the basic idea of game theory is that people value the exchanges they make with others based on the payoffs they receive. Although we may not be aware of it, we rate our relationships all of the time. Say a couple reunites after a long day. The man gives his wife a broad smile. She sends back a half-hearted one. Each of them is going to "rate" the other's response. In other words, they are going to compare this smile with others their partner or somebody else (even an imagined "other) has flashed at them. The wife is likely to think, "What a big smile he gave me. I can't imagine any other man being this happy to see me." But he may be thinking, "I've gotten bigger smiles from her before. And I sure can imagine a happier greeting from somebody else."

If we stick numbers to these ratings, we can devise a little chart like the one below, similar to the one we created in chapter 1 for Al and Jenny and their cleaning dilemma. We call this type of table a payoff matrix. It indicates each person's payoff in the exchange.

We'll use a scale of -5 to +5. The wife thinks her husband's smile was great, so she gives it a +5. But he rates hers at -3.

	Her return smile
His smile	Payoff = (-3, +5)

Game theory analyzes behavior through the use of such charts. It creates different scenarios, or "games," and then calculates the relative pay-offs each player receives, depending on the strategy they pursue. One such game is called The Stag Hunt. It is a cooperative game, rather than a competitive one, so it fits nicely here.

Hester and her husband, Victor, enter a forest. They have a choice between tracking rabbits or a stag. They must make a simultaneous decision, without discussing their choices. Here's how the game is scored: It takes two people to stalk the stag. So if one chooses to capture rabbits while the other goes after the stag, the rabbit catcher will get all the rabbits (+2), and the stag pursuer will get nothing (0). If they join forces and chase the stag, their cooperation earns 3 points. If they go after the rabbits together, they share the catch, so they each get one point. This scoring is represented in the following payoff matrix. (The first number between the brackets indicates Victor's pay-off. The second is Hester's.)

	Hester chases the stag	Hester chases the rabbits
Victor chases the stag	(3, 3)	(0, 2)
Victor chases the rabbits	(2, 0)	(1, 1)

To analyze this game, let's begin by looking at the situation from Victor's perspective. Since Hester's payoffs are not relevant to us right now, I've indicated them with a question mark in the following chart.

	Hester chases the stag
Victor chases the stag	(3*, ?)
Victor chases the rabbits	(2, ?)

The stag is worth more points than the rabbits, so we put an asterisk next to that choice. In game theory parlance, we say that chasing the stag "strictly dominates" the choice of rabbits for Victor. It is clearly the better option.

Now, let's create a chart that indicates the payoffs Victor receives based on Hester chasing the rabbits.

	Hester chases the rabbits
Victor chases the stag	(0, ?)
Victor chases the rabbits	(1*, ?)

Under this scenario, rabbits strictly dominate the choice of stag for Victor.

Let's now look at the choices from Hester's perspective. Again, the best option is for her to chase the stag if Victor does as well.

	Hester chases the stag	Hester chases the rabbits
Victor chases the stag	(?, 3*)	(?, 2)

Here's her situation if Victor chases the rabbits:

	Hester chases the stag	Hester chases the rabbits
Victor hunts the rabbits	(?, 0)	(?, 1*)

If we combine these minicharts into one table, the result looks like this.

	Hester chases the stag	Hester chases the rabbits
Victor chases the stag	(3*, 3*)	(0, 2)
Victor chases the rabbits	(2, 0)	(1*, 1*)

Notice that there are two boxes, or cells, where *both* numbers have an asterisk—this is where the players' best outcomes coincide. We call these double-asterisked cells the game's *solutions*. Why? Because they indicate the scenario in which neither player can do better by making any change by him or herself. For example, let's look at the cell in which both go after the stag (3*, 3*). If Victor switched to rabbits, his payoff would go from 3 to 2, not a good option. Hester would have the same result. The (3*, 3*) cell is called a "pure strategy" *Nash equilibrium* of the game: Neither player can do any better by shifting to a different strategy on their own.

The other "solution" cell (1*, 1*) is also considered a pure strategy Nash equilibrium of the game, even though it gives both players a lower score. If Victor swung to capturing the stag, his score would move from 1 to zero, not a good strategy. It would be an equally bad choice for Hester to make a shift on her own.

Now that we have the basics down, let's see what happens if Hester and Victor play this game over and over, and mix up their strategies. That situation of repeated play is a little more like an actual relationship where partners keep having the same exchanges over and over again. For example, they could both select stag and rabbits half of the time. But we can actually solve for the best repeated strategy (called a "mixed strategy") from each player's perspective.

Let's assume that Victor decides to hunt the stag with probability σ_{stag} (the "σ" represents the probability) and play rabbits with probability $(1 - \sigma_{stag})$. Then, if Victor played stag with probability

σ_{stag}, and played rabbits with probability $(1 - \sigma_{stag})$, the expected payoff (EP) for Hester if Hester played stag would be:

EP- for Hester if she plays stag $= (3) (\sigma_{stag}) + (0) (1 - \sigma_{stag})$.

If Hester played rabbits:

EP- for Hester if she plays rabbits $= (2) (\sigma_{stag}) + (1) (1 - \sigma_{stag})$.

Now if we set $EP_{stag} = EP_{rabbits}$, then Victor's actions are indifferent with respect to Hester's payoffs with Victor's mixing of choices. So Victor's mixing choice is acceptable to her (her indifference point has been reached).

$$(3) (\sigma_{stag}) + (0) (1 - \sigma_{stag}) = (2) (\sigma_{stag}) + (1) (1 - \sigma_{stag})$$
$$3\sigma_{stag} = 1 + \sigma_{stag}$$
$$2\sigma_{stag} = 1$$
$$\sigma_{stag} = \frac{1}{2}.$$

Therefore, Hester does not care if Victor plays stag with probability ½ and rabbits with probability ½. His choice does not affect her payoffs. So that mixing strategy for Victor can lead to a mixed strategy Nash equilibrium, not a pure equilibrium.

To get the equilibrium, a similar computation shows that the mixing strategy works the other way around. It is indifferent to Victor's payoffs whether Hester chooses stag with probability ½ and rabbits with probability ½. So when each player chooses stag and rabbits with ½ probability, those choices are a mixed strategy Nash equilibrium.

Zero-sum games

In a "winner take all" game, every cell in the payoff matrix will hold a winner and a loser. In the example below, two players simultaneously move poker chips across the table:

	She moves Left	She moves Right
He moves Up	(3, -3)	(-2, 2)
He moves Down	(-1, 1)	(0, 0)

This game has no pure strategy Nash equilibrium—there is no way for the players to reach their maximum benefit at the same time.

However, let's now look at mixed strategy equilibria, where each side plays its options at a certain probability. (We again assume that this game has many rounds.) He uses a coin toss to decide whether to play Up or Down. The result will be his randomly playing each option 50% of the time. Therefore, her expected payoff for playing Left would then be:

$$EP_{Left} = (.5)(-3) + (.5)(1) = -1.$$

For playing Right, her expected payoff would be:

$$EP_{Right} = (.5)(2) + (.5)(0) = 1.$$

So, if he flips an unbiased coin to decide whether to play Up or Down, she should play Right as a pure strategy, because her expected payoff is higher than playing Left. Since he knows this, he is not going to randomize his choices with a coin toss.

As we already saw, game theory analysis allows us to use algebra to compute what would be an ideal mixed Nash equilibrium. Again, we identify the opponent's *indifference point* between the other's pure strategies. The probability that he plays Up becomes an unknown, σ_{Up}, that we solve for. If he plays Up with probability σ_{Up} we already know that he must play Down with probability $(1 - \sigma_{Up})$. So we compute the expected payoffs for the other player ("she") as follows.

$$EP_{Left} = (\sigma_{Up})(-3) + (1 - \sigma_{Up})(1) = -4\sigma_{Up} + 1$$

$$EP_{Right} = (\sigma_{Up})(2) + (1 - \sigma_{Up})(0) = 2\sigma_{Up}.$$

We now want to set $EP_{Left} = EP_{Right}$ to find the value of σ_{Up} that makes her indifferent to what he chooses. We compute:

$$EP_{Left} = EP_{Right}$$

$$-4\,\sigma_{Up} + 1 = 2\,\sigma_{Up}.$$

$$1 = 6\,\sigma_{Up}$$

$$\sigma_{Up} = \frac{1}{6}$$

To summarize, if he plays Up with probability $\frac{1}{6}$, and Down with probability $\frac{5}{6}$, she remains indifferent to these choices in terms of her expected payoff. She can't do any better by playing Left or Right when he uses this mixing strategy.

Now let's flip this and look at her action perspective and his payoffs. Let's now compute the probability that she should play Left, σ_{Left}, and the probability that she should play Right, $(1 - \sigma_{Left})$, so that he will be indifferent to her mixing strategy. We start by asking what his expected payoffs will be.

$$EP_{Up} = (\sigma_{Left})(3) + (1 - \sigma_{Left})(-2) = 5\,\sigma_{Left} + 2, \text{ and}$$

$$EP_{Down} = (\sigma_{Left})(-1) + (1 - \sigma_{Left})(0) = -\sigma_{Left}$$

Next, we find his indifference probability of σ_{Left} with this equation:

$$EP_{Up} = EP_{Down}$$

$$5\sigma_{Left} + 2 = -\sigma_{Left}$$

$$6\sigma_{Left} = 2$$

$$\sigma_{Left} = \frac{1}{3}$$

We have discovered that he will remain indifferent to her mixing strategy if she plays Left with probability $\frac{1}{3}$ and Right with probability $\frac{2}{3}$.

When we connect the mixing strategies of both players, we get the mixed strategy Nash equilibrium for the game. Therefore, even though there was no pure strategy Nash equilibrium, the game did allow for a mixed strategy equilibrium.

This mixing strategy makes some sense in a relationship where the behaviors (like smiling, eating dinner, or offering to have sex) are exchanged frequently with some probability. It is exciting that a Nash equilibrium solution to the game may exist even when the pure strategy game is unsolvable. We can apply that to accepting and refusing invitations to have sex within a relationship.

Accepting or Refusing Sex

Let's get back to Amy and Ian. Everyday, one of them attempts to initiate sex with the other. Assuming their pay-offs are identical, the payoff matrix looks like this:

	Amy accepts sex	Amy refuses sex
Ian accepts sex	(5, 5)	(-1, 1)
Ian refuses sex	(1, -1)	(0, 0)

Ian and Amy each give the highest rating (5, 5) to both of them accepting sex. They like sex and want to have a lot of it. They also give a low rating (0, 0) to them both refusing sex. That makes sense. In the mixed cells of the table, if Amy accepts and Ian refuses, she is unhappy, feels a little rejected, so she gets a payoff of -1, and Ian gets a 1. This would indicate that she feels a bit rejected, but he is okay. This outcome is symmetrical—if Amy refuses and Ian accepts, she gets a 1, and he gets a -1. This seems to be a reasonable psychological configuration of this repeated set of possibilities. It fits the situation for our hypothetical couple.

Okay, so are there pure strategy Nash equilibria—ways for them both to receive their best outcome? Actually, there is only one. Let's look at the choices from his perspective:

	Amy accepts	Amy refuses
Ian accepts	(5*, ?)	(-1, ?)

The 5 clearly gets an asterisk. Here's the table if he refuses:

	Amy accepts	Amy refuses
Ian refuses	(1*, ?)	(0, ?)

The 1 gets the asterisk here.
From her perspective:

	Amy accepts
Ian accepts	(?, 5*)
Ian refuses	(?, -1)

The 5 clearly gets the asterisk.
If she refuses sex:

	Amy refuses
Ian accepts	(?, 1*)
Ian refuses	(?, 0)

The 1 gets the asterisk this time.
So, putting this all together we see:

	Amy accepts sex	Amy refuses sex
Ian accepts sex	(5*, 5*)	(-1, 1*)
Ian refuses sex	(1*, -1)	(0, 0)

Therefore, only one pure strategy Nash equilibrium has them both accepting sex. That's not much of a surprise.

So far that all makes sense. But now we need to know the *probability* that each of them will accept sex and also the expected *frequency* of sex for this couple.

We can compute Ian's indifference point from the matrices:

	Amy agrees	Amy refuses
Ian agrees	(5, ?)	(-1, ?)

And

	Amy agrees	Amy refuses
Ian refuses	(1, ?)	(0, ?)

$$\text{EP for Ian}_{\text{Amy Agrees}} = 5\,\sigma_{\text{Agree}} + (-1)(1 - \sigma_{\text{Agree}})$$

$$\text{EP for Ian}_{\text{Amy Refuses}} = 1\,\sigma_{\text{Agree}} + (0)(1 - \sigma_{\text{Agree}})$$

Set $\text{EP}_{\text{Agree}} = \text{EP}_{\text{Refuse}}$, the Ian indifference point.

$$5\sigma_{\text{Agree}} - 1 + \sigma_{\text{Agree}} = \sigma_{\text{Agree}}$$

$$5\sigma_{\text{Agree}} = 1$$

$$\sigma_{\text{Agree}} = \frac{1}{5}$$

Amy will agree to sex only $\frac{1}{5}$th of the time and refuse $\frac{4}{5}$th of the time to have Ian indifferent to her mixing strategy in terms of his expected payoffs. Now what about his mixing strategy?

	Amy Agrees
Ian Agrees	(?, 5)
Ian Refuses	(?, -1)

	Amy Refuses
Ian Agrees	(?, 1)
Ian Refuses	(?, 0)

$$\text{EP}_{\text{Ian Agrees}} = 5\,\sigma_{\text{Agree}} + (-1)(1 - \sigma_{\text{Agree}})$$

$$\text{EP}_{\text{Ian Refuses}} = 1\,\sigma_{\text{Agree}} + (0)(1 - \sigma_{\text{Agree}})$$

Set $\text{EP}_{\text{Ian Agrees}} = \text{EP}_{\text{Ian Refuses}}$, the Amy indifference point.

Appendix 3

$$5\sigma_{\text{Agree}} - 1 + \sigma_{\text{Agree}} = \sigma_{\text{Agree}}$$

$$\sigma_{\text{Agree}} = \frac{1}{5}$$

If Ian uses a mixing strategy of agreeing to sex $\frac{1}{5}$th of the time and refusing $\frac{4}{5}$th of the time, Amy will be indifferent in terms of her payoffs. Okay, great, we have a mixed strategy Nash equilibrium. Hooray!

How often will they actually have sex with this payoff matrix? Since they both have to accept for sex to occur, the mutual acceptance rate will be $(\frac{1}{5})(\frac{1}{5}) = 1/25 = .04$, or 4%. At 365 days a year, they will have sex about 15 days a year (about once every three weeks). That is a surprisingly low rate for this couple, given that they have set up a reasonable matrix psychologically. What's going on here?

Now we get to the good stuff. Let's take another look at the initial game theory matrix, and vary the payoffs for *refusing sex*, making it a variable, call it r:

	Amy accepts sex	Amy refuses sex
Ian accepts sex	(5, 5)	(r, r)
Ian refuses sex	(r, r)	(0, 0)

The mixing equations for her become:

$$5\sigma_{\text{Agree}} + (r)(1 - \sigma_{\text{Agree}}) = (r)(\sigma_{\text{Agree}}) + (0)(1 - \sigma_{\text{Agree}})$$

$$\sigma_{\text{Agree}}(5 - 2r) = r$$

$$\sigma_{\text{Agree}} = r/(5 - 2r)$$

If we want $\sigma_{Agree} = 0.5$, then r must $= 1.25$. For him, the mixing equations are the same, so if we set $r = 1.25$, they will have sex at a rate of $(\frac{1}{2})((\frac{1}{2}) = .25$, so that will mean that with $r = 1.25$, they have sex 91 times a year—about 1.8 times a week.

That's amazingly close to the reported national average. If r is set higher (i.e., there is a bigger payoff for refusing), then they will have sex even more often! For example, if $r = 1.53$, then $\sigma_{Agree} = .80$, Amy agrees to sex 80% of the time, so they will have sex $(.8)(.8)(365) = 233$ days a year, or about 4 times a week. That feels a lot better to Ian and to Amy.

These results suggest that, for a couple to have sex often, it has to be really okay—slightly rewarding, even—for either of them to refuse it. There must actually be a *positive payoff* to saying, "no." That conclusion may be surprising, but it is mathematically sound.

I know many people find this very confusing and complicated, but the solution we just calculated is not at all complex. This game theory analysis leads to a simple strategy for couples who are coping with a decline in desire. If you make it more than okay for either of you to say "not tonight," there will be many more nights when you both say, "yes." No need for a female Viagra. Just a little sensitivity.

Acknowledgments

Almost all of my work for the past four decades has been made possible by a miraculous lifelong collaboration with my best friend, Robert W. Levenson, who was also best man at my wedding. Nothing can compare with this great blessing of friendship, love, and camaraderie that has endured and enriched our lives for so many years. Based on learning and laughter, Bob and I have enjoyed the great gift of deep and lasting friendship. At every talk, I acknowledge Bob's contribution. This book, however, was written without Bob's careful and insightful eye, so, I take all the blame for any errors.

For the past sixteen years I have been working with my jewel, my dear and beautiful wife, Dr. Julie Anne Schwartz Gottman, friend, colleague, and companion. Thanks to Julie, I actually get to be part of a great relationship, instead of just studying them. Together, we work and research, argue, learn to love, heal the wounds we create along the way, and create methods that train clinicians in approaches to helping marriages that are scientifically based and also honor practice-based evidence. Without Julie's expertise and wisdom, the therapies based on my research and/or Bob's would have been empty of deep understanding, empathy, and sensitivity to people's pain. Thankfully, after a while it has become hard to recall who invented what in our collective work. Julie is also a natural editor and writer. She patiently helped Nan and me make the concepts in this book clearer. Her strength, intuition, imagination, and keen intellect have vastly enriched my life. I cherish you, Julie Anne.

I would like to acknowledge the contributions to my work made by interactions over the years with my dear colleagues Steve Asher, Carolyn and Philip Cowan, Paul Ekman, Jean Goldsmith, Mavis Hetherington, Susan Johnson, James Murray, Bill Pinsof, Ross Parke, Steve Porges, Ed Tronick, Dan Wile, and Jeff Zeig.

I would also like to acknowledge the work of my many talented students, laboratory staff, and colleagues who have made this work possible. They are: Julia Babcock, Renay Bradley, Kim Buehlman, Sybil Carrere, Jim Coan, Julian Cook, Jani Driver, Sharon Fentiman, Dan Friend, Bill Griffin, Carole Hooven, Vanessa Kahen-Johnson, Neil Jacobson, Lynn Katz, Itziar Luzarraga, Tara Madhyastha, Howard Markman, Kim McCoy, James Murray, Eun Young Nahm, Cliff Notarius, Jennifer Parkhurst, Regina Rushe, Joanne Wu Shortt, Cathryn Swanson, Kristin Swanson, Amber Tabares, and Dan Yoshimoto. It's been a long and mostly very pleasant journey, and I am grateful for their hard work and creative energy.

The Gottman Institute that Julie and I founded with Etana Kunovsky about sixteen years ago has been a vital fountain of sustained support. Etana's optimism and creativity kept us from going under many times. Thank you, Etana. Whenever I speak at a talk or workshop, I think about how lucky I am. What professor has an entire energetic company and an enthusiastic, hardworking staff to support him? I would like to mention Jaime Bradley, Kristi Content, Lee Culverwell, Belinda Gray, Allie Guerrero, Kyle Morrison, Michelle Plackett, Kate Ramsburgh, Ann Scranton, Carol Snyder, Stacy Walker, Cynthia Williams, and Linda Wright. Thankfully, after a while it became hard to recall who invented what in our lab's and the Gottman Institute's collective effort to help couples and train clinicians.

Very recently Alan Kunovsky agreed to become the CEO of the Gottman Institute. He brought to this task decades of being a great businessman in South Africa, wisdom, a sense of calm, enthusiasm, drive, and great compassion and creativity. He also brought to us his love for motorcycles. He and his wife Etana have become our great traveling companions as we meet therapists and researchers all over the world who are interested in the same questions we keep asking.

I would like to acknowledge our Gottman-Certified Therapists and colleagues Lisa Baker-Wilson, Christina Choi, Peck Cho, Connie Foits, Ken Fremont-Smith, Marcia Gomez, Andy Greendorfer, Barbara Johnstone, Bob Navarra, Dave Penner, Michael Rediger, Trudy Sackey, Ruth Saks, Maureen Sawyer, John Slattery, Olea Smith-Kaland, Terry Sterrenberg, Lawrence Stoyanowski, Mirabai Wahbe, Darren Wilk, Pat Worthy, Ray Varlinsky, and Lynda Vorhees. Our therapists have also been a source of understanding and inspiration, as well as challenges. They have greatly enriched our lives, and share our dream of interconnected relationship clinics worldwide that help make relationships more effective at loving. They have taken our work farther than we could ever have done, innovating and creating lovely new ideas and applying our ideas to problems we would never have thought of.

I would also like to thank my steady sources of research

funding, the National Institute of Mental Health for grants and a twenty-year Research Career Scientist Award, the Kirlin Foundation, the Talaris Research Institute, Mathematica, and the Federal Administration of Children and Families. Research is an expensive and slow enterprise. It is getting harder and harder to obtain funding for this work in the United States, and without farsighted private patrons, we would, unfortunately, simply have to stop.

So many people's contributions have made our work possible over so many years. The greatest of all these contributors are our valiant research subjects, who volunteered for the sake of science and helping others. I am forever grateful to them.

Nan and I would like to thank our agent, Katinka Matson, for her encouragement, support, and expertise. We are also indebted to our editor, Ben Loehnen, for his enthusiasm, knowledge, sharp eye, and helpful suggestions.

—John

Index

Index

Index

Index

Index

Index

Index

negative modes of communication
blocking, 38–41
preemptive, 117
of regrettable incidents, 33–34, 46
of sexual relationship, 181, 188
Responsibility, 111, 124, 247
accepting, 33, 39, 73, 107, 131, 136–37,
143–44, 154–55, 162, 218, 254–55
for betrayals, 166, 170
for decisions, 97, 104
moral, 167, 239
in sexual intimacy, 181
Roach motel for lovers, xvi–xviii, 29–41, 47,
212, 237
absorbing negativity of, 104
infidelity and, 48, 52
negative modes of communication leading
to, 37–41
Ruef, Anna, 127
Rusbult, Caryl, 49–50, 177

Same-sex couples, 14, 104, 219, 249
Satisfaction, 8, 76, 77, 147, 204
versus disappointment, 220–22
sexual, 179, 185–87
Schneider, Jennifer, 63
Schwartz, Pepper, 14n
Science of Sin, The (TV program), 153
Secrets, xvii, 63, 70, 174, 235, 238
infidelity and, 45, 47, 54–58, 163
Self-disclosure, 107
Selfishness, xvii, 6, 40, 44, 52, 79, 81, 119,
235, 255
accusations of, 111, 115
attributed to partner, 33, 36, 44, 57, 74, 223
in sliding door moments, 33
Seven Principles for Making Marriage Work
(Gottman and Silver), xv
Sex addicts, xvii, 60–62, 81
Sexual interest
game theory analysis of, 256–70
gender differences in, 59–60
lack of, 75–76
Sexual relationship, 173–99
in aftermath of infidelity, 171–72

assessment of romance and passion in,
185–88
communication about needs and desires
in, 178–84
enhancing enjoyment in, 196–98
Love Maps in, 189–95
pillow talk and, 198–99
Shadow Tag (Erdrich), 243
Sliding door moments, 32–35, 51–52, 102,
104, 110
negative, 48 (see also Negative COMPs)
turning away versus turning toward each
other during, 74, 99, 101, 166
Sound relationship house, 56, 58, 69, 162
Specific Affect Coding System (SPAFF), 10n
Stag Hunt Game, 259–62
Star Trek (TV series), 127
State of the Union meetings, 110, 119–24,
128–29, 137, 140, 145, 188
Stonewalling, 10, 31, 38, 40–41
Story of Us, 202, 203, 217, 222–26
Struggles, 20, 44, 76, 122, 135, 223
glorifying, 215–20
Syme, Len, 231

Tabares, Amber, 105, 148
Talk Dirty to Me (Tisdale), 198
Terkel, Studs, 203
Theory of Games and Economic Behavior (von
Neumann and Morgenstern), 2
Therapist, choosing a, 152–59
Tisdale, Sallie, 198
Tolerance, 114, 117–19, 124, 134
Touching, intimate, 179, 189, 192, 197, 198,
240
Transparency, 164–65, 235
Triggers, 33, 52, 67, 79, 84, 117, 142–44,
253–54
childhood origins of, 43, 116
of defensiveness, 115, 119
of flooding, 30, 114
of posttraumatic stress, 147–48, 162, 163
of vulnerabilities, 116, 128, 166
True love, definition and assessment of,
237–43

281

Index

About the Authors

World renowned for his groundbreaking work on marital stability and divorce prediction, **DR. JOHN GOTTMAN** has earned numerous major awards, and published over 190 academic articles. He is the author or co-author of forty books, including the bestselling *The Seven Principles for Making Marriage Work*, *The Relationship Cure*, *Why Marriages Succeed or Fail*, and *Raising an Emotionally Intelligent Child*, among many others. Co-founder of the Gottman Relationship Institute with his wife, Dr. Julie Schwartz Gottman, John is also the Executive Director of the affiliated Relationship Research Institute. He is a professor emeritus of psychology at the University of Washington, where he founded "The Love Lab" at which much of his research on couples' interactions was conducted.

NAN SILVER is a writer and editor based in the New York area. This is her third collaboration with Dr. Gottman. Visit her at www.nansilver.net.

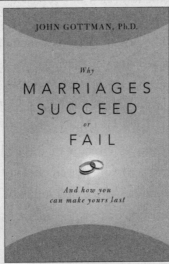